A history
of
Robert Sayle

Revised edition 2008

published by: **John Lewis Cambridge**
10 Downing Street
Cambridge CB2 3DS

Book design and layout by Olivia Daly

Cover photographs courtesy of Mark Mackenzie, Kevin Sansbury
and the John Lewis Partnership Archive

ISBN: 978-0-9558950-0-5
Published by John Lewis Cambridge
Printed by Advantage Digital Print, The Old Radio Station,
Bridport Road, Dorchester, Dorset DT2 9FT

Foreword to the third edition

The opening of the transformed Robert Sayle as John Lewis Cambridge in the Grand Arcade in November 2007 marked a new phase in the development of the shop that had opened in St Andrew's Street in 1840. This book, the third edition of the Robert Sayle history, is celebrating the 167 years of trading under the Robert Sayle banner. I am delighted that Olivia Daly, who was assistant editor of the weekly in-house magazine, the Robert Sayle Chronicle, from 1993 to 2000, has undertaken the task of writing the final chapter. We are most grateful to her and to Jenny Josselyn, Registrar 1997-2004, who has co-ordinated the production.

Over many generations the premises of Robert Sayle and the many hundreds of Partners employed have underpinned a brand name and a reputation in Cambridge. Throughout our history we have tested the boundaries of flexibility and ingenuity, which in turn produced a consistently profitable piece of retail space that was the envy of many. The enterprise that saw the business set up in 1840 has been mirrored with contemporary resourcefulness to deliver a modern department store, back on the original site of our first shop.

As we celebrate and appreciate the contemporary landscape of the new John Lewis Cambridge shop, we do so with great pride and a full recognition of the intervening years. We have installed a plaque inside the main entrance commemorating our history, because we wanted to acknowledge publicly the debt we owe to those previous generations of Robert Sayle Partners. Today we remain as dedicated as ever to first-class retailing in the heart of Cambridge. In reading through the book I hope you will be – as I have been – encouraged that so much of what we value today has been the heart of our trading principles throughout this period.

Robert Hallam
Managing Director, John Lewis Cambridge

Foreword to the second edition

We are deeply indebted to Jenifer Gooch for her dedication and commitment in producing this book, which covers a particularly eventful period in the life of Robert Sayle and brings us to the eve of one of the most significant events in our history as we prepare for our temporary relocation to Burleigh Street.

This shop has served us well, generations of Robert Sayle Partners proving that flexibility coupled with ingenuity could overcome the challenges presented by its physical shortcomings to produce sales densities and profitabilities that are the envy of many. But time has moved on and, at long last, we have an opportunity to showcase our merchandise in an up-to-date and more comfortable environment, as deserved by both Partners and customers.

For the next three years, through our sojourn in Burleigh Street, we will again be faced with fitting a gallon into a quart pot, but with the comfort of knowing that we will soon be returning to a new home in St Andrew's Street. There is one thing that we must not leave behind, however, and that is the camaraderie and dedication that has been a feature of this shop for so long. In reading through the following chapters I have been reminded of how much of what we value today is the reward for the hard work of our predecessors, and I hope that we can continue to carry this tradition with us.

Jenny Tomley
Managing Director, 2004

Preface to the 2004 revised edition

The History of Robert Sayle from 1840 to 1969 was written by Louise Sieveking and was first published in 1974. Miss Sieveking was connected with the Partnership from 1922 onwards and was Registrar at Robert Sayle from 1950 to 1960. She died in 1979. At the end of her history she noted that considerable changes took place during the two years after she finished writing in 1969. In fact, change has rarely been absent from Robert Sayle and its pace quickened considerably during the following 35 years.

Now, in 2004, Robert Sayle is set to undergo a major redevelopment as part of 'The Grand Arcade' in the centre of Cambridge. It therefore seems an appropriate time to bring the history up to date from 1969 to 2004 and to record what has happened to the shop in the context of retailing in general, the expansion of the Partnership's department store division, the story of shopping in Cambridge and the continuing success of Robert Sayle itself.

The inspiration for publishing the updated history, and combining it in one volume with Miss Sieveking's, came from Simon Fowler, Managing Director of Robert Sayle from 1995 to January 2001, and Jenny Josselyn, Registrar from 1997 to January 2004. When I retired in 2001 after 22 years as Clerk to the Branch Council, I was pleased to take on the project of researching and writing the history from the point at which Miss Sieveking had left it.

Miss Sieveking's book has been reproduced as Part I, with minor corrections and typographical amendments and the addition of some illustrations. Where she talks about "the present" she is referring to the time when she was compiling her history. All the information pertaining to the history since 1969 is freely accessible in the Gazette of the John Lewis Partnership, the Robert Sayle Chronicle and the proceedings of the Robert Sayle Branch Council. Some information relating to Cambridge city-centre developments was sourced from the archives of the Cambridge Evening News, copies of which can be found in the Central Reference Library.

Jenny Tomley, Managing Director since 2001, and the Robert Sayle Retirement Committee have been responsible for enabling us to bring the project to its conclusion this year. Karen Lord, General Manager, and Jenny Josselyn have helped in its production. Judy Faraday, the John Lewis Partnership Archivist, traced many of the original photographs.

Thanks must also go to all the other Partners who have contributed in many varied ways to this project.

Jenifer Gooch, 2004

Contents

Part I: 1840-1969 by Miss L M Sieveking

Part II: 1969-2004 by Jenifer Gooch

Part III: 2004-2007 by Olivia Daly

A history of Robert Sayle

Part 1
1840-1969

by
Miss L M Sieveking

first published 1974 by
Information Services
John Lewis Partnership

**The view of
Cambridge from
Castle Hill, 1840**

Acknowledgements

This study could not have been written without the help of a great number of people, to whom most sincere thanks are gladly offered for their kindness and patience in answering innumerable questions as well as producing photographs and documents of all descriptions.

The idea of researching into the history of Robert Sayle & Co was initiated by Mr Lewis Smith, then General Manager of the shop. He asked his assistant, Mr E E Greenhalgh (now Director of Trading in the John Lewis Partnership) if he would like to undertake it, but Mr Greenhalgh was transferred to new work soon afterwards and was unable, therefore, to find time for the project. Before leaving Cambridge, however, he got in touch with some members of the Sayle family, and it was through the friendly co-operation of one of these that I was able to make a start when Mr Smith proposed that I should take on the work, the suggestion having been ratified by the Robert Sayle Branch Council.

Commander A R W Sayle RNR, a grandson (and also great-nephew, his parents being first cousins) of Mr Robert Sayle, was so kind as to lend me certain family papers containing details of his ancestry.

The shop is built on land owned by two Cambridge Colleges – Jesus and Emmanuel – and the Archivist of both gave unstinted facilities for examination of documents concerned with the ground, its leases and its history.

Mr B E N Fawcett MA, Head Master of the King's School at Ely, took a great deal of trouble trying to verify the family tradition that Robert Sayle had been a pupil at the School – unfortunately without success, as no records exist for the years in question.

Miss Enid Porter, Curator of the Cambridge Folk Museum, very generously allowed me to see and quote from the diary of Josiah Chater, who lived from 1828 to about 1911 and who kept a very detailed account of current events in Cambridge. Miss Porter is editing the diary for publication.

Through Mr Philip Lloyd, the present manager of the Carpet, Bedding and Furniture Departments at Robert Sayle & Co, I was so fortunate as to make the acquaintance of Mr S G Bailey OBE, FR Econ Soc, who was employed at the shop from 1902 to 1907 as a junior in the Wholesale Department, and was later moved to the firm's subsidiary, Samuel L Pulham in Hills Road, until he resigned in 1909. Mr Bailey lived in the Robert Sayle hostel and he supplied much of the detail about the way of life in those days.

The Managing Director of Messrs Hitchcock, Williams & Co, Mr R H Wurr, most kindly gave me the references existing in his firm's records of the dates when the young Robert Sayle was employed there during the early years of the nineteenth century.

Mr G V M Bainbridge, Managing Director of the Newcastle shop of that name, and Mr John Cawley, General Manager of Caleys in Windsor, were good enough to provide me with much of the material for Chapter 3.

Mr C A Thurley, Senior Librarian in the Central Reference Library at Cambridge, and his assistants with untiring patience carried heavy files of old newspapers and fetched books and maps from the dark recesses behind the Reading Room. Their knowledgeable help was invaluable over

Miss Sieveking

a period of close on three years. I also wish to thank the Librarian at the London Guildhall for furnishing some details concerning Robert Sayle's London office.

For help over the mysteries of heraldry in 'translating' the Robert Sayle trade mark, I am very greatly indebted to Mr C W Scott-Giles, who among other distinctions bears the title of Fitzalan Pursuivant Extra-Ordinary at the College of Arms. He delved into the background of the coat of arms that forms the centre of the trade mark, and together with Miss H Peek, the University Archivist, spent a morning poring over the faded painting that hangs in the General Manager's office in St. Andrew's Street. The results of his investigations are given in Appendix D. The Chinese symbols were transliterated by Mrs L E Jackson MA.

Of private friends to whom I showed the draft for their opinion I would like particularly to remember Lady (DI) Roberts MA and Miss P Woodham Smith MA, both historians to whose helpful encouragement I owe very much. To these I would add Mr Maurice Newbold, who not only read the typescript most carefully but also enlightened me on

some technicalities; and Mr I H Colquhoun, General Editor of the John Lewis Partnership's journalism, who spared the time and trouble in a very busy life to act as critic from the professional standpoint.

Finally, I have to thank most warmly many Robert Sayle Partners: young ones, such as the clerks in Registry, who saved me hours of labour by knowing where to put their hands on current information; and older people, some of them pensioners, who had worked in the business for long years and without whose wonderful memories the story might well have become an arid chronicle of dates and figures. It would be impossible to name all of these; some are referred to in the course of the narrative, and if I mention only three here no lack of gratitude is implied to all the others. These three are: first, Miss Emma Taylor, from whom I learnt much of the background history of the shop, which she knows better than many because her father too was connected with the firm for some 45 years; second, Mrs Ethel Gould (née Beales) who had fortunately preserved the minute books and some photographs of the Victoria House Rowing Club; and third, Mr Basil Carroll, who went to much trouble to make a list of the plays produced by the shop's Dramatic Society, which is published in Appendix B.

L M Sieveking, April 1969

1: Family background

Robert Sayle, who founded the shop bearing his name in Cambridge, was the descendant of a family long established in Yorkshire, which spread southwards to Lincolnshire, Norfolk and Cambridge; ultimately also to the Far East, South Africa, America and the Antipodes.

A very early mention of the name occurs in the thirteenth century, when a small estate called "Le Sailes", situated on rising ground in the West Riding of Yorkshire, about midway between Doncaster and Pontefract, is quoted in local records as being held directly in sub-infeudation from the Lord of Pontefract Castle, and is valued at one-tenth of a knight's fee, which is to say the occupier of the land would be called upon to furnish two to three men-under-arms in case of hostilities. The exact size of the manor is not known, but there was pasturage as well as arable land, and the buildings included a good farm house and cottages for about 20 labourers. This land had almost certainly been cultivated in Roman times, and possibly earlier, being fertile and adjacent to a natural route to the north; it is registered in Domesday Book as a subsidiary of the larger manor of Kirby, later renamed Pontefract by Ilbert de Lacey, to whom William the Conqueror granted the manor and who built the castle to guard the road to the north. The little village of Campsall (Cansale in Domesday) still exists on the same site, now covering 1,776 acres.

The spelling of the family's name varied in early times according to the taste or 'ear' of the writer. When very few people were literate, anyone like a lawyer's clerk who had to write a name could only do it phonetically, as he thought his client pronounced it. In the case of the Sayle family, the name, like many of our surnames, may well be derived from that of the land occupied by them, and has been found as Saile, Sailes, Sayly, Salys, Sayll, Sale, Salle, Sayles, Sayle and there may have been other variants.

From early times the Sayles were recorded as active in political, religious, business and charitable affairs. According to Yorkshire records, Robert del Sayles, for example, was personally responsible in 1293 for ensuring that two representatives – the first members for the borough of Pontefract – attended the Parliament of that year. In 1471/72 a Thomas Sayle is known to have been a monk at the important Benedictine Abbey of St Mary in York: a friend bequeathed to him his "best psalter... to pray for [his] soul". In the sixteenth century, after the reformation, another Thomas and his wife Margaret were fined heavily for refusing to attend service in the new reformed Church, but adhering to the old ritual and going to Mass. Later again, a Captain Sayle is mentioned in connection with the first siege of Pontefract Castle in 1643 during the Civil War, on the Royalist side, for the castle was garrisoned for the king and did not fall to Cromwell's men until 1644. The castle was eventually destroyed by the Roundheads after the execution of the king, though it had in the interim been retaken by the Royalists.

Then, in 1672, after the Restoration, another Thomas Sayle, by occupation a tallow-chandler, gave £100 – a very handsome present in days when 20 pence would buy a week's board – towards the rebuilding of St Nicholas Hospital in Pontefract. He died the following year and left a legacy to the hospital of another £100 of his evidently considerable fortune. One reason, surely, for his interest in this hospice was that it had been connected with Pontefract and Campsall itself from very early times. It was already in existence in the days of William Rufus, and in 1139/40 Ilbert de Lacey II, a grandson of the first lord of Pontefract Castle, built the Church of St Clement within the castle precincts, in order that prayers might be said there for the souls of the King and all the royal family, past, present and to come, and to ensure religious teaching and the administration of the sacrament to "all within the Park at Pontefract and the Bedehouse called St Nicholas Hospital Bulhouse". The manor of Campsall was granted at the time as part of the dower of St Clement's Church.

One of the heirs of the above Thomas Sayle, a Mr Hastings (or Hastens) Sayle, was Mayor of Pontefract in 1688 and on four occasions later; and a relative, still another Thomas Sayle, described in a family document as a "cordwinder" (cordwainer?), was twice mayor while his cousin Hastings was out of office – unseated because it was alleged he acted too much on his own initiative, without consulting the other aldermen.

Naturally, an occasional reprobate appears in the family chronicle, such as another mid-seventeenth century Thomas (not the cordwinder), who lost two estates through gambling. When betting at a race meeting, it is told, he on one occasion lost even the horse he was riding, and had to walk home carrying the saddle on his own back. However, his fortunes were later restored to a more satisfactory level by a prudent marriage and he died a popular and respected old gentleman of 85. This Thomas was great-great-great-grandfather to Robert Sayle of Cambridge.

The strong family characteristic persisted. In the early nineteenth century John Sayle, who lived at Southery in Norfolk, the father of Robert Sayle of Cambridge, besides being churchwarden for over 20 years at Southery, subscribed very generously to the building of a new church in the village when the old one had fallen into hopeless disrepair, as is witnessed by a memorial tablet on the north wall of the present chancel. Then too, he became patron of the living of St Mary at Wiggenhall near Lynn, in Norfolk, which he bought when his younger daughter, Elizabeth Susan, married the Rector of that parish. John Sayle was also a member of the Commission set up in 1844/45 for reclaiming the Bedford fens.

So the Thomases, Johns and Roberts (there was always at least one Robert in every generation among the branches of the family) followed one another through the centuries – farmers, traders, clerics, landowners, lawyers, soldiers, family men – taking a full part in the life of their day. And the nineteenth-century Robert Sayle in Cambridge displayed much of the energy and enterprise, the feeling for social responsibility and the generosity that had distinguished his forebears, becoming a notable figure in the city of his adoption, with interests that ranged widely over religious and social as well as business affairs; nor did he forget the ancestral link with the soil for, over a good many years of his life, he farmed a piece of land near the Cambridge railway station which included the site now occupied by the block of flats known as Highsett. This land, covering just over five and a quarter acres, was leased to him from Michaelmas 1858 by Jesus College at £20 a year.

2: Robert Sayle – childhood & youth

Robert Sayle was born on 22nd February 1816 at Southery in Norfolk, the eldest son of John Sayle, described as landowner and farmer, and his wife Susan, née Clark. Eight children, six sons and two daughters, were born of the marriage.

This branch of the Sayles had been settled in Southery since about 1750, when John Sayle's grandfather moved there from West Deeping, in Lincolnshire, where earlier members of the family are known, from entries in the parish registers, to have lived and died for more than 100 years previously.

John Sayle farmed about 600 acres and, in the early years of the nineteenth century, added another 200; between 1838 and 1839 he also built himself a mansion on the estate, naming it Field House.

Other members of the family were domiciled in or near Ely at this time, and one of the eighteenth-century Sayles – Great Uncle Walter to young Robert – had been in business in London, where some of his numerous descendants still lived. Perhaps because of these connections Robert was sent to school in Ely – the King's School, it is thought, though this cannot now be verified, as school records of this date are not available – and, a few years later, he went on to London. Exactly what his movements were during the next years is, however, not known. It was intended at one time that he should become a solicitor. In fact, the Articles are believed to have been already drawn up, when he changed his mind and decided to go into business. It is therefore presumed that he was apprenticed, but there is no record to say where, though the writer of an article in The Cambridge Independent Newspaper of 13th October 1883 states

that "he gained considerable experience in some of the best retail houses".

The verifiable story begins again on 4th May 1838, when he was engaged by the well-known firm of Hitchcock, Williams & Co, who carried on their wholesale and retail business in drapery, haberdashery, etc, in St Paul's Churchyard, London, EC, where they remained until the second World War, when destruction by enemy action obliged them to move to other premises. He stayed with this firm, established in what was at that time the centre of the drapery trade, until 5th February 1840, just before his 24th birthday, having by then gained a pretty general experience in most sections of the business. Meanwhile, his father was making plans to set him up in business of his own in Cambridge.

It happened that a small drapery shop, owned by John Cooch at Victoria House, St Andrew's Street, came onto the market at about this time, and it was here that young Mr Sayle's new venture began. According to extant electoral rolls, it does not appear that Cooch had been in the drapery trade for longer than a year or two, but he had occupied the site as an ironmonger since at least 1834. He evidently changed over to drapery between 1837 and 1839, and no doubt the building was named Victoria House in honour of the young queen's accession in 1837. Cooch's closing-down sale was lavishly advertised on 15th and 22nd January 1840 in the local weekly newspaper, The Cambridge Advertiser and Free Press. Under blazing headlines, John Cooch urged intending purchasers to come early, so as to be sure of obtaining the REAL BARGAINS, which were such as could seldom occur, reminded customers of the limited time in which the opportunity would be available, and drew attention to the IMMENSE SACRIFICES being made by reductions that brought the price of goods down to "twenty per cent below prime cost". It is interesting to note, by the way, that during this sale the shop was open for business from 10am to 6pm only: normally hours would have been from 8am till 8 or 9pm.

A couple of months later, in the issues of 11th and 18th March 1840, an equally lavish advertisement appeared in the paper, occupying a double column of about 40 lines (which would at the time have cost not more than £2), to announce that Robert Sayle was taking over the premises which would be open for business on Saturday 21st March (see panel below). This advertisement, with minor adjustments, was repeated on 25th March, a few days after the opening of the new shop.

Cooch's had sold much the same sort of merchandise as Robert Sayle now planned to offer, except that the latter did not mention furs in his owner's trade. Robert Sayle must, however, have begun to stock them almost immediately, for an entry dated 1840 in the ledger of George Smith & Sons Ltd, furriers in Watling Street, EC – the oldest known reference to Robert Sayle's business purchases – states that they were willing to trust him for £500 or £600; it being known that his

---

Victoria House

St Andrew's Street, Cambridge

ROBERT SAYLE

begs to inform the inhabitants of Cambridge and its vicinity that he has taken the premises lately occupied by Mr John Cooch, which having undergone considerable alterations so as to afford increased accommodation, he intends re-opening on Saturday, 21st instant, with a new well-selected stock of:-

LINEN DRAPERY

SILK MERCERY, HOSIERY, HABERDASHERY

STRAW BONNETS ETC. ETC.

In respectfully soliciting the patronage of the Nobility, Gentry and Inhabitants of the Town, County and University of Cambridge, R.S. begs to assure them that, being thoroughly acquainted with the various descriptions of goods connected with his business, he will be enabled to select the best fabrics; and intends purchasing such as he can with confidence recommend, his object being to ensure the repetition of such favours as may be conferred upon him. In IRISH LINENS, SHEETINGS, etc., also COTTON HOSIERY, he will invariably avoid those fine showy makes so calculated to deceive the inexperienced, selecting only the most sterling fabrics.

The stock of SHAWLS, MOUSSELINE-DE-LAINES, and FANCY GOODS, RIBBONS, HANDKERCHIEFS etc., will be choice and select, comprising every novelty of the season.

R.S. merely adds, that he intends conducting his business upon the principle so generally adopted and approved, that of selling entirely for READY MONEY – affixing the smallest profit to each article; and he trusts that by attention and perseverance he shall receive that encouragement which it will be the height of his ambition to merit.

father had lately given him £500 and that "his friends are very respectable".

According to a contemporary advertisement in the same Cambridge Advertiser and Free Press by a furrier in Bridge Street, a fur department demanded a considerable amount of knowledge and discrimination, as well as a good deal of space, including as it did "capes, shawls, muffs, boas, gents' boas, collars, fur travelling gloves, etc.", which were procured from "the Leipsic and other Continental Fairs". Evidently, then as now, the fact that goods came from foreign parts had a snob value.

It will be noted that Sayle's advertisement lays emphasis on the principle of "small profits, quick returns", on quality and assortment and on his intention to trade for ready money and, by implication, at the marked prices. This last was a point worth mentioning, for it was not long since all prices had been open to bargaining. And in London – where Robert Sayle had learnt the business – there had been a long, sad history of unpaid bills and demands for unreasonably extended credit, which had led to distress and even bankruptcy for many shopkeepers. A further reason why the no-bargaining system took firm root was the introduction of plate glass shop windows. These were still not matter-of-course outside London when Robert Sayle established his business. Previously shop windows had been simply intended to admit light to the premises, not to help trade by the display of goods. The new windows gave passers-by a chance to see what lay behind this glass. Enterprising traders were not slow to take the opportunity to display their wares temptingly; and the next step would be to mark the prices, which obviously had to be definitely as shown if the customer was to feel any confidence in the honesty of the shopkeeper's professed maxims.

Might one guess that the more exclusive shops probably looked upon the idea of advertising their prices so openly as rather vulgar and liable to offend some of their customers, who might not wish it to be known how much (or how little) they had paid for things?

3: Shopkeeping

Retail trade, as we know it, is of recent origin. It has developed from market stalls and pedlars and fairs and tiny family businesses. Until nearly the end of the eighteenth century the great majority of the population of England – which was under nine million in 1801 – lived in country districts and purchasing power was small. Durable goods, such as furniture, were made by individual craftsmen and sold directly to customers. Clothes were mostly made at home, sometimes still of cloth spun and woven by the women of the family, as also was much of the household linen. Food was home-grown or bought at neighbouring markets. Variety of merchandise might be introduced by travelling chapmen but the great excitement of the year was probably the annual fair. Here would be found not only new-fashioned goods but also fresh ideas of all descriptions; different men and women to talk to; tales – sometimes perhaps true, always entertaining – from travellers who had been farther afield; fierce but enjoyable bargaining; as well as all the fun of the fair. Surely fairs must have provided those who visited them with subjects of conversation lasting from one year to the next, quite apart from the merchandise which was sold. Fairs were also a source of revenue to the king. He sold the licence to hold a fair to some important person or institution in the neighbourhood, who in turn let sites for the stalls and could order local shops to close while the fair was in progress.

Cambridge was the marketing centre for the shire and had no less than four fairs a year, one of which – Stourbridge, often pronounced and written Sturbitch – was considered to be not only the largest but also the most famous in all England up to the sixteenth and seventeenth centuries. It was licensed to the Leper Hospital by King John in the early part of the thirteenth century and was abolished only in 1934. The Chapel of the Leper Hospital still stands on the old fair ground.

There were virtually no wholesalers as such, though by the early nineteenth century, as readers of such books as Mrs Gaskell's 'Cranford' and Jane Austen's 'Emma' will remember, country shopkeepers – especially those in the fashion trades – might go up to London every now and then, or to one of the other large towns, to buy novelties from richer and more up-to-date warehousemen. In fact the twentieth century was well started before wholesale and retail businesses were sharply

differentiated. Robert Sayle's did a substantial wholesale turnover until the department was closed down in the middle of 1937.

Back in the earlier days, apart from open-air stalls and one-man or occasionally larger specialised businesses, there might be – particularly in a town like London or Manchester – a permanent assembly of separately-owned booths, selling a variety of goods under a shelter, rather like a modern market-hall, and known as a bazaar. It has been suggested that variety chain-stores are the modern equivalents. On the other hand, one might say that bazaars were the forerunners of today's department stores, since there was no question of self-service in them. The assertion has sometimes been made that the first actual department store was the Bon Marché, in Paris, which was opened as a small drapery shop in the early years of the nineteenth century but did not become a department store, professing to enable a woman to buy everything she needed under one roof, until 1852 or thereabouts. In fact, the idea was certainly being developed in England at least as early as in France, and indeed earlier in some cases. Bainbridge of Newcastle, for instance, founded by Emerson Muscamp Bainbridge as a small piece-goods and haberdashery shop in 1838, and now a branch of the John Lewis Partnership, was rapidly extended, and by 1849 its sales were being analysed departmentally, at which date there were separate departments for "Furs, French Fancy, Shawls, Cloaks, Fancy Dress Materials, Mercery, Haberdashery, Trimmings, Hosiery, Gloves, Prints, Drapery, Ribbons, Bonnets, Laces, Stuffs, Linens, Flannels,

Furnishing and Carpets". Records for all these still exist in the firm's archives.

Another of the present members of the John Lewis Partnership can also claim to have been early in the field of multi-departmental trading: Caleys of Windsor. Founded by a woman, Mrs M Caley, in the very early 1800s, its records show that the business moved successively up the hill towards the castle from Thames Street to Castle Street (1813) and, by 1824, to the charming house it now occupies in the High Street opposite the castle gate. Mrs Caley was an enterprising and imaginative business woman. She advertised her new season's stocks in the local newspapers every spring and autumn and was the first to stage fashion displays in Windsor. The earliest known account of one such show says that her customers were offered, on a Thursday in May 1820, the preview of a "fashionable Assortment of Millinery, Dresses, etc., including a variety of Leghorn and Straw Bonnets". The mannequins were probably lay figures, for living models were a later development. By the same year, Mrs Caley held the Royal Warrant as "Milliner and Dressmaker to Her Majesty and Their Royal Highnesses The Princesses and the Duchess of Gloucester". The warrant was granted by Queen Charlotte, the wife of George III, and it has been renewed by every one of our queens since then, excepting George IV's Queen Caroline.

As time went on, John Caley, her son, and later a second son too, came into the business and new departments were added: furs, feathers, artificial flowers, baby linen and corsets in the 30s; silks, velvets, laces and kid gloves from France a few years later. And there were, of

course, workrooms to copy the models shown in the fashion displays and no doubt to provide original creations. By 1846 the Windsor street directory gives "J. Caley, Silk Mercer and Laceman etc.", and "Mrs Caley, Milliner and Dressmaker to Her Majesty". With these, and the other sections mentioned above, the shop has a real claim to have been a department store before 1850.

The essential difference in retailing habits came, of course, with the industrial revolution, when the introduction of machinery speeded up manufacture and made it possible to standardise quality, while the invention of the steam engine was to make distribution easier both inland and overseas. Actually, owing to stubborn resistance, from 1825 to 1842, by both the Cambridge Corporation and the Cam Conservators, who feared for the age-old river-borne trade from King's Lynn to Cambridge, the railway did not come to Cambridge until 1845, when the main Great Eastern Line from London to Norwich was opened. The first train came through Cambridge on 24th July 1845 and most shops were closed that afternoon, so that, according to a contemporary diary, crowds were at the station to watch the 6.30 train leave for London. It was as a result of university pressure that the station was sited over a mile from the centre of the town. Other lines – the Great Northern, the Midland and the London and North Eastern – were opened in 1847, 1851 and 1862 respectively, so that by the mid-1800s Cambridge was linked with most of the surrounding country.

Robert Sayle, in 1840, came very near to the start of this new and exciting era. Owing largely to improvements in hygiene and methods of agriculture, there had been, since the beginning of the century, a remarkable growth of population. During the 40 years to date it had increased by some 80 per cent overall in England, and Cambridge's population at the nearest census (1841) was over 22,000. In 1801 it had been 10,087, so had more than doubled. With standards of living rising as a result of fresh opportunities of work, there seemed a good reason to expect that trade would expand proportionately.

This is not to say that all was plain sailing, though perhaps a university town might not experience the difficulties as acutely as places in the industrialised midlands and north. The agricultural depression which followed on the Napoleonic wars was bound to affect the rural districts around Cambridge and it lasted for about 20 years after 1815. Then came the so-called Chartist troubles in industry, which were at their worst during a trade depression in 1837/38 and smouldered to a greater or lesser degree during the next 10 or 12 years. The increase in employment during the mid-40s, due to the construction of the railways, improved trade again but trouble flared up once more in 1848, when business at home flagged and revolutions on the continent cut off much of the overseas exchange of goods. After this date, however, things improved and the country moved into a period of relative prosperity.

Purely as a side issue, it is perhaps interesting to note the distribution of shops in the fashion trade in Cambridge in 1840/41, as given in the local street directory (at which date, incidentally, 133 Beer Shops are listed in the town!).

Robert Sayle, "Linen Draper and Silk Mercer", had 18 competitors in his own line, including Elizabeth Eaden in Market Street, and there were in addition five concerns described as "Linen Drapers and Tea Dealers – Travelling", all of whom occupied premises in New Square. Of "Milliners and Dressmakers" there were 14, all women; while of men's tailors there were 56. "Boot and Shoe Makers" numbered 52 men, besides one woman who kept a "Shoe Warehouse", which meant that she stocked slippers to sell but did not manufacture them. Most boots and shoes were made to measure at the time and customers who had the money, or the credit, might order half a dozen or more pairs at once. Plenty of foot-gear must have been necessary, for roads were rough and public transport still almost non-existent, apart from carriers and stage coaches, which took parcels and passengers from Cambridge to London in horse-drawn vehicles every day except Sundays and once or twice a week to other towns, delivering to villages on the way as required. A charge was made for most deliveries; 'Carrying' was a separate trade and very few businesses had their own delivery vans then, even for deliveries inside the town, though sometimes an errand boy might be despatched with a package on a hand cart. The last of the regular coaches between Cambridge and London ran in October 1845, three months after the railway station had been opened in Cambridge. "We are glad to record", notes 'The Cambridge Chronicle' for the week ending 1st November 1845, "that the victor has been at least merciful, for Wilkins, the civil driver of the [coach] has been provided for by a berth upon the rail". A year or two later another stage coach started in opposition to the railway and ran occasionally for a time but the mechanical monster remained finally victorious.

The Paris Bon Marché, may, perhaps, fairly claim to have been a pioneer in one aspect of shop service – it was among the very first to give its customers the advantages of free delivery and of allowing goods to be taken on approval or exchanged.

4: The site

Until less than 200 years ago there were within the town of Cambridge a good many private houses surrounded by large gardens, even along the two main north-south thoroughfares, one of which is now St Andrew's Street/Regent Street. This road is, in fact, a section of an old Roman way, the Via Devana, which joins the Ermine Street at Huntingdon; it still to all intents and purposes follows in a straight line from the Huntingdon Road along Castle Street, Bridge Street and through the town to Hills Road, leading across the Gog Magog Hills and on to Colchester. From the Middle Ages to the mid-nineteenth century this was not, however, the most important of the town's streets. The High Street was the road branching off it at St John's College and leading to Trumpington Road. It lost its importance when the railway station was opened, and Regent Street again became the main thoroughfare. As time went on, popular usage identified parts of the roads with the nearest college or other large building, hence the changes of name that occur every 100 yards or so inside the town. But in the process of giving names to streets there seems to have been a good deal of confusion. Panton Street, for instance, was at a trial

in November 1857 referred to by four or five appellations, and the judge ordered that the surveyor should be instructed to put up name plates for all roads without further delay!

Much of the land alongside the roads was college property, sometimes having been bestowed centuries earlier by legacy or donation from pious persons to the religious institutions to which some of the colleges were the successors; in other cases colleges had bought the land themselves and from letting or farming it derived a part of their income, as they still do.

Robert Sayle's present-day premises are built on land owned by two colleges – Jesus and Emmanuel – and anyone looking at the shop from the opposite side of the road can easily see where the join comes. The ground belonging to Emmanuel is the smaller part – No 12 St Andrew's Street, next door to the Post Office. Jesus College owns the rest – that is, Nos 13-17. In both cases the property now extends to St Tibb's Row behind the shop. St Tibb's Row itself has a curious history. In mediaeval days Cambridge was in a sense a double town, inner and outer. The inner town was virtually a long narrow island, the river Cam forming part of the periphery and the King's Ditch –

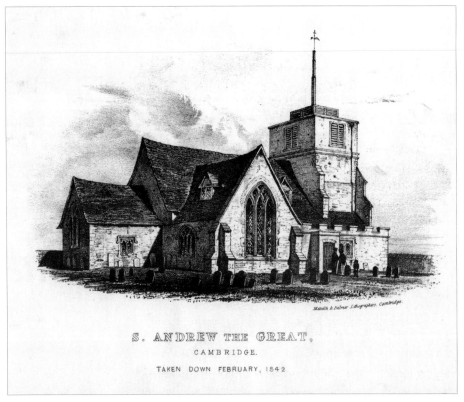

S. ANDREW THE GREAT,
CAMBRIDGE.
TAKEN DOWN FEBRUARY, 1842

The church of St Andrew the Great, Cambridge, which was demolished in 1842

an artificial watercourse – completing the circuit, where other towns might have been enclosed by walls and a moat. There were at that time two main entrances to the town across the ditch – the Barnwell Gate, where now Petty Cury joins St Andrew's Street, and the Trumpington Gate near the top of Mill Lane and St Botolph's Church. Beyond these barriers lay the outer town but it contained a number of even the oldest colleges such as Jesus and Peterhouse. As early as the thirteenth century four suburbs are mentioned: one on the farther side of each of the two gates, one across the river at Newnham, and – oldest of all – Castle End, where a settlement had existed since Roman times, and probably earlier.

It is thought that the King's Ditch was originally planned for defence against marauding 'islanders' from Ely, when it was dug at some time before the year 1200, but it soon developed into a sort of customs barrier, with the gates as toll bars, until they were demolished during the fourteenth century. For hundreds of years it remained an open trench

throughout its length, except for an occasional footbridge where it crossed a main road. The only permanently-built bridges inside the town were the so-called Small Bridge across the Silver Street weir and the Great Bridge at the bottom of Castle Street. The ditch was at least 10 foot wide, in parts as much as 15, and of about the same depth. According to old maps, its course branched out from the river at the lower end of Mill Lane, followed Mill Lane, cut across Trumpington Street, went up what is now Pembroke Street, turned in by St Andrew's Hill, running behind St Andrew's Church to the corner of Petty Cury, thence via the top of Hobson Street, through part of what now forms the grounds of Sidney Sussex College and along Park Street, to rejoin the river opposite the back of Magdalene College, roughly where the electricity works now stand. Modern street names have been used here for the sake of clarity but much of the ditch was originally cut through open country. As time went on, parts of the ditch were culverted and houses were built over it. The last sections to be covered in were those along St Tibb's Row and Park Street, after the beginning of the nineteenth century.

Actually, though believed to have been originally intended for security purposes, the ditch came to be used primarily as the main town sewer and often gave rise to complaints about its condition, especially when, as sometimes happened, it was dry and silted up in parts. It was popularly known as the Black Ditch, for no doubt obvious reasons! And this name was still used within living memory, at least as applied to St Tibb's Row, which is marked on nineteenth century maps as recently as 1874, "late Black Ditch". Older inhabitants recall that their parents used this designation.

How then, it may be asked, did St Tibb come into the story? The clue lies in Falcon Yard, which leads off St Tibb's Row and was formerly part of the site of a large and well-reputed inn called The Falcon. St Tibb, it appears, is a contraction of the name of the seventh century Saint Tibba (this name itself, some say, a contraction of Tabitha), who is buried in Peterborough and who was the patron saint of falconers; her feast falls on 6th March. When it came to renaming this part of the old ditch in the nineteenth century, what choice could have been more felicitous?

To return to St Andrew's Street: No 12 is built on part of an estate bought in 1607 by Emmanuel College from its owner, Michael Wolfe, for £130 "in lawful money" (that is, coins which had not been devalued by clipping the edges). The whole property then consisted of a capital house (Wolfe House) with gardens and outbuildings, and it was leased complete for a good many generations after the purchase. With changing social conditions, however, the place was eventually divided up and let for the erection of smaller dwelling houses, business premises etc, though in fact this did not take place until towards the end of the eighteenth century, not much more than 50 years before Robert Sayle started his shop on the site. Almost the last

tenant of Wolfe House was the Reverend Dr John Newcome, Master of St John's College, who signed a 40 year lease from 1759. He did not, however, live to complete the tenancy and it was only a few years after his death that the estate was broken up for other development.

Nos 13 to 17 St Andrew's Street had a rather different history. Towards the end of the thirteenth century the original piece of land – one acre in extent and with already some buildings on it – was given to the Cambridge nunnery of St Radegund, to be used for the benefit of that institution. Two hundred years later, as a result of outbreaks of the plague among other causes, the number of nuns had dwindled until only two remained. The Bishop of Ely, Dr Alcock, as diocesan overlord of Cambridge, obtained permission from the king to house the nuns elsewhere and to suppress the nunnery; he appropriated the lands and buildings and in 1497 founded Jesus College, using the nunnery premises. The full name of the college is to this day "The College of the Blessed Virgin Mary Saint John the Evangelist and the Glorious Virgin Saint Radegund, commonly called Jesus College". The rest of the lands, including what now covers Nos 12 to 17 St Andrew's Street, continued to be used for the support of the new college.

Years went on, and the richer people who had lived on sizeable estates inside Cambridge preferred to move further out, leaving the college landowners to let their properties to the best advantage in smaller holdings – which explains the jigsaw effect that still obtains in very many areas off the main roads. This is the background to Robert Sayle's association with the two colleges.

5: Premises and leases

In 1840, when Robert Sayle took his first lease from Emmanuel College, he did not occupy the whole of what is now included in 12 St Andrew's Street. His part went back only to about the level of the present despatch room, say 100 feet. The rest of the land and its buildings were let to other people – Mr Pink, who kept a toyshop, for instance, Joshua Harper, and later his wife, described as staymakers, and so on. It was not, in fact, until a number of years after Mr Sayle's death that the whole site came into the business. During his later lifetime, in 1873/74, the last 30 or 40 feet at the St Tibb's end were occupied by Thoday's timber yard, saw-pit and stables. A small wicket gate, opening onto St Tibb's Row, gave entry to the back premises, though this gate was actually on Jesus College land.

In the early days of Queen Victoria's reign and up to 1858 it was unusual to make a lease for longer than 40 years. Ground rent was low: for the first few years of Robert Sayle's occupancy it was between two and three pounds on the Emmanuel College land, and within his life-time rose to only about £13 a year. It was payable in six-monthly instalments, and the "Bursar of the College for the time being", as the agreement has it, was rewarded with an extra one shilling each time "for writing the acquittances". Later this was raised to two shillings.

In addition to the ground rent, a so-called 'fine' was imposed with each fresh lease. This fine was not, of course, a fine in the sense of retribution for wrong-doing but was in the nature of a premium, and was reckoned at 3 to 4 per cent annual interest on the amount of the lease's value, calculated for the length of the tenancy. During Mr Sayle's lifetime, also, the fine on the Jesus College site rose from £210 to £860, owing to changes in the value of land as well as, in this case, an increase in the area rented. Payment of the fine was, incidentally, more or less a guarantee that the lease would be renewable at the appropriate date, if required.

Although made for 40 years as a rule, it was an understood thing that leases would normally be reviewed every 14 years. During the period tenants were sometimes able, with the permission of the landlords, to sublet parts of their premises, as indeed Robert Sayle did on various occasions when he acquired the tenancy of sites that were not needed for his shop. During the early period of his tenancy the street numbers were changed. What is now 12 St Andrew's Street was originally part of No 6 when numbering was first introduced. Probably the whole of the Wolfe House estate was No 6 at that time. Early plans of the site show the land occupied by each tenant; what buildings were on it were given only as they affect the ground space. Any upper storey or storeys are, therefore, largely a matter for conjecture, except when the main features are outlined in a lease. As far as can be gathered, Robert Sayle's premises in 1840 consisted of a ground floor which contained the shop, a small yard and some outbuildings at the back, a basement used as a 'warehouse' or stockroom, and an upper storey with living quarters; most likely, too, some attics.

From contemporary street directories it seems clear that in those early days Robert Sayle lived over the shop, as most traders did; and he probably also housed some, at any rate, of his employees. At that time they would all have been men; women were not to any extent engaged as salespeople until the late 70s or 80s. Even in the five years 1874-78, 57 per cent of new engagements for the selling staff at Robert Sayle were men; 10 years later only 42 per cent, and the proportion grew less as time went on. Of arrangements in 1840 for meals and for keeping the living quarters clean nothing is known. The assistants themselves were expected to keep the shop and stock tidy.

Expansion onto the Jesus College site occurred at intervals, when suitable leases were available and when Robert Sayle needed more space. The first extension was effected in 1851, when he took on No 13. He was then dealing as "draper, silk mercer and general warehouseman". By 1865 the premises had spread to include Nos 14 and 15, and carpets had been added to the stock-in-trade. The next extension did not take place until 1874, when No 16 was taken over; an Undertaker's Department had been opened a year earlier. At this time, the average weekly cash takings in the shop were seldom less than £1,200. The last extension, to No 17, occurred in 1888, several years after Mr Sayle's death, when the business had become Robert Sayle & Co. The land being let on building leases, no alterations or rebuilding might be undertaken without prior consent of the landlords. From time to time, too, it

was stipulated that a given amount of money should be spent on repairs or improvements to existing buildings within a specified period. Nowadays a lease generally provides that the leases shall either wholly or in some part carry out repairs or other work but it does not as a rule specify the sums to be spent.

Conditions of tenancy also naturally included insistence upon insurance – especially against fire, which appears to have been a really serious hazard in Cambridge at the time – and the making of proper arrangements for general maintenance. The Emmanuel College lease of 1867, for instance, prescribed that all wood and iron work on the inside of the buildings should be painted afresh every seven years, and on the outside every four years, with "oil paint in proper and suitable colours". To cover possible damage to the show windows and other glass fixtures, the Cambridge Plate Glass Mutual Insurance Society was founded on 25th March 1851; Robert Sayle became a founder member of the society.

Furthermore, very definite engagements had to be entered into about the kinds of trade that might – and more especially might not – be carried on upon the premises. The Jesus College lease of 1874, for example, contains the following words:-

"The Lessee or any under Lessee or under Tenant . . . shall not erect or use nor suffer to be erected or used upon all or any part of the hereby demised premises any Soap Manufactory Tallow Chandlery Distillery Sugar Bakery Slaughter House Common Brew House Malt House Dye House Furnace Forge Cooks Shop Oil Shop Butchers Shop Farriers Shop Blacksmiths Shop Curriers Shop Pewterers Shop Braziers Shop Beer Shop Beer House or Tobacco Pipe Manufactory nor suffer any Inn or Public house to be kept thereon nor harbour lodge or permit to dwell therein any lewd or disorderly person or persons nor keep thereupon any hogs boars sows pigs or offensive Beasts Cattle or Animals nor suffer to be done thereupon anything which shall or maybe or grow to the annoyance grievance disturbance or damage of the Lessors or their Lessee or Lessees or Tenant or Tenants in the neighbourhood . . ."

**St Andrew's
Street, 1870.
Robert Sayle
is beyond the
first lamp post
on the right**

original little shop at No 12 St Andrew's Street; but, beginning in 1876, Nos 13 to 15, Jesus College property, were entirely rebuilt, to give a whole new front of four storeys and cellarage – the latter being arranged as a millinery showroom and workrooms. Other showrooms were on the ground and first floors. The upper floors contained bedrooms for assistants.

The college itemised very fully all the required alterations, which included not only the exterior stonework but also the types of doors and windows, some dormer windows for the attics, the locks, keys, bolts and bars, grates, chimney pieces, shelves, pipes, water closets, and other details, no matter how small. The ground floor and first floor were used for showrooms, with two spiral staircases connecting them. Fireplaces with marble mantelpieces chosen by Mr Sayle himself adorned these showrooms, and new stoves were installed in various parts of the building. New kitchens and stables brought the total cost up to about £3,500. Stables were now particularly important since the Undertaker's Department had been opened in 1873, with a hearse, mourning coach or coaches and fine black horses, the successors to which were famous in the town up to the time of the first World War, when they were commandeered for officers' chargers and never replaced.

A similar lease from Emmanuel College in 1885 demands that no "noisy noxious or noisome or offensive trade" shall be engaged in upon the premises. (Commas were seldom used in legal documents.)

Internal alterations, in addition to the prescribed redecoration, must have been carried out at fairly frequent intervals, as changes in trade required. Major structural alterations were undertaken only once in Mr Sayle's life-time, during the late 1870s and early 1880s. It was said that he had resolved never to alter or pull down what had been his

6: Public and private life

For the first years of his business life Robert Sayle, as has been said, lived over the shop. His parents were living at that time, and his father was evidently generous to him in the matter of money, so that he was spared that particular anxiety. He did not marry until August 1849, when he was 33 years old. His wife, Priscilla Caroline, was the daughter of Thomas Ginger, of Eddlesborough in Buckinghamshire. She was about eight years younger than Robert Sayle and outlived him by over 20 years. She died in May 1904, just a week before her 80th birthday. Within the first 15 years of their marriage 10 children were born to the couple, all of whom lived to grow up, except one little girl who died when she was only three years old.

As the family increased, accommodation over the shop naturally became too cramped and in about 1860 – six of the seven children by then born being alive – Robert Sayle took over from Jesus College at £42 per annum, the lease of the land on which stood Nos 10 and 11 St Andrew's Street. He had hoped for a 99-year lease, but the college would only grant one for 40 years. He bought the buildings and sub-let No 11, but No 10, which had at one time been his predecessor John Cooch's private house, he to a great extent reconstructed for occupation by himself and his family. The builders, a firm named Adcock, evidently made a good job of it; when

he sold the house a few years later to Jesus College for £2,500, their surveyors referred to it as "a good sound substantial building" and noted that it could be "easily converted to shop use". Here the family lived for eight or nine years, until they decided to move out of town, which may well have been partly on account of the very poor standard of public hygiene in Cambridge at that time.

No doubt, also, Robert Sayle felt that he and his family needed a permanent place of their own; his parents had died at Southery in 1856 within a few months of each other and the estate in Norfolk had gone to two of the younger sons, after suitable monetary settlement with other members of the family. Robert Sayle, for obvious reasons, wanted to remain within easy reach of his business. He bought a plot of land in Trumpington and built a large family residence which he named Leighton House, to which they moved in 1866 or 1869. He himself came to Cambridge every day in his carriage, which he stabled behind the

25

shop during business hours. (Nowadays Leighton House is occupied by the Preparatory Department of the Perse School for Boys.) At about the same time that he was moving to Trumpington, he had a warehouse built, on Jesus College land facing onto St Tibb's Row, with workrooms above it, and also more commodious new stables and a coach house, "with appurtenances". The shop, which by now extended to Nos 13 and 14 St Andrew's Street, was described by a contemporary local resident as having a "dashing" plate glass front and a "gateway entrance".

Robert Sayle was determined that his children should be well-educated. The girls were brought up at home, as was usual in those days; all five boys were sent to public schools and three of them went on to university. Two were at Cambridge: Arthur Willis, the eldest, who graduated in mathematics in 1876, and Robert Henry, who took a law degree in 1875, later becoming a solicitor. The youngest, Charles Edward, went to New College, Oxford, to read history, returning to Cambridge subsequently for post-graduate study. Later on he became a librarian at the University Library and,

among other work, published a catalogue in four volumes, running to nearly 2,000 pages, of early English printed documents held in the Library. He also wrote a book called 'The Art of Dining'. He is referred to in the Victorian County History of Cambridgeshire as "one of the leading members of the (library) staff". Another son, Martin Wellesley, emigrated to America in the late 1880s. The fifth son, George Moore, went into trade, and after his father's death had for a time an interest in the wholesale end of the business; it seems probable, indeed, that he worked in it before his father died but his name does not appear in this connection until afterwards. Both he and his brother Martin Wellesley drew salaries from the shop from January to August 1884.

Despite the cares of a large family and despite the expansion of trade, Robert Sayle did not find in all this a sufficient outlet for his energies. He took an active part in what was going on in the town, not only as regards civic affairs, but also in religious and educational matters. In many of his ideas he was well in advance of his time. He was a man of liberal religious tolerance. Though himself an Anglican, he felt strong interest in and sympathy for other denominations, in particular the Wesleyans. The members of this community had until very recently suffered under quite serious social disadvantages and Mr Sayle took a good deal of trouble to help in overcoming them. He not only subscribed generously to various of their projects but also lent money, free of interest, to further their religious and educational aims. He was, for instance, an intermediary in obtaining the site for the first Wesleyan Chapel in Hobson Street, which was opened in 1849, and in 1865 he helped the Methodist Conference to acquire a suitable piece of land for the building of a large chapel in Hills Road.

In the late 60s, too, he was asked by the Conference if he would be willing to give up the tenancy of his farm in Hills Road and persuade the owners of the land – Jesus College – to sell the property as a site for the erection of a Methodist school for boys. This Mr Sayle was not ready to do but it happened that he had recently been offered the chance to buy the Leys estate, off Trumpington Road, and he suggested to the Conference that this might be suitable for their purpose. After some hesitation the Conference approved the idea and the estate was bought (Mr Sayle advancing the money) and settled "for all time to be used for Methodist educational purposes under the direction of the Methodist Conference". The loan (over £14,000) was repaid

on 2nd September 1872. The school was opened in 1875. He also subscribed generously to the funds of a Wesleyan Chapel in Southery.

At about this time, too, it was being realised that more needed to be done for the education of women and girls in Cambridge, and schemes were afoot to start a girls' school to be run on the same lines as the Perse School for Boys. Robert Sayle was among keen supporters of the plan, which was sanctioned in 1873, the school being opened in 1881, under the governing body of the boys' Perse School, which appointed six managers and arranged that four more – all of whom must be women – should be co-opted.

Mr Sayle was also very much interested in Cavendish College, which had been founded as a study centre for young men near the beginning of the 19th century and had had a chequered career. About the year 1870 it was admitting students of younger than normal undergraduate age, to enable

them to take university courses as economically as possible. The university was unenthusiastic and the college was not a success; but the Senate was eventually persuaded to approve it as a hostel within the university and it was re-opened in 1873, as Robert Sayle and others had hoped and worked for. It struggled on for a time thereafter, but never really prospered and was finally closed down because of lack of funds in 1892. Soon after, the buildings were taken over by Homerton College, which moved from its earlier premises in east London to carry on teacher training for women.

Robert Sayle was one of the guarantors, too, of the YMCA buildings in St Tibb's Row, the foundation stone of which was laid on 30th March 1870, and he helped to raise funds for the purpose, as well as to secure a freehold site. He was equally concerned for the welfare of his older fellow-citizens, giving subscriptions and other aid for the erection of the Royal Albert Almshouses in Hills Road, which opened in 1859, successors to the Royal Albert Asylum for the elderly, established in 1846. He was also one of the first subscribers to "The Cambridge Improved Industrial Dwellings", an early experiment in housing, founded in 1876, and various other improvements in the amenities of the town are credited to his energetic influence.

Cambridge had in some ways hardly emerged from the housing conditions of the Middle Ages. In 1790 John Byng (later Lord Torrington) spent one summer touring in the Midlands. He arrived in Cambridge early in July, and noted in his diary that the weather seemed to have "settled in for a desperate rain". He decided to stay overnight, and put up at The Black Bull, which he found

uncomfortable in every way. "This wretched inn, with most of this wretched town ought to be burnt down", he thought. "ALL Cambridge," he continued, "is in comparison with Oxford... about a hundred years behind hand." In September 1654, the diarist John Evelyn also visited Cambridge and observed that "the whole town is situate in a low dirty unpleasant place, the streets ill-paved, the air thick and infected by the fens". Both writers agreed, at any rate, that King's College chapel was a splendid building – "It altogether answered expectation", said Evelyn. John Byng also spoke well of the Backs, which were then known as the Trinity Pieces, Clare Hall Pieces, and Queen's Green. Conditions had apparently not changed much by Robert Sayle's day. Although Improvement Commissioners had been appointed by an Act of 1788 to be responsible for the lighting, paving and drainage of towns, it would seem that Cambridge had somehow slipped through the net. A Board of Enquiry was set up under the Public Health Act of 1848 to enquire into things there, and its report, published in 1849, gives a truly horrifying account of dirt, overcrowding, lack of proper street lighting, paving, refuse collecting, or even any domestic water supply. Many people had to fetch water from a distance, and, on top of that, to pay for it – a farthing a gallon is mentioned. In fact, the only commendation the town received in this report was for its two new cemeteries – the one in Histon Road, dating from 1842, and the one in Mill Road, opened in 1848.

From the time he was a comparatively young man, Robert Sayle had been interested in the work of the Improvement

Commissioners and his name is often found as a member of various committees working to this end. To take one example: the corner of Petty Cury and St Andrew's Street had long been notoriously awkward and dangerous for traffic. In 1875 Robert Sayle bought the building at the corner – The Wrestlers' Inn, which had been one of the old coaching inns – and disposed of part of the land to the town to enable the road to be widened at that point. (The remainder of the site was sold by Mr Sayle's heirs in 1884 for the erection of what is now known as the Old Post Office building.)

Again, he took a prominent part in encouraging the provision of adequate street lighting. Although a small Gas Company had been formed in Cambridge in 1823, at first using oil gas, later coal gas, it did not produce enough power to light the streets properly; and from time to time proposals were made to extend its usefulness. It was clear, however, that the existing company was neither large enough nor affluent enough to cope with the extra amount of gas that would be

needed, to say nothing of the expense of laying pipes, erecting lamp-posts and servicing them.

By the 1860s it was evident that a new company was urgently required and meetings were called of interested citizens and rate-payers, conspicuous among whom were Robert Sayle, John Lilley, and W Eaden Lilley, to discuss the project with the civic authorities and the commissioners. After lengthy and sometimes petulant debates on the subject ("gas doesn't pay – no dividends for years from the old company – insist on these being paid up first – why throw good money after bad? – gas too expensive – inconvenience of having the roads dug up" – and so forth), tenders were invited and at last a new company, named the Cambridge (Consumers') Gas Company, was established towards the end of 1867, with Robert Sayle a member of the six-man board, quite determined that the price of gas should be reduced and that the town should be properly lit. A subscription list was opened and some hundreds of shares

The Royal Albert Almshouses, Hills Road, 1859

were issued. There was, unfortunately, still a good deal of opposition to the scheme, especially, of course, from shareholders in the old company. For the next 18 months the newspapers were full of letters on both sides of the question, in which senior members of the university also joined; and neither the town authorities nor the Improvement Commissioners seem to have acted quite fairly or consistently towards the Consumers' Company. It was not a success and was only able to carry on for another year or two. An adequate supply was not assured for some considerable time thereafter. Fifteen or 16 years later, Mr Sayle was believed to be interested in getting electricity introduced into the town. It was not, however, brought into use in Cambridge until 1892.

Newspapers also referred to his "shrewd capacity and spirited action" which resulted in the conversion of the old Corn Exchange (built on St Andrew's Hill in 1842) into a series of small business premises known as The Arcade, when the present Corn Exchange was opened in 1875. The Arcade has since been demolished – though part of it survived until the early 1950s – and the site is used as a private car park. In its day it must have been very much like one of the old bazaars. In fact, the 1860s and 70s were some of the most active years of Robert Sayle's life. His health was good and his energy and enterprise never failed, even if not all his projects were wholly successful. In 1869, being then 53 years old and not content with his very varied interests in Cambridge, he launched out in a new direction: he opened an office in London.

7: London and overseas

The earliest mention of Robert Sayle's London office occurs in Kelly's Post Office Directory of 1869, when it is listed as being situated at 174 Aldersgate EC, Robert Sayle being described as a "general warehouseman". This is confirmed for the next four years by an entry in another street directory, published by the City Press (for the City of London only). The 1874 record, however, gives fresh information. It reads: "Sayle, Robert, general warehouseman, 174 Aldersgate Street. Also at Cambridge, Hongkong and Shanghai." Trade with China, mainly through Shanghai, its largest port, had been carried on increasingly by certain European countries since the eighteenth century. By the middle of the nineteenth century, with the industrial revolution well under way, the greatest volume of this trade was with Great Britain. China's exports consisted mainly of silks, raw and woven, and of tea; its chief imports from Britain were all kinds of Manchester goods (that is, cotton materials), and these were coming more and more to be a speciality of Robert Sayle. Hong Kong had been used as a mercantile base by British traders for many years, but it came under the British Crown only through the Treaty of Nanking in 1842, after which the number of its inhabitants, and therefore the possibilities of trade, increased vastly. The opening of the Suez Canal in 1869 must have helped business in these parts very greatly, as well as in Penang and other places in the Straits Settlements, by cutting the time of the journey to and from London by about one-third.

Fashion, of course, played its part also. It is not known exactly which year Robert Sayle chose to go into the far eastern trade, though between 1870 and 1872 seems the most likely; but it was in the 1870s and 80s that the Aesthetic Movement flowered, and with it came the taste for the soft colours and materials that characterised oriental fabrics and designs, as well as for the porcelains, fans and other bric-a-brac that were imported in huge quantities for years to come. In 1874 both Liberty's and Whiteley's opened oriental departments, and other large London stores soon followed suit, as no doubt did provincial stores. By about 1880 it was possible in most places to buy the handwoven Chinese, Japanese, Malayan and Indian silks, cashmeres and cotton goods, with or without embroideries or batik designs, that were used for curtains and cushion covers, for dresses and draperies, and indeed in every conceivable way by artistic and fashionable women until the early 1900s. Robert Sayle's branch in China had a brisk two-way trade, a considerable part of his wholesale business being routed through there. This export trade extended also, though on a smaller scale, to Ceylon, Penang and Manila, where it was dealt with through agents and not, as in Hong Kong and Shanghai, under the name of Robert Sayle & Company. Apart from certain goods

produced in the Cambridge workrooms for the European community in these overseas ports, it seems pretty certain that the bulk of the merchandise exported by Robert Sayle consisted of Manchester goods, though there is now no documentary evidence left to prove this.

Robert Sayle's London office remained in Aldersgate Street for a good many years, but moved from No 174 to No 195 in 1881. In 1884, the year after Mr Sayle's death, the address became 195-196, and the firm's title was "Sayle, Robert & Sons". No 196 was given up again in 1887. From 1895 to 1900 the address was Portland House, 73 Basinghall Street, EC, and the name of the firm had been changed to "Sayle, George Moore (Robert Sayle & Son)". No further mention of the office has been found after the year 1900, nor is it known when George Moore Sayle dissolved his connection with the business.

The description of the trade carried on from the office varies from that of "general warehouseman" in 1869, when it was no doubt the London Buying Office and centre of Robert Sayle's wholesale business, to "China and Japan merchants" in 1889, and "China and general merchants" in 1892. In his will Robert Sayle is described as "trading in the Empire of China and at Victoria in the Colony of Hongkong and at Singapore in the colony of the Straits Settlements as a general merchant".

As far as can be ascertained only one of Robert Sayle's sons, Arthur Willis, the eldest, went out to the Far East; he died at Shanghai in 1878, when he was no more than 26 years old, two years after taking his degree at Cambridge. But Mr Sayle's eldest daughter married a cousin, Boardman

Bromhead Dalton Sayle, the son of one of Mr Sayle's brothers, who became Manager of Robert Sayle & Co. (Overseas); they lived in Hong Kong, where two of their three sons were born. When Robert Sayle died, Mr Dalton Sayle was appointed by the executors of his will to "administer the personal estate and effects of the said deceased in China".

Among relics known to exist of this branch of the business is a fine trade sign, composed of the royal arms surmounting Robert Sayle's own coat of arms (granted in 1874) combined with various Chinese characters, and below these a nautical device with the motto "domine dirige nos" (which is, in fact, the motto of the City of London). A facsimile of the sign hangs in the General Manager's office in St Andrew's Street, Cambridge. (See Appendix D.) There are also accounts in old ledgers which refer to the transfer of sums of money to and from the overseas branches between 1872 and 1884. Sales are recorded at about £6,750 a month in 1872, and in the following years at a little over £7,000 a month. Unfortunately, after 1884 no distinction is made between inland and overseas wholesale trading in any existing records, though a single mention occurs in 1884 of goods to the value of £1,658.8s.0d being shipped to China.

A trade card of unknown date refers to "Sayle & Co, Hongkong and Shanghai", giving the office address in London as 174 Aldersgate Street; and the names of some of the ships by which the goods were transported are known mostly from the Glen and Castle lines – Glenlyon, Glenearn, Glengyle, Cawdor Castle, Glamis Castle, among others. It is, of course, possible that Robert Sayle began

doing business with the far east before opening his London office; in fact this is suggested by 'The Cambridge Chronicle and University Journal' of 12th October 1883, which said that he extended his field of operations to China "about twenty-five years ago", which would make it before 1860; but no confirmation of this date has been found. On the other hand, small quantities of goods are understood to have been sent to China through the wholesale section of the Cambridge business as recently as 1907, though it would seem that Robert Sayle & Co (Overseas) no longer existed by then.

Victoria House was not, during these times of expansion, without its troubles. Cambridge, being built in the middle of fen country, was always subject to floods of more or less serious proportions. One of the worst of these occurred in 1879. It happened in the night of Saturday to Sunday, 2nd to 3rd August. A thunderstorm came up, frighteningly against the wind, so the papers said, at about 11 o'clock on the Saturday night, growing worse as the hours passed, and spreading all over East Anglia and the southern counties, with gale force winds and torrential rains. Trees were uprooted, houses and farms wrecked and set on fire by lightning, cattle struck and killed or drowned in dykes swollen by the rain, crops ruined. Remarkable to say, only one human being is reported to have died in the storm. The river rose about eight feet in Cambridge, with resultant damage to bridges, trees were down along the Backs, and serious flooding occurred in parts of the town, some cellars getting three or four feet of muddy water in them. Drapers' shops were among the worst sufferers, Eaden Lilley and Robert Sayle each losing upwards of £2,000 worth of stock. Next day the damaged goods were sent for sale to the Old and New Corn Exchanges, where they were quickly, though perhaps hardly profitably, disposed of. The storm continued unabated until about five in the morning, over three inches of rain being recorded in the gauges; and it was found that Parker's Piece and other open spaces had become veritable lakes. Newnham village was quite cut off from the town. People claimed to have stood on Castle Hill and watched boats being rowed across Midsummer Common. The water did not altogether subside for about a week. A mark to show the height to which the river rose was carved on King's College bridge, where it may still be seen. "The worst for a quarter of a century", it was said.

Again, some 70 years after this date, Robert Sayle suffered under one of these fierce storms that seem to hit Cambridge two or three times in each century. It was on a Saturday afternoon in the summer of 1949, and the shop was being prepared for stock-taking on the following day, in addition to the normal Saturday rush. The electricity supply failed as a result of the storm and the shop was in gloom; the basement, in complete darkness, lit only by lanterns, became flooded to a depth of six inches. Mr Walsh, the General Manager, led a team of volunteers who baled the water into bins and buckets and carried them up to empty in the yard, customers meanwhile being served from the fourth step on the other staircase.

Seven hundred years earlier, a storm of similar violence was chronicled by a thirteenth century scribe, Roger of Wendover, who died in 1238. This too hit East Anglia, starting in Bedfordshire and sweeping across the Isle of Ely "like a blast of hell", killing cattle and even birds, and "lifting the corn out of the fields".

8: The end of an era

Once the London office had been opened, Robert Sayle spent a good deal of time in the metropolis, often being away from home for two or three nights together. He evidently made his mark in the City, and according to various newspapers he was "highly esteemed" in the mercantile community for his "business capacity and integrity". He became a member of the City Liberal Club – he was a staunch Liberal all his life – and is even supposed to have been offered nomination at one time as Sheriff of London and Middlesex; an offer which, if made, he evidently did not accept. In 1873 he was appointed a Justice of the Peace in Cambridge, which was widely approved in the town; he was looked upon in all quarters as a man of sound judgement and probity.

His health had been good all his days – a single mention occurs in a letter, dated in the winter of 1862, of his absence from business on account of illness – and his nervous energy was obviously immense; but he did not live to a great age. On 11th September 1883 – he was then 67 years old – he suffered a heart attack, and was so seriously ill as to cause real anxiety. But he soon recovered sufficiently to be thought completely out of danger. He attended to his business affairs as usual, and even went to London accompanied by his wife on Wednesday 3rd October, spending the night there and returning home on the Thursday. On the following day, Friday 5th October, he was attending to his correspondence in the early afternoon, when he felt a return of the heart pains which had attacked him on the former occasion. By a fortunate chance – or perhaps Mrs Sayle had asked for the visit? – the doctor called at that very moment. But his efforts were of no avail, and Robert Sayle died within a few minutes.

Not only the Sayle family, but the whole town, was shocked by the news. At first many people refused to believe it, since an earlier rumour of his death at the time of the first attack a month before had proved to be a mistake. But soon the shop was closed, the shutters were pulled down, and a notice was posted on the doors. The newspapers reflected the general feeling of regret in the town. He was, said 'The Cambridge Express' on 10th October, "an example of what perseverance and energy will do... The large shops in St. Andrew's

Street are a proof of what industry and skill are capable of accomplishing." 'The Independent Cambridge News' of 13th October wrote that "the regret that was felt extended to all classes and to many members of the University". The paper referred to his enterprise and public spirit, and continued: "Most men who build up large commercial concerns... have devoted themselves exclusively to this work; but Mr Sayle took the liveliest interest in local matters... and some of the best public improvements that have taken place recently owed their inception and execution to his judgement and enterprise." Perhaps the finest tribute of any was that "he never gave a promise that he did not fulfil".

The funeral, which was arranged by the shop's own Undertaker's Department, under its manager, Thomas Hubbard, took place on Wednesday 10th October, at the Mill Road Cemetery, after a service at the church of St Andrew the Great, where Robert Sayle had worshipped for many years, and where a pew was always reserved on Sundays for his employees. He had been a supporter of the church in other ways too. In 1878, for instance, he had been one of a number of people who subscribed to increase the

The tomb of Robert Sayle, his widow and some of his children, in Mill Road Cemetery

endowment of the St Andrew's living, when he gave £100, as did also the Master and Fellows of Emmanuel and of Christ's College, as well as the Dean and Chapter of Ely.

The funeral cortège formed up outside Leighton House in Trumpington. After the hearse, which was laden with flowers, came six mourning coaches, carrying Mr Sayle's four surviving sons and other members of the family. In Cambridge itself it was joined by a contingent of young men employed at the shop, walking four abreast, and there were members of the Wesleyan Trust, labourers from Mr Sayle's farms, and many others. Large crowds lined the route, according to local newspapers, and at the cemetery were "several thousand persons", including the Master of St John's College, the Warden of Cavendish College, the Regius Professor of Civil Law Mr High Shield QC (who was also the Bursar of Jesus College), the Mayor and other civil dignitaries. A few young women sales assistants were admitted by ticket to the crowded mortuary chapel. Eight senior salesmen acted as bearers. The service was taken by the vicar of St Andrew's, assisted by the incumbent of Trumpington Church. In his address, the vicar of St Andrew's referred to Mr Sayle's high moral standards and to his exceptional mental ability, and spoke of all he had done for the town, more especially for the poor and for those whom he considered to be in any way oppressed. A muffled peal was rung at St Andrew's that night.

9: Under new management: Robert Sayle & Co

Robert Sayle signed his will on 17th September 1883, shortly after his first heart attack. It was proved on 13th December 1883, and his personal estate was finally sworn in October 1886 at close on £90,000. As trustees and executors of the will he had named two of his sons, Robert Henry Sayle and George Moore Sayle, together with three friends: Joseph Clark, who had worked in the business with Mr Sayle for many years; Edward Dobson Greenberry, described as mercantile clerk, also employed in the St Andrew's Street establishment; and John Groome Howes, of St Paul's Churchyard, London EC. The last named declined in the event to act, and Mr Greenberry died less than three months after Mr Sayle himself, on 20th December 1883. The remaining three executors appointed Mr Dalton Sayle, nephew and son-in-law to Robert Sayle, to act on their behalf in the Far East.

Instructions were given in the will that all mortgages outstanding on real estate, of which there was a fair amount, should be paid off as soon as possible, special mention being made of those on "the Trinity Hall or Hills Road estate" (on which the large Methodist Church was built) and on Southery House, Trumpington Street, which was at the time occupied

Trumpington Street, 1900. Charles Edward Sayle lived at No 8

by George Moore Sayle, Robert Sayle's third son, but which was bequeathed to Mrs Robert Sayle for life, or for as long as she wished to live in it and remained a widow. Mrs Sayle, who was joined by her youngest son, Charles Edward, did in fact live there until her death in 1904, and her son kept it on until his own death in 1926. After provision made in the will for the immediate family and close relatives, substantial legacies were left to Joseph Clark and Edward Greenberry in consideration of long and faithful service; and annuities, payable weekly, were left to two old employees. Except for certain provisos about reinvestment of money, the disposal of Robert Sayle's business and other property was left to the discretion of the trustees. They decided that, as long as suitable purchasers presented themselves, the shop in St Andrew's Street might be carried on under the old name, if the new owners so wished. Joseph Clark was himself anxious to acquire a share in it and a friend, Arthur Edward Chaplin, was found to join him. It was realised, however, after the accounts had been analysed, that a third partner would be needed if the price required by the trustees were to be paid, and since Mr Clark, one of the intending purchasers, was also one of the

trustees, the terms of the sale must be approved by the Court of Chancery.

Among applicants to join this partnership was Mr Hugh William Porter, Managing Director of a linens business in Belfast. He made full enquiries by post about the kind of trade carried on, the class of goods sold, the turnover and amount of stock held in each department; and, of course, he wished to have personal details about the other two partners, as he was unable, on account of illness, to come to England for definitive discussions until early July 1884. There was some delay over the monetary terms, but finally the partnership was accepted, the articles being drawn up by Mr R H Sayle, in his capacity as solicitor. It was agreed that the business should be carried on under the style of Robert Sayle & Co, and that, if one of the partners were to die, the partnership should continue as to the survivors. The sale was made final on 7th August 1884, on the sanction of Mr Justice Chitty, one of the judges of Her Majesty's High Court of Justice (Chancery Division).

Business had, of course, proceeded at the shop under the aegis of the trustees during the months since Mr Sayle's death, but the official change of ownership to Robert Sayle & Co did not take place until the last week in August 1884, although the sale was then back-dated to 19th January of that year, from which day all goods sold in the shop or bought from suppliers were to be reckoned as on account of the new owners; book debts contracted before that date to be for the account of the vendors. The rent paid for the shop premises to the executors by Robert Sayle & Co for the period was £725.

Among the items mentioned in the Articles of Partnership as payable to the trustees were: £5,000 for the goodwill; purchase of leases and buildings £14,500 (subsequently apportioned as £5,000 for Emmanuel and £9,500 for Jesus College property), the money to be paid not later than a year after the transfer of possession; valuation of the merchandise as at stock-taking on 19th January 1884, less certain discounts, £27,252; furniture, fixtures and rolling stock (but not including horses) £3,355. Elsewhere six horses are mentioned at £22.10s.0d each.

Conveyance of the leases to the new owners was, of course, subject to the approval of the college landlords, who licensed the executors of Robert Sayle's will to assign the premises and latest leases to Robert Sayle & Co. The sale was not to be made effective until payment in full had been received by the trustees. The most recent leases – 1873 from Emmanuel and 1875 from Jesus College – were eventually transferred to Robert Sayle & Co between 1885 and 1888. The governing body of Emmanuel College was ready to let the old lease run for the remainder of the term, but proposed converting the fine into an increased ground rent. In the end, half the fine (£198) was so converted, and the rent raised from £13.3s.0d to £43.12s.0d a year. Jesus College offered a new lease to date from October 1889, with also a considerable advance in rent and a fine of £910 (later lowered to £860). At the same time the college authorities agreed

that Joseph Clark should arrange a mortgage on the business to pay off the trustees. Meanwhile, a circular had been drafted and sent to customers, with a covering letter from Mr R H Sayle, introducing the new proprietors and inviting continued support. Suppliers were also, of course, given official notice through solicitors of the change of ownership and asked to transfer their accounts accordingly.

Each of the three new owners-directors of Robert Sayle & Co was an interesting and in some ways unusual character; and they all carried on the tradition started by Robert Sayle himself of taking a prominent part in the life of the town, displaying a more genuine social conscience than one tends to associate with many business men of the period.

Mr Hugh Porter, the latest comer to the business, was new to Cambridge. He was born in Coleraine, Northern Ireland, in January 1845, the son of a Presbyterian Minister and descendant of a family whose members included many soldiers and clerics. He is said to have been endowed with a fine soldierly bearing and a particularly friendly and straightforward disposition. He was a lover of books, and a keen Liberal in politics. He was married and had two sons, one of whom read history at Christ's College and the other law at Emmanuel; the latter became a Law Lord in after years. Mr Porter's business life began at the York Street Spinning Company in Belfast; when he had completed his apprenticeship he moved on to Messrs Milling & Co in Leeds. Some years later he returned to Belfast and became, ultimately, Managing Director of the General Drapery and Manufacturing

Warehouse of Lindsay Brothers. In 1884 he joined Robert Sayle & Co as part-owner. A man with excellent business qualifications, he also took a great interest in local affairs. He became an Elder of St Columba's Church in Downing Street, and was a promoter and director of the University and Town Fire Insurance Company. He was appointed a Justice of the Peace in Cambridge in 1897. He seems, however, never to have enjoyed very robust health.

Mr Joseph Clark, the senior partner, was well-known to all the employees in the shop and certainly also to a good many of the customers, having spent the whole of his working life at Victoria House. He was born in Cambridge on 17th August 1843, and came into the business as a boy of 14 in 1857. It has been said that he was a nephew of Mr Sayle's on his mother's side, but he was in fact no relation. By 1883, when Mr Sayle died, he had been working in the shop for close on 27 years, and Mr Sayle had come to rely on him in many ways, treating him more as a partner than an employee. Mr Clark was married and had two sons and two daughters, none of whom came into the business. While still very young, he had been among the earliest to join the Cambridge Volunteers after the movement had been started in 1859, largely as a result of the Prince Consort's encouragement, to strengthen forces available for home defence. Mr Clark was evidently a man with something of the same temperament as Robert Sayle himself, participating energetically throughout his life in public service of various kinds. He was a strong churchman, and the building of St John's Church in Hills Road was held to have been due

largely to his efforts. He was also particularly interested in Addenbrooke's Hospital, and was for a number of years a member of the Weekly Board, which managed the hospital's affairs before it was reorganised in 1898. He continued to take an active interest in the institution even after he ceased to be a member of the Board. In later life he was appointed Justice of the Peace for Bottisham.

The third partner, Mr Arthur Edward Chaplin, was about a year younger than Mr Clark. He had in earlier days also spent some years at Victoria House. He was born in 1844, the son of an Ipswich wine merchant, and in 1858 was apprenticed to a draper in Walthamstow. This may have been a family business, for in 1890 his brother, Mr Charles J Chaplin, authorised him to sell his (Charles's) drapery business in Walthamstow. When he had finished his apprenticeship, he came to Robert Sayle, where he remained until in 1870 he proceeded to Leytonstone to start in business on his own account. In 1884 he sold his shop and returned to Cambridge as partner in Robert Sayle & Co. At some time he was made a freeman of the city of Ipswich, as his father had been before him. Among his outside interests was Free Masonry. In 1896 he was Master of his Lodge, the Scientific No 88, and later Treasurer. He was also a leading member of the Royal Arch Chapter of Pythagoras.

Although relations between managers and the managed were much more formal than they have since become, Mr Chaplin evidently evoked not only respect but also liking in his employees. His appearance was impressive; he was a man of very strong character and is well remembered 30 or more years after his death by people who knew him in their young days. "He had a tremendous personality", one of these described him, and he was "very downright". But although he was a firm disciplinarian and was regarded as an exceptionally shrewd man of business, Mr Chaplin was nevertheless held to be fundamentally kindly and thoughtful for the well-being of his staff. He made no difference, one is told, in his attitude to selling and non-selling personnel, which was unusual in those days. As he pointed out, although the sales-people actually sold goods to their customers, that was not the end of the transaction. The 'after-care' – such as delivery of the goods, alterations to a garment, fitting a carpet, keeping the shop clean and pleasant – was all part of the service, and was just as important for goodwill as the original sale. Mr Chaplin married Miss Alice M Bales in 1875 and had two daughters and two sons, the elder of whom was later taken into partnership in Robert Sayle & Co.

These three men, then, became joint proprietors of what had formerly been the strictly one-man business of Robert Sayle. They did not, however, remain the only people financially interested in the prosperity of the shop. Though not for many years in name and in law, it very soon became to all intents and purposes a company with a number of shareholders. A good many others besides the partner-directors put money into the concern, either on loan or deposit, and drew interest on it at the rate of 5 per cent per annum. The actual capital account, by far the largest part of course, stood in the names of Messrs Clark, Chaplin and Porter, but other interested persons invested by no means inconsiderable sums, and within four or five years the number of depositors had increased fairly widely, including friends and relatives of the proprietors, and later some of the employees.

Mr A E Chaplin
Joint Proprietor
1884-1919
Governing
Director
1919-1934

10: The turn of the century

In the 1880s the shop was certainly busy, although, according to a business letter, gross profits in 1883 seem to have been only 19 per cent. A boost must have been given to retail trade at this time by the fact that, when the revised University Statutes were published in 1882, all Fellows of the Colleges were, for the first time in the history of the university, allowed to marry; until then the terms of their appointment had obliged them to forego the wedded state and, normally, to live in college, except in a few cases in which colleges had waived the rules earlier. After this, there must have been quite a number of new households to be furnished, as well as new brides-to-be catered for.

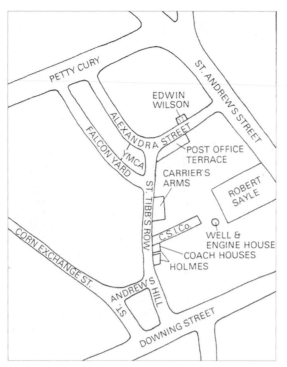

**The area around
St Tibb's Row
at the end of the
19th century**

Robert Sayle enjoyed a high reputation in the town and the need for its premises to be kept up to standard was therefore all the greater. Extra capital, even in relatively small amounts from private depositors, was no doubt welcome for financing the immediate payments for reorganisation which became necessary with the change of ownership. Workrooms, new and old, were built or repaired in 1882, 83 and 84; coach houses, harness-room and stables at about the same dates. With the new leases came also increased ground rents and premiums. Legal expenses had to be met – though it must be added that, comparatively, these last appear to have been very moderate. Five cottages on St Tibb's Row, bought privately by Robert Sayle in 1855, were purchased by Emmanuel College from the trustees of his will and, in 1884, leased to Robert Sayle & Co, who relinquished them when the new Post Office was opened in St Andrew's Street in 1934. The site of the cottages is now occupied by some sections of the Post Office and Telephone Exchange.

Part of the shop's premises were sub-let. One such part, on the north-western side of the yard and facing onto St Tibb's Row, was let to the Cambridge Scientific Instrument Company – the first of its kind in the British Isles, incidentally. This concern had been founded in 1881 in a couple of rooms at the back of Robert Sayle as an experimental workshop by Mr A C Dew-Smith MA, of Trinity College: its premises were extended by Robert Sayle in 1882 and in 1883 at a cost of about £700. In 1883 Dew-Smith went into partnership with the youngest son of Charles Darwin, Horace Darwin, who then became designer of the firm and later its chairman. Actually, this company really put England 'on the map' as regards the special type of precision instruments manufactured, which had until then been mostly imported from Germany. Among the best-known of their inventions was an apparatus for cutting infinitesimally thin slices of animal or vegetable tissue for microscopical examination; they also made the first electro-cardiograph. The establishment was formally registered as a limited liability company in 1895, and was soon obliged to move to more adequate premises than could be afforded in Robert Sayle & Co's yard. The company transferred on more or less the same site as their present works, though of course the premises have been greatly enlarged since those days. Another part of the shop's site, also facing onto St Tibb's Row, was let by Robert Sayle & Co to Lacon's Brewery for 40 years from Michaelmas 1887 for The Carriers' Arms public house, together with stables and sheds adjoining. Lacon's were to pay a ground rent of £12.10s.0d a year, offsetting most of Robert Sayle & Co's rent of £12.12s.0d to Emmanuel College for this piece of the land.

In those days Robert Sayle & Co was listed in the local directory as "Manufacturers, Wholesale Warehousemen, General Retail Drapers, and Undertakers". They sold all kinds of clothes for women's wear, made-to-measure, and even some ready-made or partly-made garments leaving only the main seams to be stitched; also furs and lingerie, hats and bonnets, stockings and gloves, ribbons and laces, maids' caps and aprons, and, of course, haberdashery; as well as carpets, linen and cotton goods, dress and furnishing materials of all descriptions. On the fashions side, the Millinery, Blouse, Gown and Mourning Departments enjoyed a particularly high rating in the town. There was no Shoe Department: footwear was still almost entirely a specialised craftsman trade. And men's wear sections were as yet in the future, for at that time men's and women's clothing were not sold in the same shop. As regards household linens: – "It was the first place everybody went to" is quoted by the grandchildren of the customers of those days.

The last department in the directory's description of Robert Sayle's business – the Undertaker's – was given a second, separate, advertisement, and must certainly have been one of the most profitable sections, directly and indirectly. The service implied more than merely conducting funerals. It meant that the shop was ready to supply all necessary mourning wear, which could bring a great deal of trade to the shop as a whole. A dressmaker and milliner usually accompanied the undertaker to attend on a bereaved household, to make all proper arrangements. Mourning was elaborate; it was sometimes worn for years at a stretch, graduating from the deep unrelieved black of a widow's weeds, through black with touches of white, to violet or some similar shade, before it was correct to wear ordinary clothes again. The demise

of the reigning sovereign was also marked by the wearing of some form of mourning by loyal subjects, even if it were only a black crepe armband. King Edward VII was the last to whom this token of respect was generally shown.

Coffins were made by Robert Sayle's own carpenters. For an elaborate funeral there would be an inner casket of lead, which was then enclosed in a strong wooden shell, generally of polished oak or elm, often richly adorned with brass ornaments and handles. Occasionally, if someone happened to die at a distance from home, and the body was to be sent back for burial, it was first embalmed, though this was not carried out on the premises at Robert Sayle. Miss Emma Taylor, whose father was one of the firm's coffin-makers, remembers being told by him that on one such occasion, when the remains were to be sent overseas, a sheet of glass was let into the leaden casket to show the deceased's face. At every funeral each of the bearers was presented with a new pair of black gloves.

A 1923 advertisement from a local newspaper promoting the Robert Sayle funeral service

41

On the manufacturing side of the business, in addition to garments made in the workrooms for customers and for the wholesale trade, an interesting local craft was the making of so-called swansdown trimming. This was for very many years a favourite adornment to all kinds of dresses and lingerie. It was by no means a new idea when the shop became Robert Sayle & Co in 1884, for among the rebuilding undertaken in the previous three years were two new down-rooms as well as alterations to an old down-room, so the trade had evidently been flourishing for a long time before then. The art of making the trimming was handed down from mother to daughter for several generations. According to someone who spent many years in the firm's employ and who saw the trade in being about 35 years after this date, metal-lined bins were ranged along the walls of the down-rooms, which were built above the stables and are now part of the Linen Department's stock rooms. On Saturday mornings young and old from the surrounding country districts used to bring in quantities of down (from ducks and geese as well as swans) which had been collected and washed during the week. It was weighed and recorded and the workers were paid according to the amount handed in by each family. Some of them then used to get down-proofed cambric and were given an allotment of down to take home and make into strips of the trimming; they were paid a few pence a yard for their labour. Quantities dealt with must have been quite large, for book entries of payments to 'downers', as they were called, averaged over £70 a month before the year 1900. There was also at least one member of the Robert Sayle workroom who made up this kind of trimming and checked what was brought in by outworkers. Large quantities of the strips were sold to wholesale houses, much of it going to London and to China. The trade continued at the shop for a number of years after Mr Sayle's death, but gradually faded out during or soon after the first World War.

Also among Robert Sayle's wholesale products was beer, which was brewed on the premises. It had originally been made for consumption by the employees, part of whose maintenance included a certain quantity of beer each day. Intermittent workers were, in addition to their wages when actually employed, given a ration of bread and cheese with a pint of beer at midday. In later years it was recalled by a man who had spent over 50 years in the business, that "in the old days" – it could have been before 1900 – each man received a quart of Robert Sayle & Co's home-brewed Old Audit Ale on Christmas Eve for his own consumption. On Christmas Day there was a staff party to which wives and children of employees were invited. The menu included stuffed goose with the usual accessories, Christmas pudding, mince pies, etc. White Bordeaux was served with the meal, and port followed. Afterwards there was a big Christmas tree for the children.

Some of the beer was exported to Robert Sayle's far eastern trading posts and possibly elsewhere, as well as being consumed on the premises in Cambridge by managers and directors in addition to other members of the staff, as is witnessed by certain journal entries. In 1888 there was a "Beer Retailer" in

Littleport, Ely, named Robert Sayle but it is not known whether he had any connection with the Cambridge establishment. The beer was brewed in the space now occupied by the carpet showroom; above this was a water tower which, as an invoice shows, had been repaired and made higher in 1877 at a cost of £22. The water was pumped up from a well in the yard and, in 1889, a gas engine was installed to work the pump, which was sheltered by a little round red brick house, the whole thing costing £120. It was demolished in 1964, the well not having been in use for many years. The water came from Hobson's Conduit, that is to say ultimately from springs in Shelford, and was considered to be exceptionally pure. The supply was never known to fail. When the brew house was pulled down in the late 1930s, during rebuilding operations, a poster was found which read "Robert Sayle, licensed to brew beer for export". Legend has it that when the last lot of beer was brewed half-a-dozen bottles were buried somewhere within the shop's precincts in memoriam.

Other exports were, of course, the various drapery and general goods that went to China and other distant places through the London office. Not that the wholesale trade was confined to London and overseas. A great part, in fact probably the major part – and increasingly so as time went on – went to smaller shops in Cambridge itself and in the villages and market towns in the neighbourhood. These customers were looked after by Robert Sayle's two travellers, who called on them and were responsible for following up the orders. The travellers also personally collected

payment of some of the accounts each month: their own income was derived from 1.25 per cent commission on the sales in addition to a small retaining fee. Orders were also at times – in fact until after the end of the first World War – brought in by one or another of the carriers, who often acted as buying agents for people living in the country. Each of their drivers used to be given a Christmas Box of one shilling every year by Robert Sayle, which was accepted with gratitude (and no doubt liquidated at The Carriers' Arms).

The wholesale turnover was at that time further inflated by the fact that goods purchased for sale in the shop were first entered to the wholesale branch of the accounts and transferred, as required, to the retail side. Two clerk/packers were permanently on duty in this section. The firm's van, horse-drawn at first, later a Ford motor, went up to the station every morning at 10 o'clock precisely, to collect any orders or packages that might have come in by train and to despatch parcels of goods to the London office and to any other places that could now be reached more easily by rail than by road.

Business went on steadily and generally satisfactorily during the 10 or 12 years after Mr Sayle's death but it was found that relatively minor alterations to the premises were not going to be permanently enough to keep up with expanding trade and changing ideas. Accommodation became inadequate, fixtures and fittings were unfashionable, and the general layout of the building awkward; a good deal of space was used wastefully for offices when it might more profitably have been used for selling.

The demolition of Victoria House, 1905

Obviously a thorough overhaul and comprehensive rebuilding would soon have to be undertaken.

Unfortunately, during the second half of 1897, Mr Hugh Porter's health broke down altogether. He was obliged to be away from business for over six months, and he died on 27th April 1898, at the age of 53, shortly before he was to have been appointed Deputy Lieutenant of the County. A memorial service was held at St Columba's church in Downing Street on 29th April, the shop being closed for two hours during the time, as a mark of respect and to give employees the opportunity of attending. The body was afterwards taken to Belfast for burial. Mr Porter's death naturally occasioned some rearrangement of financial matters as between the executors and the two remaining partners in the firm. However, a part of his share in the

shop property was left on deposit in the business, the family drawing interest on it, according to the articles of the partnership agreement.

The college lands were revalued in December 1898, and negotiations were already in progress with the owners for the usual 14 year review of the leases: Emmanuel's was due in 1901 and Jesus College's in 1903. Some very thorough-going changes were envisaged. The Jesus College property now covered a front of 92 feet on St Andrew's Street, about the same as at present, and ran back some 290 feet to St Tibb's Row; Emmanuel College's frontage on St Andrew's Street was between 34 and 35 feet and also extended to St Tibb's Row, including the area occupied by The Carriers' Arms.

The layout of the premises was roughly as follows: all the St Andrew's Street front consisted of showrooms, on the ground and first floors. Carpets and Household Linens took up most of the area now used by the Carpet and Hard Furniture Departments. The carpet showroom was the largest in the shop, measuring something like 90 feet by 30. Dresses, coats and suits were sold on the first floor, but some of the smaller fashion items, such as blouses, were on the ground floor. The basement was used chiefly by certain of the wholesale departments. Behind the front shop were a packing room and the "cloth room", where mourning and other materials and accessories were sold to wholesale customers. Beside it was the Counting House and a few steps led up to the staff dining rooms, below which were the kitchens. On either side of the yard were a large woodshed and coal bunker, stable, coach houses, and coachman's quarters, and above these the down-rooms, workrooms and so on. Resident members of the staff were housed on the two upper floors of the main building.

Emmanuel College proposed that its new lease should, as before, be made for a term of 40 years, dating from 29th September 1901, with an increase in rent after the first year and a half, plus a premium. It was also required that Robert Sayle & Co should block up all doors, windows and other communications between their premises and those next door, that is to say between No 12 and No 11 St Andrew's Street (the latter of which, it will be remembered, had at one time been part of Mr Sayle's private property), so that the lessees of No 11 should not be overlooked or in any way disturbed. Also at about this time Robert Sayle & Co transferred the lease of the buildings of The Carriers' Arms to Lacon's for £1,500, though the firm would continue to draw the ground rent of £12.10s.0d a year from the brewery company until the old agreement ran out in 1927.

Discussions about a new lease from Jesus College, though not due for review until 1903, had been started in 1896, and Mr Hugh Porter had been much involved in the negotiations up to the middle of 1897, when the onset of his last illness had prevented his taking much further part in the business. The current lease from this college still had about 26 years to run after 1903 and the college proposed that the rent should be continued at the old rate until 1915, with an increase for the following 14 years, and that thereafter a new lease should be granted, with a fine of £1,100 – and, presumably, another increase in rent.

After further deliberations, the college offered to waive the fine and raise the rent immediately to a more realistic figure, with a 60 year agreement to date from 10th October 1903, on condition that the tenants should spend £6,000 on improvement within the next two and a half years (that is, by the end of 1905). This was accepted by Robert Sayle & Co in June 1903, except that they asked that the period for completing the alterations should be extended to 1908. After some further discussion the college agreed, providing that at least half the work should be finished by 1905. It was also agreed by both parties that, before the lease ended in 1963, all communications with adjoining buildings on Jesus College land should be blocked up. This was necessary because, since 1889, Robert Sayle & Co had occupied premises behind No 18 St Andrew's Street. The furnishing workrooms and offices below these, also parts of the present carpet showroom and of the soft furnishing showrooms above, are still on this site, which is fronted on the main road by an independent business. There is no basement to this part of the building.

During the alterations which, to judge by a photograph taken in 1905 of part of the work, must have been very extensive indeed, business is reported to have been carried on as usual. The difficulties must have been enormous, for the picture shows what appears to be nothing more than a large hole in the ground with some hoardings in front. The photograph was taken in September 1905 – this part of the new premises was opened in July 1906. It just shows what can be done!

11: Pay and conditions of work

In the beginning of the twentieth century, as at the end of the nineteenth, social conditions had changed remarkably little from what they had been 40 or 50 or more years earlier. A good many employees at Robert Sayle & Co, as elsewhere, lived in, if only because public transport was inadequate to make practicable a daily journey of any length. Bicycles had, it is true, been invented – the first one was seen in Cambridge in 1869, it is said – but they ran on solid tyres until 1885, were expensive to buy, and to a great extent, certainly in the 80s and early 90s, belonged to the domain of sport rather than of utility. Women, who were now coming more and more into business life, did not look with any enthusiasm on the idea of riding to work alone every day, in all weathers, possibly from several miles outside the town, apart from the fact that it might well have been considered unfeminine. In any case, the working day was too long to make an active journey at each end anything but a strain.

Two other forms of road transport were available inside the town towards the latter part of the century. First, the Street Tramway Company, founded in 1879, which ran two rather infrequent lines of one-horse trams – one from the depot in East Road to Market Square, via Gonville Place, Lensfield Road and Trumpington Street; the other from the railway station along Hills Road to Christ's College. And second, the Cambridge Omnibus Company, established in 1896, whose two-horse buses linked the station directly with Market Hill. (Both companies were closed down in 1914.) Considering current rates of pay, it is clear that even a penny or twopenny fare each way, six days a week, would take too much out of the wage-packet. Besides, the area covered by the buses was very limited, and country buses were unknown since the carriers had gone out of business. As far as most shop-workers were concerned, it really had to be a case of "walk or live in".

Living in may not have been ideal – according to present day standards conditions would be thought very austere but, against the background of the period, the system was adequate and met a need. From an employer's point of view, too, it was useful. He wanted a fine impressive building which would do him credit, but passenger lifts were still something of a luxury outside London, so that the upper storeys were of little use for selling-space, though they could well serve as a hostel. Also there was no trouble about getting people home if they happened to be working later than usual.

Living quarters at Robert Sayle – men's and women's strictly in separate parts of the building, of course – were very simple. Bedrooms often had to be shared and amenities were few. Everyone had to be in by 10 o'clock at night (girls by nine), with an extension to 10.30pm once a week for men only (for 'courting'). There were senior and junior sitting rooms, the sexes separate, and there was, naturally, a kitchen and a dining room, which were in the same position as they are now, the latter divided in two by a partition, so that men and women also ate separately. The dividing wall has gone, though it is still obvious where it stood. A permanent cook and kitchen-maid were employed, also a boy to carry the coals, and a housekeeper to look after the hostel, with several maids. Apart from these there was no domestic staff, except that a carver was engaged to come in every day to distribute the meat ration. The directors' dining room (known as the 'Firm's Room') was on the first floor, where the main rest room is now, above the staff dining room. There was a maid to wait on the directors – more strictly 'proprietors', though employees always referred to them by the other title – and a service lift, which is still in use, was installed between this room and the kitchen. It was solidly and handsomely furnished in the taste of the period. Of the shop's staff, only those who lived in were allowed access to the dining rooms; everyone else went out for the midday meal. An hour's dinner time was given but there were no coffee or tea breaks, though employees were sometimes able to snatch a few minutes out of their departments during the afternoon to swallow a glass of beer and a piece of bread and butter, which were laid out on the long dining tables – the beer in its barrel standing on the floor.

Meals were of good quality and plentiful, according to the testimony of people who worked and lived at Victoria House in the first few years of this century. Breakfast usually consisted of tea, porridge, bread and butter with jam or marmalade, in unlimited quantities; twice a week eggs and bacon or sausages etc were served. The midday dinner was the main meal, at which meat or fish was provided, with vegetables, a pudding, cheese and beer. Supper consisted of bread and cheese and beer, laid out as it was during the afternoons, and to which people helped themselves as they wished. There were cupboards in which they might keep any extras they cared to provide for themselves. In old books mention is sometimes made of beer for breakfast, but this was most unusual after 1840 and certainly was not customary by 1900.

Leisure time was catered for by the provision at the management's expense of a reading-room (called 'the library) — which was mentioned as being in existence in 1889 – and a billiards room, both on the premises. They were intended for those who lived in and were situated on the first floor. Full use was made of them, at least by the men of the establishment. The library did not contain books, for which it appears there was no demand, but pretty well all the daily and weekly newspapers were available, serious and otherwise. It is recalled that one man won a prize of £500 in a competition in Titbits and that he deposited the money in the business; with interest being paid at 5 per cent, this would have given him almost 10 shillings a week extra income, which was worth having. The reading room was kept tidy and up-to-date by one of the younger men, who received a small addition to his wages for looking after the place. The billiards room was comfortably furnished and contained a miniature table with all necessary equipment. All in all, and in comparison with many others, conditions at Robert Sayle seem to have been remarkably liberal. The story goes that in the very early 1900s a cricket pitch was contrived in the basement. Anything is, of course, possible! The cellars were otherwise used at the time by Millinery and some of the wholesale departments, both as stockrooms and for receiving customers.

Perhaps the most popular recreation was provided by the rowing club, known as the Victoria House Boating Club at first, but in 1904 renamed the Victoria House Rowing Club. It had its own club colours – pink, navy, and sky blue stripes (changed to green, black and white in 1900) – and is first mentioned in a minute book recording the accounts of the 1890 season. Races were then usually tub pairs and scratch fours; eights were added later. Prizes, as well as the cost of hiring and servicing boats, were paid for out of the subscriptions, which varied from four to five shillings a season for rowing men, and from one shilling to half-a-crown for honorary (non-rowing) members. Any surplus funds were spent on a club dinner at the end of the summer. The club was much encouraged by the directors and other senior men. Mr Clark was its president for some years, and in 1898 presented a challenge cup to be rowed for each season by members of the club. It is on record that the directors felt that "every young man in the house should support the club". (But it is permissible to wonder if some of them were put off by the prospect of daily training periods from six to eight in the summer mornings!) From 1907 to 1914 Mr Chaplin's elder son Hugh was the club's president. At his suggestion it was agreed in 1908 that "any young ladies in the house" might be "admitted members of the club at the usual subscription". It is not thought that all the girls who joined at that time were actually rowing members, though undoubtedly some were, for they took part in a regatta a few years later.

Some of the colleges, notably Pembroke, Jesus and Downing, were helpful in allowing the hire of their boats and boathouses, and in providing a coach at times; and in 1913 it is mentioned that the Jesus style of rowing (on sliding seats, which were a novelty then) was practised in the eights. The

club's first regatta – it was intended that it should become an annual event – was held on Thursday 26th June 1913. Twenty-three races were on the programme, and the president acted as judge. A month later the club entered for the Cambridge Rowing Association's races and made two bumps in the four days' racing. After the last race a bump supper was held at The Blue Boar. The second annual regatta took place on 2nd July 1914, and this time some of the lady members entered in the mixed double sculls. The winners were a Miss Rogers and Mr S Osler, with Miss G Fox and Mr G T H King coming second. The club continued in being up to the middle of 1915 when, after a meeting held on 18th June, it was decided that, since most of the men had joined the forces, the activities of the club should for the time being be suspended.

Pre-war, meanwhile, life went on as it had done for the best part of half a century. Money wages were low, but up to perhaps 7s.6d or 10 shillings a week more might be reckoned for living in. The pay of the selling staff was increased by a commission on sales (threepence in the pound), so seniors might do quite well, but the younger ones must have found it hard to make much extra; and the system could tend to create bad feeling among the staff, because the order in which assistants might approach a customer was jealously guarded – 'first sales', 'second sales', and so on – nor was it altogether a good idea from the customer's point of view, for it was apt to make for 'high-pressure' selling, which many people find annoying or embarrassing. Distinctions of rank and priorities were strictly preserved and shop-walkers, who were, so to speak, in charge of deportment and general discipline in the shop, saw to it that no rules were broken. All the same, strict or not, present-day customers who knew the shop as children 50 or more years ago still remember how pleasant it was to go there with their mothers or grandmothers, and how much they enjoyed the ceremonious greeting of the shop-walker or a buyer – a bow from the waist, with the left hand behind the back.

Wages were not paid weekly but on the 15th day of every month, unless that happened to be a Sunday, when they were paid on the Monday morning following; any necessary adjustments, such as commission, payment for breakages (which was usual up to the 1920s), settlement of a house account, were made at the same time. One great concession enjoyed by those who lived in at Robert Sayle, and by a very few others among the employees, was that of being allowed to buy goods in the shop at the wholesale price. This privilege was continued until someone suggested that the Truck Act was being infringed; thereafter they could buy at 5 per cent, later 7.25 per cent, above this price.

Records show that a man's basic wage in the days of Robert Sayle himself and later of Robert Sayle & Co might be from £70 to £80 a year, living in, occasionally as much as £90 or £100. An experienced saleswoman could earn £60 or £70 a year in the 1890s, that is to say £5 or £6 a month. A boy just out of his apprenticeship started at about £20 in 1900. Untrained juniors might get only their meals with, at best, a shilling a week for the first year, rising to another shilling or so a week for the next two or three years. The parents of an apprentice usually had to pay a premium for the training, and most apprentices lived at home, not in the hostel. The Counting House was staffed almost entirely by men; not until the 1914 war made it necessary were women admitted to any responsible positions in this male stronghold.

Holidays, if any, were unpaid, and so was sick leave. Bank holidays were introduced in 1871 but they were not – and in fact still are not – a statutory entitlement for all employees. The weekly half-day was made compulsory in retail trade only by the Shop Acts of 1911 and 1912. In 1846, so a contemporary diarist noted, Robert Sayle was closing at 7pm, Eaden Lilley having set the fashion a year earlier. By 1871 Cambridge shops used to close at 4pm on Thursdays during the summer, but only up to September. There was in those days no extra pay for extra hours worked. An employee was considered not as having been engaged to work a certain number of hours in a day or week but to deal with a particular section of the business; if for any reason, such as stock-taking, it was necessary to work beyond the usual time, that was all part of the job. As in most shops, normal working days up to the turn of the century lasted from 8am to 7pm at least, and later on Saturdays, anything beyond that must have been heavy going. The struggle for the eight-hour day in retail trade went on from 1880 to 1914 or later. Oddly enough, an eight-hour day (48 hours a week) is believed to have been general, according to Trade Guild regulations, in the Middle Ages. It was in the eighteenth and nineteenth centuries that the very long working day became the rule.

In considering the figures for wages, it must of course be remembered that a straight comparison, pound for pound, with present-day money does not make sense. It was quite possible for a single person to live on £1 a week without any particular difficulty. Conditions of work and rates of pay changed very little from the time when Robert Sayle started trading until after the first World War. It has been calculated that between 1840 and 1914, the purchasing power of the pound sterling fell by only five pence. Between the end of that war and the present day the value has dropped by at least 17 shillings.

There was little change in business dress until after the 1920s either. It was always black, including women's stockings, even after light-coloured hose became fashionable. Senior saleswomen and women buyers wore long silk or satin gowns, often with a train to give added dignity; men wore black suits, with frock coats for seniors, stiff white collars and cuffs to their shirts, and black ties. They had to be well turned out to keep their jobs. The younger men used to take it in turns to sweep and clean the shop before opening time – these boys were known as 'squadders' at Robert Sayle. Directors, shop-walkers and senior buyers used to wear resplendently shining top hats as they moved around the premises – chiefly, it was believed by irreverent juniors, to take off with a flourish to important lady customers. Mr G H Doggett, the manager of the Counting House, always wore a 'square bowler' in business. His name first appears on the firm's books in February 1884, that is a few months after Mr Sayle's death. He was from the beginning a 'salaried', as distinct from a 'wage-earning', member of the staff, and he remained in the business for just over 50 years.

The training of juniors was taken very seriously. Mr Robert Mutten, for instance, the buyer of the Manchester goods department, used to make his apprentices learn to recognise the quality and fineness of materials by touch, as well as by counting the number of threads to an inch with the help of a powerful magnifying glass, testing over and over again until it became second nature. "He was a wonderful trainer," says one of his trainees, who worked in this section from 1902 to 1907, "he really inspired his apprentices." And other department managers, each in his own way, were equally meticulous, so that an assistant really came to understand his stock and could talk to a customer and give advice with authority based on knowledge. An intelligent youngster would grow up with an interest and a genuine pride in his work, and certainly also with the feeling that he was a member of a team and of importance to the business.

Any dishonesty was severely punished. One hears stories, dated not so very many years before 1900, of young delinquents being taken before a magistrate and given six weeks in prison and/or a sound birching for taking a shilling from the till. The nineteenth century was hard on crime. Justice was not only done, but was seen to be done. As lately as 1850 two people were publicly hanged in Cambridge. That was fortunately the last time an execution took place in public here. As a corollary to the story, a contemporary diarist noted that all the rest of that day there were enormous numbers of drunks about the town.

According to records, staff turnover in the latter part of the nineteenth century at Robert Sayle – as no doubt also elsewhere – was apt to be fairly rapid, though there was always a considerable nucleus of people who stayed on for years – up to 30 or 40 or more – and made their whole career in the shop. A surprising number of both men and women came to work in Cambridge from places that seem very far away – from London and Manchester and Southampton, for instance; from the Isle of Wight or Exeter or Sheffield or Bath; even from Edinburgh. For these, a residential hostel had obvious advantages. A good many such immigrants stayed in Cambridge for no more than a few months, or possibly for as long as a year or two, and then moved on. Those who had come from London tended to return to the bright lights but others apparently hoped for more from the smaller towns and went on to some place like Norwich or Colchester. Reasons for departure are seldom mentioned; occasionally the record says "married" or "dismissed" and – once only – "left under a cloud", though no hint is given to indicate the blackness of the cloud. Otherwise only dates are shown, and the names of the firm to whom references were sent and from whom they had been received in the first instance. One odd little mystery is left unexplained: £10 was paid every six months over a number of years to an employee "in consideration of good conduct and keeping steady". It was cancelled one half-year; resumed the next half-year; and once more after that. Then the name disappears from the register for ever.

12: Mainly about people before and during the First World War

In addition to the building programme that had to be carried out in the first years of the new century, Robert Sayle & Co took over Samuel L Pulhams, a small drapery business operating at Hale House, 17 Hills Road, which they held until about 1912 and then sold again. It is even possible that they had owned it before 1900, but no proof exists. No doubt it was used to eke out selling space while building was going on in St Andrew's Street. Beyond this fact, nothing is known about this little shop, except that it has a link with another of the branches of the present John Lewis Partnership. A boy of 13, named W E Thirkettle, was engaged as an apprentice in Robert Sayle & Co's Silks Department on 1st February 1887; on 6th February 1892, at the end of the apprenticeship, he left and obtained a post with Messrs E Hide & Co of Southsea. His name was mentioned some years afterwards as having become manager of the Hills Road shop in Cambridge but no details have survived. Some 50 years later, in 1949, his son, Mr W C S Thirkettle, was manager of the Ironmongery Department at Knight & Lee of Southsea, when this shop joined the John Lewis Partnership.

**Miss A J
Chipper
in 1959**

Of great personal interest to Robert Sayle & Co in 1902/03 was the appointment of Mr Chaplin's elder son, Arthur Hugh Bales Chaplin, to a partnership in the firm. "Mr Hugh" was about 27 years old at the time, good-looking, keen on sport, friendly and energetic, and was very popular both among the staff and outside the business. From boyhood he had been, and still was, an enthusiastic member of the Cambridge Volunteers, and he did much to encourage the younger men in the shop to join the corps too. Like his father, he was a Free Mason, and later became Junior Warden of his Lodge, the Cantabrigia. He married Miss Elizabeth Joan Tizzard, a lady from Ipswich, and in due course a son and a daughter were born to them.

Others, whose names are still familiar to many connected with the shop, also come onto the scene during those days, the oldest and most widely known of them being Miss Amey Jane Chipper. Miss Chipper was born on 24th October 1864, and was first engaged at Robert

Sayle & Co on 10th September 1894 at £35 a year, having previously been employed at a shop in Bournemouth. There is no record of her leaving Robert Sayle within the next years, but she did, in fact, leave twice, for very brief periods, for reasons unstated. It is noted in the staff register that she 're-entered' on 1st March 1897, her pay now being £60 a year, and that she re-entered yet again on 9th September, this time at the princely salary of £100 a year. She always lived in the hostel.

She is recalled by people who have known the shop for a long time (some of them still working there in 1968) as the highly successful buyer of the Blouse and Lace Departments. She stayed to complete close on 40 years of service before retiring in November 1934 to live, first, in a house off Brooklands Avenue in Cambridge and afterwards in a bungalow at Worthing. She always kept in touch with old colleagues at the shop, and her last visit to Cambridge took place in June 1959, when she attended, as guest of honour, a luncheon given by the General Manager, Mr Lewis Smith, for men and women who had spent 25 years or more in the business. Miss Chipper insisted on living alone and managing her own affairs, including her garden, until her death in August 1961, within two months of her 97th birthday. She was a delightful old lady, small and slight, of immense personality and with a splendid sense of humour. Like most successful men and women of her era, Miss Chipper had the reputation of being strict in her professional capacity, but she was known also to do very kind things. One stormy day, for instance, she noticed that the firm's errand boy was wearing a very shabby, inadequate pair of shoes. She made enquiries and, finding that he came of a really necessitous family, she bought him a new pair herself. All through the 1914-18 war she used to go in the evenings, after the shop had closed, to help at the First Eastern General Hospital, which had opened at the Leys School on 6th August 1914; later it moved to Trinity College and was finally established in Burrell's Walk, between Queen's Road and Grange Road.

Another well-known character linking the present with the past was Mr Oliver Charles Johnson. Born in 1882, he joined Robert Sayle & Co at the age of 19 on 21st October 1901; he remained with the firm until 31st October 1951, his membership being broken only by service in the 1914-18 war. He joined the army in March 1916 and was demobilised, unscathed, three years later almost to the day, in March 1919. He returned to the shop 10 days or so afterwards. He enjoyed nothing better in later years than talking about his wartime adventures. In business, 'Johnny' was widely experienced, mainly as a 'piece goods' man; for quite a long time he was on the wholesale side, both as a salesman and traveller. Later he moved into the retail Silks Department of the shop and grew to be a familiar figure to customers – "a real landmark in Cambridge", as someone put it. He was a little man, and had a way of spreading both hands on the counter and leaning over it with a confidential air that was quite irresistible. Incidentally, he could boast an amazingly good health record. He was absent on account of illness on a single occasion, for a fortnight, in all his 50 years at Robert Sayle, and he lived to

enjoy nearly 13 years of retirement. He died on 1st May 1964, at the age of 82. In his younger days he was a lively member of the Victoria House Rowing Club; he is mentioned as vice president in 1903 and captain in 1907; and he coxed the boats on many occasions.

Another well-remembered man, who started with Robert Sayle & Co in that pre-war period, was Mr John William Pretty, who came into the business in 1909, succeeding Mr Robert Mutten as buyer of Cotton Materials and Fancy Goods, Blankets and Hosiery. He had previously worked at Cavendish House in Cheltenham, and he entered Robert Sayle at what was, for those days, the considerable salary of £180 a year. He was very much liked by the staff, who never doubted that he was to be respected as a sound businessman, but also found him very approachable, unusually so for that time – "you could talk to him," and "he entered into things", say those who knew him as young people, still with a sense of almost awed surprise. He stayed in the business for the rest of his working life, ultimately becoming Managing Director, and seeing two further changes of ownership.

The year 1911 brought to the firm the loss of someone who must have seemed a permanent institution. The senior partner, Mr Joseph Clark, had for several years been gradually failing in health, and had latterly suffered more serious disablement, though it was only for the last few months of his life that he found it impossible to attend at the office. In the end he was confined to bed for no more than a matter of days, and he died at his home in Hills Road on Monday 14th August 1911, a week before his 68th birthday, having spent 54 years at Robert Sayle. He was buried at Cherry Hinton cemetery on the afternoon of Thursday 17th August. Mr A E Chaplin – the only survivor of the three men who had taken over the business after Mr Sayle's death nearly 30 years earlier – was now left as joint proprietor with his son Hugh of the shop and its outside interests.

Mr Clark's decease naturally made monetary rearrangements necessary again, as his will, in accordance with the relevant clause in the original articles of partnership, allowed only a certain proportion of his share in the shop property to remain invested in the firm, while the rest was to be paid out to his heirs or executors. Members of his family, however, deposited some of their personal money in the business, so the finances did not suffer too sudden and severe an upheaval. The current leases from the colleges (1901 and 1903 respectively) presented no difficulties, for they stated that if either of the two signatories – Mr Clark and Mr Chaplin – were to die, the survivor and executors, or their licensed assigns, should be entitled to carry on as tenants without alteration to the conditions.

There was a capable and efficient team of buyers – mostly men – for both the wholesale and retail sections, and their senior assistants were also thoroughly experienced. Miss Chipper and Mr Pretty have been mentioned. Mr Pretty's senior salesman was Mr J C Struggles, who had first come to Robert Sayle & Co in 1894 and who stayed with them for just 30 years. Then there was Mr Percy Norrington, in charge of the largest and most lucrative of the retail departments – Carpets and Furnishings.

He had joined Robert Sayle & Co from the Hastings branch of Plummer Roddis Ltd in 1905; in due course he became a director of Robert Sayle & Co Ltd and retired, for health reasons, in 1934. His senior assistants were Mr Horace Prime and Mr Walter Papworth, both in the business since 1905; both, too, were among those of Robert Sayle's staff who enlisted during the 1914 war, and survived to return when it was over. Both names, too, appear on the shop's "active" list in 1934 and after. Mr Prime in his young days also functioned in the Victoria House Rowing Club as a cox.

Another of Robert Sayle & Co's pre-war stalwarts was Fred Cowling, originally one of Mr Norrington's porters, who first came into the business in 1909. The porters at that time used to help in carpet and linoleum laying at customers' houses, so could do much for the shop's goodwill. Later Mr Cowling concentrated solely on this part of the work. He volunteered for war service in 1914, but failed to pass the medical examination; the following year he presented himself again and was accepted: "They weren't quite so strict over the medicals by then," he says. Later that year he became a casualty, when a shell explosion buried him in his trench for a short while. After a fortnight in hospital he had, so he says, a very pleasant five weeks convalescing before returning to the front, during which time he represented his brigade at football. He came back to Robert Sayle & Co in 1919, and soon became what he called a "full-blown fixer", ultimately rising to be head planner and layer of floor coverings. He spent altogether 50 years on Robert Sayle's books, before retiring on pension in April 1959. Much

579 years of service at Robert Sayle: This picture was taken in 1920, just after Robert Sayle had become a Limited Company, and the four Directors thought they would like to be photographed with those of the employees who had been longest with the firm. Each of the men had spent fifty years there.
From left to right are: (standing) Mr Turner (Commercial Traveller); Bill Rayner (Van Driver); J B Rampling (Director); Arthur H Clark (Director, and Manager of the Fashion Departments); J W Pretty (Director); J Struggles (Manager, Linens Department). (seated) A Holliday (Head of Wholesale Department); D Clark (Foreman, Wholesale Packing); G H Doggett (Director, Head of Counting House); S Fromont (Foreman, Despatch), H Harvey (Driver and horse-keeper to Mr Chaplin, the head of the firm)

of his leisure time was devoted to cricket and football; he played cricket until he was well over 60, and afterwards was much sought-after as an umpire.

Workroom staffing during the war was evidently very sketchy. Miss D I M Seargeant, who joined straight from school six months before the war ended and completed close on 44 years before retiring from full-time work in 1962,

recalled that the whole of the work – carpet-sewing, upholstery and soft furnishings – was tackled by her and one other young girl, together with an elderly carpenter, under the supervision of the buyer, Mr Norrington. This had the advantage, from Miss Seargeant's point of view, that there was plenty of variety in the work and she learnt about sewing curtains etc as well as carpets, though

A Victorian hook, used for tethering horses, in an exterior rear wall at the shop

she ultimately specialised in the latter, becoming yet another of the shop's goodwill ambassadors when she visited customers' houses.

Another notable man among the buyers was Mr J E Rampling. He had been with Robert Sayle & Co since March 1890 and he remained in the business until 1934 – a matter of 44 years. He became a director and was head of the wholesale division, controller of purchases in bulk, the most valuable section of the trade. His son (never at Robert Sayle) opened a shop for surgical appliances in Market Street, which was later transferred to its present site on Rose Crescent.

The 'heavy fashions', which were known as Gowns, Mantles and Costumes at that time, were bought by Mr Joseph Clark's son Arthur, who, as time went on, also became a director. Millinery, a few years later, came under Miss K Wheatley, one of whose claims to fame was that she designed hats for performers in the Footlights revues; the 'actresses' were, of course, all men in those days, as women were not yet admitted to membership of the university nor, therefore, to membership of the Footlights Club. Her creations, it is said, were much admired. In charge of a subsidiary, but important, section – artificial flowers and feather mounts – was Miss E Geller, an immigrant to Cambridge from Forest Hill, London, who joined in March 1887 and did not leave until she retired on pension in September 1931. Clearly, although a good many workers were restless and changed jobs frequently, quite a fair proportion of Robert Sayle &

Co's employees found conditions in Cambridge to their liking. A photograph taken in 1920 (shown on p55) shows four directors with seven men who had each spent more than 50 years in the business in various capacities from groom and coachman to senior salesman.

But now the quiet days of the early 1900s were drawing to an end and, although few could have imagined it at the time, a change was on the way that was to alter conditions in the whole world. War, totally unexpected, was about to break out – a war that was to affect not only Britain and Europe but every country on earth. Earlier wars, even the long-drawn-out Napoleonic Wars and the more recent Boer War, had been fought mainly by professional soldiers and sailors, and the lives of the majority of people had hardly been touched. This was to be 'everyman's' war and there was, in the beginning, a feeling among the young of romance, of chivalry, almost of crusade about this war which came to be called "the war to end wars". No-one foresaw the long, dragging tragedy of the next four years, nor the utter disintegration which was to follow. "It'll be over by Christmas!" they said confidently.

When war broke out on 4th August 1914, Hugh Chaplin was among the first to report to the local recruiting office, and he took with him as nearly as possible every man of suitable age in the business. He was commissioned as captain into the Cambridgeshire Regiment, and acted as adjutant in the recruiting campaign. It was not long before he was posted to France. After about six weeks there, he fell ill with a bad attack of pneumonia and was sent home to recuperate. He returned to the front as soon as he had recovered. Two years later, on 14th March 1917, he was seriously wounded in the left arm, leg and foot. After treatment at a base hospital in Boulogne, he was taken back to England, where he died on 21st May, aged 42. He was buried at Trumpington with full military honours.

Four months later, on 26th September 1917, Mr Chaplin's younger son, Charles Montague, was reported missing, believed killed. He was not known at Robert Sayle as his elder brother was, for he had studied as a surveyor and in 1906, when he was about 24 years old, he had emigrated to Canada to become a farmer. Soon after the outbreak of war he had come back to England with the Canadian forces, as a private in Princess Patricia's Light Infantry. In November 1916 he was wounded and, when he had recovered, was posted to a cadet school, from where he was commissioned as Second Lieutenant and attached to the Cambridgeshires. He was sent overseas immediately and survived only six months. He was unmarried.

In the course of the war the pattern of employment in retail changed radically. With all the younger men in the forces – many of them never to return – women were engaged in greater numbers and to more responsible positions than ever before. From August 1914 to December 1918 about 75 per cent of new engagements at Robert Sayle were women; male staff engaged were either boy apprentices or men who for some reason were ineligible for military service. From early 1919 on, a certain number of men returned after demobilisation, but the overall change

had come to stay. Except in those sections where the handling of stocks required greater physical strength, women had taken over, especially in the fashion departments, and behind the scenes clerks were now predominantly feminine. Even in such work as the packing and despatch of goods and (temporarily) transport driving, not to mention the Counting House – all previously looked upon as wholly and obviously for men only – women had buckled to and had shown, most successfully, what they could do.

There were other changes. Robert Sayle's splendid black horses, as has been said, soon went, commandeered by the army. They were replaced, for routine transport, by a couple of one-horse vans and a small Ford motor van, the latter of which was driven by Miss Goodwin, the daughter of the Bursar of Jesus College, who took on the work from 4th December 1915 to 31st December 1918, and was paid at the rate of 25 shillings a week. For funerals, the Undertaker's Department now hired a hearse when required. After the war, returning transport men acted as bearers.

Changes in minor matters included the suspension 'for the duration' of the Victoria House Rowing Club and other amenities. Food shortages were more severe and rationing less efficient than during the second war. On the other hand, civilians were hardly involved in danger, except to a very limited extent when zeppelin raids occurred and later during a few visits by enemy aircraft carrying machine guns. Casualties resulting from these attacks were insignificant. Cambridge itself was not touched.

13: Post-war: Robert Sayle & Co Ltd

The end of the war came at last, with an armistice on 11th November 1918. The year 1918 also brought a serious epidemic of influenza, which began a few weeks before the armistice was signed and which was so bad that it was spoken of as another Black Death. Certainly few escaped the outbreak in 1918 and an enormous number of people died of it, not only in England but also on the continent. No doubt this had a detrimental effect on the social and economic climate, which was unsettled enough in any case, after over four years of storm. Thankful as everyone must have been that the slaughter had come to an end, the nation was weary and depressed, people felt flat and discouraged; sad, despite the titular victory, once the first days of wild rejoicing were past. There was hardly a family that did not mourn the loss of a husband or father, sons, brothers or friends; to say nothing of thousands of men permanently disabled.

Other distresses followed. Soldiers returning from the front were demobilised and found no work. Many were young and had not learnt a trade before being called up to the forces; some had enlisted straight from school, or after perhaps one or two years at a university and had not even finished their education. Industrial concerns had switched over to the production of war material and it took time to bring them back onto a peace footing. International trade was chaotically disrupted. The gaiety of the "bright young people" in the early post-war days and the 20s was, in its feverishness, symptomatic of the unrest and anxieties of the time. Unemployment was wide-spread and it

was seriously worse among men than among women, so that they felt bitterly that the horrors they had gone through, the dangers and the sacrifices, were now forgotten or thought of no account. Fortunate were those who had their old work to come back to – although they generally found that they returned also to the same rate of pay they had been receiving pre-war. Women who had taken over men's jobs were not always ready to give them up again. Many a one had lost her husband and needed the money to keep herself, and possibly children. Nor, for that matter, were employers necessarily anxious to change back, except no doubt where former members of staff returned. Women had helped through the war years and had proved loyal and efficient, as well as being willing to work for lower wages than men. It was a tangled situation and it prompted attempts to secure equal wages for men and women doing similar work – efforts that were sometimes founded less on any principle of abstract justice than on the hope of preventing the employment of women in preference to men for purely monetary reasons.

The death of his two sons in the war had left Mr Chaplin the sole proprietor of Robert Sayle & Co, his family now consisting of two daughters, a son-in-law, a daughter-in-law, and three grandchildren. It seemed unlikely that any of these would wish to carry on the business in the future and, when peace had been restored, Mr Chaplin decided after discussions with all concerned that the most satisfactory course would be to turn Robert Sayle into a limited company – as had already been considered in 1909, though nothing had come of it at the time. A scheme was put into effect on 1st August 1919, and the shop became "A private Company not issuing Shares to the Public". Mr Chaplin remained as Chairman, or Governing Director, and always the final authority in what was now Robert Sayle & Co Ltd, but he handed over the executive directorship to Mr J W Pretty. He appointed his son-in-law, Mr F S Scruby, a director of the company on 1st August 1925. In March 1921 Mr Chaplin celebrated 40 years of connection with Robert Sayle by giving a dinner for the staff.

The new company's nominal capital was issued in the form of 12,000 preference shares, carrying a fixed dividend of 6 per cent per annum, and 73,000 ordinary shares, both types being of £1 face value. Majority shareholders were Mr Chaplin, his family and friends, and some of the senior employees also subscribed. Shares were allotted to Mr Arthur Clark and the two sons of Mr Hugh Porter, as residuary legatees in each case. On 21st October 1919 5,000 shares were deposited at Lloyd's Bank against payment of certain debts; they were redeemed on 16th February 1924. The total number of shares taken up initially was 8,400 preference and 41,000 ordinary; the remainder could be issued later if additional capital should be required. A further 300 preference shares were in fact issued in 1928, making a total of 8,700.

In the early months of 1919 a number of Robert Sayle & Co's men returned after demobilisation, generally – like most other people – to the old rate of pay, at least to begin with. But whereas £60 or £70 a year had been a living wage in 1914, it was no longer the case four and

a half tempestuous years later, especially if a man had married meanwhile. Time passed before this was generally realised: wages had been stationary practically for as long as anyone could remember. Thus there was discontent and restlessness everywhere; people were afraid to give up any work they had, yet found that they could not live decently on the wage they received, scarcities of all sorts having forced prices up.

Throughout the 10 or 12 immediate post-war years the majority of new engagements at Robert Sayle – 74 per cent of them – were now women. This is not to imply that the owners were heartless or grasping, but simply that women had been found to be thoroughly suitable for the many varieties of work connected with the drapery and fashion trades. Nevertheless, as far as wages were concerned, it was 1921 before any woman was engaged at Robert Sayle at a salary of over £100 a year; while it was 1923 before a newly-employed man's drawing-rate in the shop was as high as £250 a year. The greater number of initial salaries shown in the firm's records of that time were still somewhere between £50 and £80 a year for male employees and between £45 and £70 for girls and women. As, however, there is seldom any indication in these records of the age or extent of experience of a newcomer, nor whether he or she lived in or out of the hostel, nor how soon any increase was paid, it is difficult to assess conditions quite fairly. The highest starting salaries recorded as being paid to anyone at Victoria House between 1920 and 1930 were £300 to a man and £170 to a woman, both towards the end of the decade, but these were exceptional

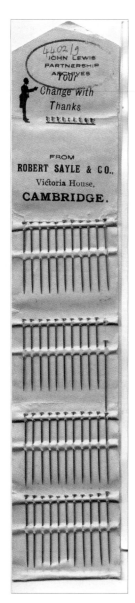

and most were considerably lower.

A small indication of alteration in the value of money is given by the fact that farthings were still coins to be reckoned with in 1919. They were freely used in pricing goods and change of one farthing on a bill was often given in a draper's shop in the form of some small gift, such as a paper of 50 or 60 pins – well worth the trader's while monetarily, it appears – or of a token usable as a farthing in another purchase at the same establishment. An example of such a token – a small envelope into which a bill could be slipped – has been preserved at Robert Sayle and is to be seen, framed, in the General Manager's office. Last used in 1925, it was obviously an inexpensive kind of advertisement, at a tiny charge to the firm's stationery account, with an encouragement to a customer to return to the shop (if only so as not to waste a farthing!). If a customer chose, she could of course have the actual coin. A good stock of farthings was always kept in the cash office at Robert Sayle, though other money was banked twice a day. One night thieves broke into the shop, evidently in search of money only, for no stock was taken. They picked up a bag of coins (all there was in the safe), and climbed out with it over the back wall. They must have been sadly surprised to find that they had helped themselves to the next day's provision of farthings. (Another burglary in the shop, in 1857, had had a different ending. Large quantities of silk handkerchiefs and shawls were stolen, the culprits were discovered and brought to trial. The judge, however, refused to pass sentence on them because he said the evidence

was given "in malice" by a female accomplice who had a grudge against one of the men!)

In the country generally, unemployment and other labour troubles grew increasingly acute, so much so that in some quarters fears of revolution were expressed. The climax came in May 1926, with a general strike. The immediate cause was the miners' dispute over changes in their pay and working conditions. Other unions came out in sympathy, the stoppage beginning at midnight between 3rd and 4th May. All forms of public transport came to a standstill but certain essential services were carried on by volunteers, acting on plans outlined by the government. The Post Office would accept only six parcels a day from Robert Sayle but some goods went by passenger trains, which were run by volunteers. Actually, the amount of disruption to life in general was less than might have been expected: people walked more or were given lifts in private cars; newspapers stopped publication, except for an occasional issue by means of amateur helpers, but their place was taken by bulletins pinned up in publishers' or distributors' windows. One newspaper was, in fact, published through the combined enterprise of The Morning Post and Winston Churchill. The Morning Post offered its premises, which were accepted by Mr Churchill, and The British Gazette was launched. The paper was produced by members of the office staff, and distributed by volunteers all over the country in cars and by plane. The sales increased during the strike period from about 230,000 on the first day to near 2,250,000, and the publication was believed by many

A packet of pins (above), given in place of a farthing in change – now in the Partnership's archives – and a farthing token (below)

people to have had a considerable effect in bringing the trouble to an end. Its issue ceased with the end of the strike. There was little shortage of food. In Cambridge, undergraduates – tutors permitting – were delighted to act as volunteer porters, booking clerks, etc, on the railway, or as bus drivers and special constables. "Effervescing" was how the newspapers later described these enthusiastic auxiliaries.

Robert Sayle's business was, of course, affected in common with everyone else's: profits for the half year fell by over 20 per cent. Much of its trade being wholesale, it was dependent to a very considerable extent upon the postal and railway services. Its own transport system was not geared to a wide area of delivery. Under the government scheme, moreover, two of its three vans were mobilised with their drivers, Fred Haynes and Fred Blunt, for food deliveries between Cambridge and Norfolk. This left Robert Sayle with a single van, and customers carried their own parcels if at all possible, heavy or unwieldy goods being delivered 'as and when'. Two undergraduates acted as driver and porter on this remaining van, and thoroughly enjoyed it, from all accounts. On 13th May the strike was called off by the TUC, which felt that enough had been done to demonstrate sympathy, although the miners' troubles had not yet been resolved. By 19th May about 70 per cent of the strikers were back at work.

About this time too, certain of Robert Sayle & Co's out-of-business activities were resumed: a staff outing was arranged each summer, and the Victoria House Rowing Club (VHRC) was revived in 1928; the ladies' section a few months

afterwards. Stimulation of interest in the club among the ladies was to a great extent due to Miss Ethel Beales, who had joined Robert Sayle early in 1914, some six months before the outbreak of war, as a clerical junior, and who ultimately became chief credit clerk. Miss Beales was a member of the Cambridge Town Rowing Club, and in 1928 she succeeded in encouraging 24 of the Robert Sayle girls to join the VHRC besides herself. Mrs J W Pretty, the wife of the Managing Director, consented to become president of this section, with Miss Beales as secretary. After the election of officers and a club committee at the first meeting, held on 11th March 1929, a uniform was decided upon – black shorts, white blouse with a bow tie in the club colours, black gym stockings, black low-heeled shoes and gloves. Newnham College was approached and agreed to provide boats and boathouse facilities.

A general meeting of the men's section of the club had been called on 23rd April 1928, with Mr Pretty in the chair. Officers and a committee were elected and plans made for hiring and servicing boats and for training crews. Mr O C Johnson, as a former cox, undertook to supervise the training of his successors. The old club colours – green, black and white – were retained and the use of writing paper, headed with the club crest of crossed oars, was approved. Subscriptions were necessarily above the 1914 level, and were agreed at 10 shillings each season for rowing members (7s.6d for ladies) and from five shillings for honorary members. The men's uniform was now to include a blazer and, for the first time, a cap with the club badge instead of the

The Victoria House Boat Club in 1933: the first team (top) and second team

pre-war "white washable hat" which had then been worn for paddling down. The club's house flag still exists.

Only annual general meetings were as a rule recorded in the minute book and the next entry is dated 10th April 1929. At this meeting the proposal was made, following a suggestion from Mr Pretty, that a house regatta should be held during the season, as had been done in 1913 and 1914. The idea was received with enthusiasm and, to organise it, a sub-committee was chosen consisting of the captain and secretary of each of the two sections of the club, men's and women's, together with one ordinary member from each. Training was taken very seriously; a physical training instructor was appointed and smoking and the consumption of alcoholic drinks were forbidden for a week before the races. One relaxation was granted: the time of the early morning practices was changed to last from 6.30 to 7.45 instead of 6-8 as it had been in pre-war days. The regatta was duly held in June 1929, and the lady members took a full part in it. In addition to the usual races, the events included men's tub pairs coxed by women, women's tub pairs coxed by men, and mixed tub pairs, drawing for cox. The ladies also put up crews for the

president's fours and there was a veterans' race for men over 40. Names of winners have not been preserved but, from the accounts of some who were present at the festivities, a good time was enjoyed by all.

Among the lady rowing members at that date was, in addition to Miss Beales, Miss Annie Brown, who later became a department manager and retired in 1963, after over 47 years in the business, and, among the men, Mr William Asplen, transport driver, who retired in 1966, with 37 years to his credit; Mr O C W Smith, a member of the shop's transport section, who retired in 1970; and Mr T E Potter, now Robert Sayle's Outside Representative. Mr Ronald Gould, who completed close on half a century in the firm, was for several years club secretary. In 1934 Miss Beales became Mrs Gould and retired from business life, until she came back to do part-time secretarial work many years later. A house regatta was held each year until 1933, followed by tea at The Plough, but by 1934 'natural wastage', that is to say, members leaving or at any rate retiring from rowing, had reduced the number of active participants very considerably and replacements were apparently not forthcoming. Efforts had been made in 1932 to keep things going by allowing a few outsiders, both men and women, to join the club, but this had not been found to be a workable solution and in June 1934 it was regretfully decided to wind up its affairs. There was a good financial balance in the club's accounts, and this was expended over the next two years in social functions for the remaining members of the club. As in pre-1914 days, some of the college boat

clubs, Selwyn and Pembroke in particular, had been very friendly and helpful to the VHRC, allowing the hire of boats, boathouses and boatmen, and at intervals they had provided speakers to give talks on subjects connected with rowing. The club had entered for various of the town boat races and had done sufficiently creditably to have been expected to finish in a good position on the river in 1934. Its demise was sincerely regretted by the members who were left but the club has never been resuscitated.

Victoria House Ladies' Boat Club, late 1920s

14: Some changes during the 1920s and 1930s

Although by the end of the 1920s the Great War had become almost ancient history to many, its effects remained painfully evident at least to the generation who had grown up before 1914. The country was still in an uncomfortable, unsettled condition economically and emotionally. The post-war trade slump affected every aspect of life; wages and money values generally were in a state of flux and unemployment was a more serious problem than ever. Great Britain had gone off the gold standard in 1914; but – to the dismay of a good many economists who thought the pound was over-valued, though to the satisfaction of much of the general public who felt safer when the currency was backed by gold – it returned to the gold standard in 1925, while Winston Churchill was Chancellor of the Exchequer. For a time retail trade picked

Entrance to the Old Counting House
Taken about 1924 showing the entrance to the Old Counting House at the foot of the stairs.
The double doors to the right of the clock led into the 'Manchester' Department (linens)
and beyond was the marking-off room and stairs to the Wholesale Department. All
goods were marked off personally by the Buyer or a Director and coded. The code
was MANIFESTORY. Thus 12/- was MA/-. The Handbag Department is in the foreground
with Ribbons and Haberdashery next to it

up, though spasmodically. Nonetheless, there followed five or six years of unease, from which most of the western countries suffered. The international monetary situation was reduced to little short of chaos, culminating in the collapse of banks and stock-markets in Europe and America between 1928 and 1931. This was a main contributory cause of Britain's decision to go off the gold standard again in 1931. It was feared that if it were not done further reductions in wages could not be avoided and possibly an even greater amount of unemployment must be expected. All this naturally affected

trade both local and international.

Robert Sayle's leases came in for another review during this time. The very recent one granted by Emmanuel College in 1925 was surrendered for a new one which, in consideration of the large amount of money spent by the firm on improvements since then, was extended by 30 years, to run for 86 years from Michaelmas 1929 at the relatively moderate increase in annual rent to £315. On 13th August of the same year, the agreement made by Jesus College with Mr Clark and Mr Chaplin in 1903 was simply reassigned to Robert Sayle &

First Floor Gowns

Taken on a Thursday afternoon (early closing) in 1933 approximately a year before Selfridges took over. The picture shows the three wells which gave daylight to the ground floor and which have since been closed to provide a larger Fashion Showroom. The plain partitions on either side of the nearest well concealed the fitting rooms; at the far end was the Ladies' Hairdressing Department. Five of the six central pillars were purely decorative and have also since been removed. On one of them to the right appears a notice advertising the Funeral Department

Co Ltd without further modification. Despite – or perhaps because of – post-war difficulties, inflation, strikes and unemployment, the directors felt that it would be wise to increase Robert Sayle's scope by branching out in a number of new directions, to use its selling space in fresh ways in the hope of counteracting some of the adverse influences.

A Ladies' Boot and Shoe Department was opened in September 1927, under Miss L Blowman, who left Oxford's Elliston and Cavell to work in Cambridge. The department was sited on the first floor, in the space now occupied by the inexpensive gowns section, and Miss Blowman started off with three sales assistants. At about the same date, Mr David Neave and his brother John, together with eight girls, were engaged to organise a Ladies' Hairdressing salon, in more or less the same position as it is at present. According to some of the few advertisements published in the press by Robert Sayle in those days, a full permanent wave cost from 37s.6d to 45s.0d. Prices actually went down soon after this date and the 'perm' cost no more than 25s.0d to 30s.0d. The department did quite well from the outset, though the figures may sound unimpressive in comparison with present-day values. During the first full year's trading it took nearly £3,000; by 1931 it was taking well over £4,500. In 1934 the figures dropped to £3,850, but that was a bad year all round and, in the main, the department must have been sufficiently profitable. Its accounts on the balance sheets were for a time kept separately from those of the shop as a whole, so figures are more readily available than for other individual sections. (Owing to pressure on space, the department closed early in 1970.)

Also in the year 1927, The Times Book Club rented a space on the first floor, and on 3rd October opened a branch of its library. In addition to the rent, a small commission was paid to Robert Sayle on books sold, in return for service given by the shop in packing and delivery when necessary. The turnover seems never to have been large but the amount of commission paid increased steadily during the years for which figures are now available, showing that it came to be pretty well used. In the same busy year 1927 comes the first mention of the 50 gallon petrol pump erected in Robert Sayle's yard. It cost £50. The stables had by now become garages or stock rooms; a figure for "stabling" last appears in the balance sheet for 31st January 1927.

Some two years earlier, during the first half of 1925, a carpet-beating factory had been installed on part of the ground previously occupied by The Carriers' Arms. Surveys of the site and buildings were carried out in 1924 and the adaptation of the buildings for the new venture was completed by Messrs William Bell & Sons of Cambridge during the latter part of 1924 and the first few

months of 1925, at a total cost of £833.6s.9d. The electrically-operated beating machine was made by Alexander Orr, an Edinburgh firm of engineers. The cost of this was £367.16s.0d and the factory was ready to go into action by June 1925. The beater was a remarkable, but efficient, contraption. Carpets to be cleaned were stretched over two heavy rubber rollers, 15 feet wide. Dust was beaten out of them by noisy wooden and metal clappers, after which the carpets were reversed and any loose dust on the underside was mechanically brushed off into bins behind the machine, which had at intervals to be cleared by hand – an understandably unpopular job. Another drawback was that the draught caused by the machine in action was apt to blow dust via a staircase and any chinks in woodwork, or through an open door, into an upper room which was used by upholstery workers – who also complained that they were deafened by the noise when the beater was in use. However, the factory continued its active life for over 35 years, and was not dismantled until the spring of 1961. The fair was in progress on Midsummer Common at the time, and the electric machine was bought by the proprietor of a merry-go-round.

During these times of change and expansion, the responsibility for everything in the firm's life rested, as before, wholly on the directors. They had to make all the necessary decisions and had to adapt themselves, as well as the business, to what must have seemed a total reversal of ideas and ways they had believed in for all their long and in the main successful lives. By 1930 Mr Chaplin, the Governing Director, was 86 years old; two of the other directors were less than 10 years junior to him. They had grown up and become middle-aged during the reigns of Queen Victoria and Edward VII, when it had been unthinkable that anything could go permanently wrong with the country and its institutions. Difficulties, yes – but they would be no more than passing troubles. Life in the 1920s and 30s must have seemed to these men like something out of a bad dream.

Mr Chaplin had enjoyed good health, but since 1914 he had suffered shattering blows in his private life. Not only had he lost both his sons in the war, but also his unmarried daughter had died in 1926, and his wife and brother two or three years earlier. He had become subject to recurrent attacks of bronchitis. For 50 years since Mr Sayle's death he had been first part-owner and then senior director of the business. He had taken his responsibilities very seriously and had surrendered neither to his personal tragedies nor to advancing years. But in the summer of 1934 he was obliged to give in to a particularly severe attack of bronchitis. He was ill for several weeks, and died on 17th August at his home in Chaucer Road, aged 90. The funeral service was held at Trumpington Church on 20th August. On 23rd August the body was taken to Golder's Green in North London for cremation, as there was at that time no crematorium at Cambridge. The ashes were returned for burial at Trumpington.

15: 1934-35 Selfridge Provincial Stores – a merger

Shortly after Mr Chaplin's death negotiations were started by Selfridge & Co with the remaining directors of Robert Sayle – Mr J W Pretty, Mr J B Rampling, Mr Arthur H Clark and Mr F S Scruby. Selfridges were in the market for a number of shops of more or less the same type as Robert Sayle to add to their subsidiary group, known as Selfridge Provincial Stores (SPS). Mr Gordon Selfridge was Chairman of this company, and his son, Mr H Gordon Selfridge Jnr, its Managing Director. This sale went through before the end of 1934 and it was decided to keep the old name, as indeed was done with all the units in this group. By 1st February 1936 SPS owned, in addition to Robert Sayle, the Bon Marché and Axtens in Brixton, also Pratts of Streatham. Outside London they had George Henry Lee in Liverpool, Cole Brothers in Sheffield, W J Buckley & Co in Harrogate, A H Bull in Reading, Blinkhorns in Gloucester and Stroud, Caleys in Windsor, Trewin Brothers in Watford and Thomsons in Peterborough.

Offers to acquire the shares in Robert Sayle & Co Ltd were sent to shareholders on 19th November 1934; by the end of the month all had been transferred. The preference shares were bought at par. The ordinary shares went at a premium, for 27s.6d each; in 1925, when hopes of a trade recovery had still been high with the return to the gold standard, they had been valued at 30 shillings. People who had deposited money in the business were given the option of leaving it in the new company at 4.5 per cent per annum, with six months' notice of termination on either side, or of withdrawing it on 31st December 1934 with interest paid up to date at the old rate of 5 per cent. Some decided one way and some the other.

At the take-over, the Emmanuel College lease remained unchanged from its last renewal – for 86 years from 29th September 1929 – and was reassigned to Selfridges. Jesus College made a new agreement, backdated to March 1934, granting the lease for a term until Michaelmas 2015, thereby bringing the termination of the leases from both colleges to the same date. With the renewal of the leases, repairs and alterations to the premises were again required, the agreement with Jesus College having been concluded on the understanding that £4,000 was to be spent on this property within the next two years and a further £2,000 in the four following years. One of the first changes made by SPS was to open up the inside of the shop by breaking through the main wall between the premises built on the land belonging to the two colleges; that is, by making the throughway between what is now the Dress Materials Department (which had until then been occupied by the Counting House) and the Fashion

Accessories Department, as they now are, and at the other end of the shop, between the Men's and Boys' Wear sections. It was at this time, too, that the shop front was turned into an arcade, with consequent increase in window and display space, at a cost of about £3,000. The second and third floors – that is, the living quarters – were entirely reconstructed, the cost of this last being in the region of £7,000. Mr Pretty remained as manager of the shop under the new owners and in September 1935 Mr F W Haley was transferred from Thomsons in Peterborough to be his Assistant Manager.

Certain fresh ideas in system and organisation were introduced by Selfridges. Perhaps the change which made the most immediate impression was that buying for most sections was thenceforward to be done centrally; a decision which led some of the local buyers to feel that they had been demoted, being no longer in full control of their departments, their stocks or their finances. Moreover, departmental heads were now known as "junior executives"; the only "senior executive" locally was the manager of the shop. Some of the buyers were no longer young and they found the new ways embarrassing. For this and other reasons a number of them, as well as some of the other more senior employees, resigned either immediately or soon after the beginning of the new year. Familiar names disappear from the books. Mr S H Doggett, the Secretary of the old company, left before the end of 1934; he lived in retirement in Cambridge until his death on 25th November 1940. His son, Mr Frank Doggett, a clerk in the Counting House since September 1923, stayed on with SPS for several more years. Miss Chipper went on 30th November 1934. Miss Blowman remained until 8th June 1935 and Mr Norrington 'til 15th August. Mr Rampling and Mr Arthur Clark retired in 1934; others at various times up to the middle of 1935. Some of those who chose to resign might in any case have been asked to do so under SPS regulations, according to which the retention of any member of staff aged over 65 had to be sanctioned by the central office and was agreed only in exceptional cases. At the other end of the scale, the engagement of any new personnel aged over 40 was discouraged.

Long-range management can never be quite the same as a purely personal form of control. For 94 years Robert Sayle had been a personal business; even when turned into a limited company it had been run by familiar people on familiar lines. It was now becoming one unit among many in a widely-spread concern; it would live, some people felt, under an impersonal and unfamiliar rule that was bound to be different, however benevolent its intention. SPS had, necessarily, its regulations and, equally necessarily in so composite a group, these regulations had to be codified to ensure a measure of uniformity. Any departure from them must be referred to and agreed by the central management. The code of regulations, which went into very minute details, was issued to the senior executive in each branch and was further elaborated by a book of so-called "sermons", a set of memoranda giving some guiding lines, which might be superseded or added to at any time if it should be found desirable; they

explained and perhaps softened the edges of the code, but did not encourage a casual approach or woolly thinking. Thirty-five years ago such a code was something of a novelty. The very fact that it was written down and published in book form – statutory law rather than common law, so to speak – could be worrying to people who had grown up under a less formal system. The regulations, as was to be expected, dealt with all aspects of the shop's life: merchandise management; engagements; terminations; staff contracts; staff training; entitlement to holidays and sick pay; promises made to customers; relations with travellers and suppliers (particularly those local ones who must now in many cases be dropped); wages; promotions; character references in and out; the responsibilities of individuals vis-a-vis the central offices, etc, etc. Those who lived with these rules no doubt soon found that, taken all in all, things went on much as before, with only relatively minor changes affecting the staff's life. Selfridges themselves felt that the take-over in Cambridge was carried through particularly smoothly and in the spirit of friendly co-operation.

Wages to some extent increased. Staff discount was standardised, being granted at the end of a short probationary period after engagement at the rate of three half pence in the shilling (12.5 per cent) to rank and file, and 20 per cent to those of executive status, whether "senior" or "junior". A year or so later it was decided that a penny in the shilling should be allowed to families of members of the staff. No discount was to be given to anyone whatever on the first day of the summer and winter sales. Shopping cards

DRESSES

The shop opened up: The Dress Piece Goods Department in 1935, the Silver Jubilee Year of King George V's Accession. Note the walls removed on the left and the three wells admitting daylight in addition to the far-end rooflight

were valid, normally, for not more than three months and were reissued only on 1st February, 1st May, 1st August and 1st November. They were usable in any of the SPS branches. Living in was reckoned at 20 shillings a week (raised to 30 shillings for seniors in 1938), with an allowance of 15 shillings a week during absence on holiday. Meals taken regularly in the canteen counted as 7s.6d a week. A short break was now allowed during the afternoons. A barrel of beer still stood in the men's dining room.

Increased emphasis was laid on health and general fitness. New entrants were expected to have a medical examination, either by the regular SPS doctor in London or by a local practitioner approved by the company. Sick pay was granted after one year's service, provided that the employee had been graded 'A' by the doctor; partial sick pay might be awarded in some other

cases at the firm's direction. Annual holidays were reckoned from 1st February. One day's leave on full pay was given for each month an employee had been in the business before that date, with a minimum of six days in a year and a maximum of 12; so anyone engaged before 1st February was allowed a week's paid holiday during his first year, even if he had been in the place for only a month or two before the decisive date. Anyone engaged between 1st February and 1st March was granted four days' paid holiday during the first year. (This was, of course, before the present statutory regulations about holidays were in force.) An extra week's holiday with pay was given to anyone attending a Territorial Army camp. Thursday remained closing day. Normal business hours were from 9am to 5.30pm and six o'clock on Saturdays.

Early in the new year, 1935, a great Clearance Sale was held. "Under our new business conditions," ran an advertisement in the 'Cambridge Independent News and Chronicle' on 4th January, "all merchandise which has been in the establishment for three months or over MUST BE CLEARED, regardless of original cost. Never have we been in a position to offer such genuine bargains." Men's wear was offered at less than half price. Silks by the yard were selling at 1s.6³/₄d, 2s.0d and 2s.3¹/₂d. Carpets, 7 feet 6 inches by 9 feet, were reduced from 98s.6d to 52s.6d each. A week later, linen sheets, 70 inches by 108 inches, were marked down to 20 shillings a pair, with linen pillow cases at 1s.6³/₄d and 2s.3¹/₂d each. In the July Sale that year, a three-piece suite, hide-covered, could be bought for 19 guineas, and a mahogany bedstead for 69s.6d.

Advertising was now to become more frequent than under the older managements. Robert Sayle himself and his immediate successors in Robert Sayle & Co had never believed in spending much money on it, preferring to rely on recommendation by customers. After the 1914-18 war, and especially after the business had become a limited company, press publicity came to have rather greater importance. The summer and winter clearance sales, at any rate, were regularly advertised, as also was the arrival of new seasons' spring and autumn fashions and occasionally other events. During the years from 1919 to 1926 an average of about £450 a year had been spent with the newspapers. In 1929 the figure jumped to over £1,000 and for the next four or five years it

remained at an average of more than £850. The extra advertising was no doubt to some extent due to the opening of the various new departments at Robert Sayle in 1927, but something may perhaps also be ascribed to the fact that the slump was at its worst in those years, when every means had to be tried to keep trade at an acceptable level. Nonetheless, unlike other Cambridge shops of comparable standing, whose advertisements appeared in local papers throughout the year, Robert Sayle seldom advertised more than once a month – except that there was always a discreet little notice on the back page to remind readers of the Undertaker's Department. Under SPS advertisements were more widely spread and more flamboyant. Play was made with the name – "The Sale of Sayle's" was one – to catch the eye. Not only were announcements inserted more often in the local dailies or weeklies and even occasionally in a national newspaper, but the net was gradually extended to include more specialist publications like the 'Varsity Weekly' and 'The Oddfellow's Handbook'. By 1939 they were also appearing in some of the college magazines – Newnham, Girton and St John's – and notices were displayed at the Festival Theatre from time to time and inserted in the Poppy Day magazine.

Subscriptions and gifts were sent to numerous local and trade charities, including among others the Commercial Travellers' School, the Drapers' Schools, the Easter Counties Asylum, Addenbrooke's Hospital and the Hunstanton Convalescent Home, as well as to the local branches of some national societies such as the Cancer

Research Fund, the Salvation Army, the YMCA, the YWCA and the British and Foreign Bible Society. In 1939 the Air Defence Cadet Corps was added to the list. Under the earlier managements no lists had been kept, at any rate none have survived, of such subscriptions, most of which seem to have been made personally rather than part of the business expenses.

Another change under SPS was an increase in the strength of the pensions fund. In the old days pensions were not in any way an obligatory part of an employer's duty to his staff; nor was there any public monetary assistance except a parish rate to give sporadic help to the indigent until, from 1st January 1909, under Lloyd George's government, a national pension of five shillings a week was payable to old people with very small means. (This last was not in any way connected with personal insurance.) An employer might, as an act of grace, grant a pension to a long-service employee, as Mr Robert Sayle had done in his will and probably also during his lifetime, but in general it was expected that people should, by care and thrift, make provision for their own old age. If this had not been possible, and if they had no relations who could look after them, there was always the workhouse, though this was considered to be something of a disgrace in a family. Actually, some of the workhouses in Cambridge had quite a good reputation for their standards of food and comfort; one of them was the building facing onto St Tibb's Row beyond St Tibb's cottage, which was originally the workhouse for the ward of St Andrew the Great.

A small pensions fund had been started by Robert Sayle & Co Ltd in 1922. Annual increments were added to it as profits permitted and interest at the rate of 5.5 per cent was always reckoned on the capital sum. As time went on records show that retired employees enjoyed its benefits, payable twice a year normally, and varying between five shillings and £1 a week. On what basis the amount was calculated is not clear. Some £2,700 in this fund was carried over to SPS.

Compulsory personal insurance was a later development; though a semi-voluntary form of insurance to which only those below a certain level of income were obliged to subscribe, it was introduced in Great Britain in 1911. Employers had been required, under the Employers' Liability Act of 1880 and the Workmen's Compensation Acts of 1897 and 1906, to pay some indemnity to members of their staff for accidents occurring to them while at work. To cover such liabilities policies were taken out with insurance societies. Under a staff scheme, one such policy, arranged by Robert Sayle in 1932 with the Colonial Mutual Life Assurance Society Ltd, allowed from £19 to £154 to be claimed by the victim of an accident. National insurance against unemployment and loss of earning power through sickness or old age was still only partially compulsory after 1918. Something, also, could be privately organised through funds established on a mutual basis by Friendly Societies – whence the expression still sometimes used about anyone drawing the national sickness benefit: "he's on the club!". The present system of full national insurance dates from 1948.

16: An inventory

At the time of the changeover to SPS, a magnificent inventory of the fixtures and fittings, trade utensils and rolling stock of Robert Sayle & Co Ltd was compiled by a London firm of valuers. It is a most impressive volume, bound in navy blue leather covers, gold-tooled, each nearly half an inch thick, containing 287 pages. The whole book measures 12 inches by 13 inches by 3 inches and weighs 14 pounds. In this inventory the living quarters are described as well as the business sections. A great many alterations to the structure and internal arrangements have since been made, but a general idea of the layout in 1934/35 can be gained, before the important changes made by SPS in the next year or two.

As regards the shop premises, the basement contained a furniture showroom, but otherwise only stockrooms. Of these last, the greatest amount of space was allotted to haberdashery and knitting wools, together with some of the Display Department's equipment. The remainder was taken up by reserve stocks of ironmongery and drapery.

On the ground floor were selling departments for furniture and floor coverings, and there was also a carpet stockroom, as well as the Soft Furnishings and Household Linens Departments, all of which were sited in the area now containing the carpet and furniture showrooms. Carpets had formed an important part of the shop's trade for about 70 years; Furniture was as yet building up from small beginnings. At this time, this part of the premises was still separate from the rest of the shop; a slype or roofed passage between Nos 16 and 17 St Andrew's Street led from the main road through the building into the yard. A glass door on either side of the passage gave access to the two parts of the shop. The passage was closed at night by heavy gates on the street side. In 1953 it was incorporated in the shop to be used as extra display space, thereby doing away with the segregation of the furnishings departments from the fashion sections.

The remainder of the ground floor selling area was occupied by haberdashery, knitting wools, small accessories such as gloves, stockings, ribbons and laces, by materials by the yard, and by the men's wear sections. The Wholesale Department was also on the ground floor, behind the present Men's Wear departments and extending into what is now the receiving dock. An extra stockroom for wholesale goods was on the first floor. Also on the ground floor were the various sections of the Counting House, taking up the whole of the space where now dress piece goods are sold; and further back were the receiving, marking off, and despatch rooms, the telephone exchange, a small advertising office, and the manager's room, (known as the Private Office). Carpeting on floors in selling departments and in the offices was fawn Axminster bordered in crimson and black, but the wholesale part had bare boards, except for one small piece of coconut fibre matting.

On the first floor was another furniture showroom, also The Times Library. Apart from these two sections, which were above the ground floor furnishing departments in No 17 St Andrew's Street, the first floor was devoted to ladies' and children's fashions, with five fitting rooms. Beyond these was the Hairdressing and Manicure salon, containing 12 cubicles, in seven of which central hot air drying was installed; this meant that a flexible tube could be plugged into the wall of a cubicle to convey hot air from a central heater, while the operator stood by her client to dry the hair by directing the nozzle of the tube onto the head. Adjacent were a hairdressing laboratory and stockroom. Marcel waving was still popular, and curling-iron stands are mentioned as part of the equipment. Permanent waving was carried out on the Eugene and Macdonald systems, both of which remained in vogue for a good many years to come. Floor coverings here were of inlaid and bordered marble-patterned linoleum. Carpets in the fashion departments were Axminster, with a multicoloured foliage design on a black ground, and there was a parquet-patterned linoleum surround. Heating throughout the shop was by means of hot-water radiators. At this date, the cost of water, lighting and heating (excluding coal), came to between £700 and £800 each half year.

Living quarters for the staff occupied a part of each floor. The kitchen and larder, a store room, and a comfortable sitting room for the maids were in the basement. On the ground floor, a few steps above the level of the shop floor, were two dining rooms, men's and women's still separate and furnished much as they had been 30 years earlier, except that the men's room now contained a piano. The Principal's dining room was, as before, on the first floor.

On the second and third floors were, on the women's side, 26 bedrooms, including the housekeeper's, a sitting room each for the housekeeper, the seniors and the juniors, a cloakroom for day girls, a linen cupboard, three bathrooms and lavatories. In the attic was a bedroom for three maids who slept on the premises. Assistants now living in mostly had single rooms, each of which was furnished with a three-foot bedstead, a chest of drawers, a washstand, a towel horse, a chair and a mirror. Mention is made of hanging space only in some cases, usually in the form of a curtain across a corner, though a wardrobe is listed in two of the rooms. An electric light pendant with a shade gave illumination; the electricity was turned off each night at 11 o'clock. On the floors were linoleum and a couple of rugs. When rooms had to be shared, all furniture was duplicated and a screen was provided to give a measure of privacy. Usually about 30 lived on this side, shut in at night on each floor by heavy doors at the end of the corridor opening onto the stairs. The maids' room in the attic was comparably furnished but the staircase leading to this room was reported to be dilapidated and altogether in poor condition. This, with the rest of the living quarters, took first priority for renovation when SPS acquired the property.

On the men's side there were, in all, 13 bedrooms – two on the first floor, five on the second, and six on the third. On the first floor, too, were a smoking room, a bathroom and a box room. There were no married quarters. The smoking room was evidently the descendant of the original billiards room, for it contained a quarter-sized billiards table, with cues, markers and other equipment, and plenty of comfortable seating. It was lit by a large, 16 inch, shaded hanging lamp. Eight, in all, of the rooms in the living quarters on both sides of the house had gas fires with coin slot meters.

At the back of the premises were outbuildings, one of which, on the ground level, south side, was arranged as a mortuary chapel with an altar, crucifix and other suitable furnishings; there was also an undertaker's store, with grave linings, imitation grass, oak coffin trestles, a purple and gold rug, etc. The rug was stolen once but was recovered soon after from a stall in the market. A furniture store room and a carpenter's shop were above the mortuary and on the other side of the yard were the carpet- beating factory, the upholstery workroom, white wood, and carpet-sewing rooms. All workrooms were heated by slow combustion stoves.

Finally, there were the garages. One held the hearse – a motor vehicle bought in 1925 for £741; it was sold in 1938 for £2.15s.0d and not replaced. Others contained a saloon car, a large lorry, a 10 hundredweight Ford van and one 13 hundredweight, three smaller vans and three runabout cars. In the balance sheet of 1934/35 they had been valued at £990 total. The vans were sold on 1st February 1940 for £14. The shop windows on the St Andrew's Street front were all carpeted with grey felt and were lit by electric lights with silvered diffusion reflectors. Ten windows are listed and an island showcase, with every imaginable kind of display stand.

17: Selfridge Provincial Stores – following on from Robert Sayle & Co Ltd

Certain fairly complete records have survived covering most of the shop's finances for the 15 years during which the business existed as Robert Sayle & Co Ltd. We know something about turnover, profits and other money matters but the figures have not been broken down departmentally. For the last few years of its life as a private company, up to the end of November 1934 when the shop became a member of the SPS group, we also have details of the names, departments and salaries of the indoor staff. Unfortunately no similar lists have been found for the tradesmen, transport,

maintenance and workroom personnel of those days, though an occasional note has come to light. Selfridges' principle was to save only a minimum of records: – "Destroy, almost ruthlessly, records that those who want to retain them cannot show a specific, up-to-date, need for", runs a memorandum. "With other pieces of junk [they] contribute to mental clogging that saps initiative and elasticity." It was, of course, agreed that Counting House records had to be kept, but even most of these for no longer than from one to 18 months; a few for two to three years. Only legal documents were to be preserved, for any time up to 10 years. So it was probably only by chance (or illicit hoarding!) that any old Robert Sayle papers have come down to us. Some were understood to have been destroyed at the time of the rebuilding during the second half of the 1930s. All remaining important documents were handed over to John Lewis & Co Ltd in 1940 and it may well be that many perished during the bombing of Oxford Street that year.

It was a matter of great satisfaction to all members of staff in 1934/35 that Mr Pretty stayed on as manager of the shop under the new regime. A good many of the other senior people retired, as has already been mentioned. Although very few individual names occur in the books from 1935 onwards, the earlier records show that, in 1934 just before the take-over, there were exactly 70 salespeople in the business, 25 of whom were men (including two in the Wholesale Department and one traveller) and 45 women and girls. Departments for men's wear and those with heavy stocks to handle – carpets, silks, linens and other piece goods – were all staffed by men and there were two male assistants together with three girls selling hosiery. The other departments – women's fashions, shoes, ribbons, laces, gloves etc – were run by women, though Mr Arthur Clark was, up to the end of 1934, responsible for the fashion showrooms and was succeeded in 1935 by Mr D Stout, who held the post until his death in May 1943. The tailoring sections were then taken over by Miss A A Callaghan, who later became Mrs Piper. She retired in February 1969 after a very successful career. Haberdashery, always a very busy

and profitable section, came under female rule and employed eight salespeople, the largest number in any departments of the store.

The Counting House was, in 1934, managed by Mr G H Doggett, who was also the Company Secretary; under him were two male clerks (one of them his son Frank) and nine young women. In addition there were three girls in the cash desks. At the time of the transfer to SPS the secretaryship was merged with that of the parent company; Mrs H B Parsons, who was with Selfridges for a number of years as Chief Accountant, became secretary of SPS and Mr Frank Doggett was made manager of the Robert Sayle Counting House when his father retired.

Quite a number of the salespeople and others of the immediately pre-SPS days are still familiar figures to the present generation of the shop's workers and customers. Some have progressed from being lively juniors to being managers of departments and some have – only within the last year or two – retired, after keeping up the traditions of the business through all the changes and chances of the last 30 or so years.

The hostel was fully occupied in 1934/35 and continued to be so for a good many more years. It was run by a housekeeper, who had eight or nine maids to help her, their pay ranging from £16 to £50 per annum. This was later increased slightly, the minimum being £20; the maximum was raised to £60 in February 1938. It seems to have been generally agreed, by female residents at all events, that the hostel was a pleasant enough place to live in, especially after it had been refurbished by Selfridges. Some of the men were more doubtful – being perhaps usually less practical in ensuring their own comfort? Small drawbacks, like not being allowed to be out after 10 o'clock at night (nine o'clock for junior girls), were not seriously resented and were welcomed by the parents of the younger female residents. A late pass could on occasion be obtained for a dance or a theatre engagement and some of the male residents took it in turns to act as doorkeeper when necessary; if the merrymakers were very late in returning, their reception by a sleepy Janus might be a little tart. Food was good. No charge was made for living in. From February 1938 employees might, if they wished, draw cash in lieu of board and lodging or of regular canteen meals, at the rate of 20 shillings and 7s.6d a week respectively. Most wages and salaries in 1934, prior to the change of ownership, were still being paid monthly and adjustments were made, as before, for purchases on a house account and so on; from time to time this might make budgeting difficult and not much money would be left to draw, especially for younger people, so that recourse to a kindly friend or an indulgent parent might be necessary for a loan to keep the wolf from the door until the next pay-day. "But we managed!" one is told with a reminiscent twinkle. "Make-do-and-mend and all that. We had fun!" After the shop came under SPS, weekly payment was the general rule; but Selfridges considered that it was more suitable for executives to be paid by a monthly cheque and encouraged this, though without insisting on it.

Judging by the records of pay-rates in 1934, girl juniors on the selling staff received from £12 to £18 a year (£1 to 30 shillings a month); a boy might get 7s.6d a week. Women seniors drew £96 to £180 a year; men from £100 to £250. A short list headed "Buyers, etc", all of whom were men, shows that salaries in this grade ranged from £400 to £550 a year. The two male clerks in the Counting House were paid £225 per annum each; their female colleagues from £25 to £115, according to age and experience. In addition, the clerks and some of the buyers enjoyed commission twice a year, based presumably on the half-year results and the presentation of the accounts. Commission in wholesale departments was paid as part of the wages and on the amount of contract sales. Selfridges operated on a so-called "drawing-rate", whereby anyone due for commission as well as fixed pay might, at choice, draw up to an estimated amount of commission for one period in advance; any miscalculation would be rectified on the succeeding pay-day.

Under Robert Sayle & Co Ltd, in 1934/35, members of the Carpet Department, whether salesmen, porters or workroom staff, had been the best paid in the shop, a minimum of £3 a week being normal. A girl in the millinery workroom might, at the age of 20, earn eight pence an hour; an adult man in the upholstery workroom collected nine pence halfpenny an hour and a boy five pence three farthings an hour. Transport workers were paid from 45 shillings to 55 shillings a week. When Selfridges acquired the business, wages of the selling staff were, as far as one could tell, increased but, as figures subsequent to this date are seldom given in accounts that have survived, except as totals under headings such as "General Selling", "House", etc, and the numbers of staff involved are not stated, it is not possible to form an accurate idea of details. A separate list was kept of those drawing their pay monthly, which shows that in several cases the salaries were increased more than once during the next years by quite appreciable amounts; it is unlikely that these were the only lucky ones.

Although the figures for Robert Sayle retail trade had been going down steadily during the last years of its independent existence, they took a slight turn for the better after the shop joined the Selfridge group. Since 1920/21, when the short-lived optimism of the early post-war period had made Robert Sayle into a limited company and sent figures rocketing up to £184,314 (of which £144,941 was retail and £39,393 wholesale), trade had been gradually falling off by some thousands each year, until at 31st January 1935 – when the accounts of the final year of the old company were published – the retail trade was worth £94,149 and the wholesale £11,858, making a total of about £106,000, a drop of over 40 per cent on the earlier figure.

In 1935/36, with the change of ownership and of trading policy, and the retirement of much of the senior personnel, some further decline in turnover might have been expected, even if only temporarily, while staff and customers adjusted to new ways and different merchandise. In fact, the retail trade very soon began to improve again, especially with hire-purchase sales becoming popular. Cash and credit sales, excluding wholesale transactions, recovered in the next three years to £96,000, £103,000 and £105,000

respectively; in the following year, that is to say 1939/40, the total turnover was reckoned to be just over £125,000. A real decline, however, came in the wholesale business during the same period. It was intentionally run down because Selfridge's policy was to concentrate on the retail side. In the first half of 1936 the Wholesale Department had been worth nearly £4,700, in the second half it had dropped to £2,200. After this it contributed progressively less, until its figures appeared for the last time in the accounts at 31st January 1938; the department had been closed down at the end of the previous half year and the final balance, about £500, was shown in the profit and loss accounts for that year. The two salesmen were transferred to retail departments.

After the wholesale trade had been given up, several new departments were opened up in the space now available. At the time when SPS bought the business, the trading value of the departments was fairly evenly divided between the fashions and the furnishings sections and this trend continued throughout the Selfridge period. Under the earlier managements neither china and glass nor lampshades and electrical goods had been stocked and departments for both these groups now made their debut. Hardware had been sold previously but turnover was small and remained so; until 1939 it was worth less than £1,000 each half year.

Also at this date, 1937/38, mention is first made in the accounts of sections for jewellery, trunks, handbags and other leather goods, all of which became permanent and useful parts of the branch's trade. After 1937 certain changes were made in the organisation of the fashion departments too. Inexpensive dresses, coats and costumes were sold in "five-price" sections, the frocks becoming very popular at the expense of model gowns, but the cheaper tailoring capturing very much less from the better end of the trade.

18: 1939-40 – another change

Although trade had to some extent recovered at Robert Sayle between 1936 and 1939, Mr Selfridge and his son evidently came to the conclusion that the group had not turned out to be altogether the kind of business that suited them, especially in view of the more and more unsettled social and political conditions. The SPS company had been founded in 1926 and for some years had been fairly successful. But in February 1940 The Financial News referred to "the rather dreary post-1930 record of the Selfridge Provincial group and the gradual weakening of its financial position". The total turnover of the whole concern in 1939 was only just over £3,250,000.

Added to internal business difficulties, the world political situation was growing more than ever harassing and nerves were taut. Hitler's Germany was an ever-present menace, increasingly so from 1937 onwards. Relief had been enormous all over the country when, in the summer of 1938, the Prime Minister had come back from Munich and proclaimed that "Peace in our time" was assured. Unfortunately he was wrong and after a further year of anxiety, with trouble piling up all over Europe, war broke out once again between Germany and this country on 3rd September 1939.

Selfridges now decided definitely to dispose of the SPS group. The John Lewis Partnership, under its founder and Chairman, Mr John Spedan Lewis, stepped in at once to make an offer for the shares. Negotiations began with a letter addressed to SPS Ltd on 15th October 1939 and it was hoped to complete the deal by the early part of January 1940. Various last-minute hitches delayed the matter from one day to another but it was finally concluded towards the end of the month and control of the (at that time) 15 branches of SPS passed to the John Lewis Partnership effectively from 1st February 1940, with an enormous number of the SPS two shilling shares being transferred to John Lewis & Company Ltd at three pence each. This was, incidentally, a comparatively satisfactory price for the Selfridge shareholders, for the shares had not long since been quoted on the Stock Exchange at one penny. The total amount of money that changed hands over the deal at this time was between £30,000 and £40,000. "A bit of a gamble", some thought, but it turned out to be an investment whose value soon proved to be undoubted. Other SPS shares, at £1 face value, including the 6 per cent preference shares in Robert Sayle & Co Ltd held by a number of people from earlier days, were dealt with later. An

THE GAZETTE

(First issued 16th March, 1918)

OF

THE JOHN LEWIS PARTNERSHIP

begun in 1914 with Peter Jones, Sloane Square, London and now including also John Lewis and Company Limited of Oxford Street, London, Clearings Draycott Avenue, London, Jessop and Son Limited of Nottingham, Lance and Lance Limited of Weston-Super-Mare, Knight and Lee of Southsea Tyrrell and Green Limited of Southampton, Crawford Street Garage Limited Crawford Street, London, John Lewis Properties Limited, John Lewis Building Limited, The Odney Estate Limited, Cookham, Berkshire, Waitrose Limited of 19-23 Gloucester Road, S.W.7, 286 Fulham Road, S.W.10, 3 The Parade Ealing, W.5., Castle Hill, Windsor, 158 Ewell Road, Surbiton, 450 Finchley Road, N.W.2, 14 Victoria Parade, Muswell Hill, N.10, 18 Golders Green Road N.W.11, 7-9 The Highway, Gerrards Cross, and John Lewis Partnership Limited

THE PARTNERSHIP

is intended to secure happiness for its members in any way that it can but chiefly by acquiring the greatest amount of capital for their separate property in the proportion of their separate parts in the collective effort of the team. Within such limitations, as may arise from their general sense of social obligation, the Partnership is to be conducted always wholly and solely for the benefit of its members present and future. Each Partner is to hold his place in the team so long only as its efficiency will not be increased by his standing down but, once in, he is to be given all possible help to keep his footing.

THE GAZETTE

is intended to play in all of the affairs of the Partnership the part that a Free Press plays in all of the affairs of a Nation. Except where this is clearly indicated, views expressed in it must not be taken to be the views of the Management.

The Gazette *is intended to maintain closer touch between the different sections and individual members of the Partnership's total team, especially between the Management and all the rest, than can exist without some such means. You can write to it whatever you like and sign your name or not, just as you please.*

The postal address is " The Editor, The Gazette, *7 Holles Street, W.1 " (Telephone: Mayfair 7711). For the Partnership's own letter-boxes envelopes can be marked simply " The Gazette."*

The Gazette *can be supplied to subscribers outside the Partnership. Such subscriptions must be paid in advance. Each issue is twopence post free. Contributions, signed or unsigned, of any kind and from any quarter, are welcome.*

Copyright in this paper is reserved without registration at Stationers' Hall, such registration being by the Copyright Act of 1911 unnecessary.

FIFTEEN NEW BRANCHES

1. The Partnership has just acquired the controlling-interest in each of the following fifteen businesses. The figures of turnover are for the year that ended on the 31st January 1939. It must be remembered that they probably include a good deal of trade that we should not consider sound business and that our policy will sacrifice. It is obviously impossible to put into the first notice everything, that seems likely to interest some Partners, about these new branches. Further notices will appear in due course, including probably a general account of each separate branch.

IN LONDON

		£
1. Bon Marché Ltd.	of Brixton	
2. Quin & Axtens	of Brixton	
3. Pratt's	of Streatham	

These three are all one company. For the year mentioned their combined turnover was 969,644

			£
4. H. Holdron Ltd.	of Peckham	..	.. 357,490
5. John Barnes & Co. Ltd.	Finchley Road	..	.. 282,712
6. Jones Brothers (Holloway) Ltd.	of Holloway	..	.. 248,531

OUTSIDE LONDON

			£
7. George Henry Lee & Co. Ltd.	of Liverpool	..	.. 519,892
8. Cole Brothers Ltd.	of Sheffield	..	.. 346,819
9. A. H. Bull Ltd.	of Reading	..	.. 191,708
10. Robert Sayle & Co. Ltd.	of Cambridge	..	.. 105,011
11. Blinkhorn Ltd.	of Gloucester	..	.. 79,480
12. W. J. Buckley & Co. Ltd.	of Harrogate	..	.. 77,552
13. Caleys Ltd.	of Windsor	..	.. 45,950
14. Trewin Brothers Ltd.	of Watford	..	.. 42,983
15. Thomsons (Peterborough) Ltd.	of Peterborough	..	.. 33,443

£3,301,215

2. It was hoped that in this notice our *Gazette* would achieve that supreme desire of newspapers, to have all to themselves some announcement of great interest and

offer was made to those who still had deposit accounts at Robert Sayle to repay them at the agreed six months' notice, or after a shorter period if preferred, but anyone who wished to continue leaving the money on loan to the new company was at liberty to do so, though at a reduced rate of interest. Most withdrew it before the end of 1940; the last few were paid out in May 1943.

One of the conditions of the sale of the Selfridge subsidiary was that the title should be changed: it was renamed Suburban and Provincial Stores Ltd – and thereby retained the old initials SPS. Each of the component branches kept its former name. For the time being, Mr H Gordon Selfridge Jnr and two other members of the SPS company remained on the board of Suburban and Provincial Stores Ltd, with Mr Spedan Lewis as Chairman. They withdrew a few months later.

Mr Lewis had been interested in the SPS group ever since Selfridges had just forestalled him in buying some of the units in 1934/35. He had been particularly sorry to miss Robert Sayle, as he had always wanted the John Lewis Partnership to be represented in the two older university towns. The Partnership already owned four shops outside London in addition to the two – John Lewis and Peter Jones – in London and had had good experience of selling through branches. There were, therefore, sound reasons for the Partnership to hope that the new expansion would be a success, though doubts were expressed in some quarters about the timing of the purchase. 'Women's Wear News' remarked at this juncture that "it says a good deal for faith in the future that a business transaction of the size of John

Lewis and SPS should have been even contemplated in times like the present". And it continued in a later paragraph: "It will be interesting to see whether the staffs of these stores can become 'partners' in the same sense that employees of the existing stores in the John Lewis group are partners." The question was also put whether an early return on the investment could be expected. "But no doubt the size will in due course improve the organisation as a whole, from both buying and selling points of view", the writer concluded. The John Lewis Partnership was, in fact, determined that, as far as possible and as quickly as possible, the new branches should become full members of the organisation and their employees 'partners' in every sense. Very few changes of personnel would, it was hoped, be necessary in cases where members of the staffs themselves wished to remain. Mr Lewis described the 4,000 new 'Partners' in an issue of the company's weekly newspaper, The Gazette of the John Lewis Partnership, as "a thoroughly decent crowd and just our sort". At Robert Sayle & Co Mr Pretty – who had lately been appointed a borough councillor – agreed to continue as General Manager; his doing so was a great help in making this second, unexpectedly rapid, change of ownership easier for the rest of the staff. Many other seniors also stayed on but Mr Haley, the Assistant General Manager, was transferred back to Peterborough as General Manager of Thomsons almost immediately.

Civilians were from now on being brought into the war effort to an ever increasing extent and, sooner or later, most people under 40, and many older ones too, were mobilised in one service

(opposite page)
**The Gazette of
3 February 1940,
covering the
Partnership's
takeover
of Selfridge
Provincial Stores**

or another, whether in the armed forces, Home Guard, Special Constabulary or, very importantly, as members of the Auxiliary Fire Service. This service organised wardens for every street and every large building. At first it was done on a local and purely voluntary basis. It was not until 1941 that the government introduced compulsory fire-watching for all shops, factories, etc; by then Robert Sayle, in common with the rest of the Partnership, had already had fire-watching arrangements in being for over a year and had been congratulated by the authorities on its efficiency.

In Cambridge the Auxiliary Fire Service was an absolute essential. Being overcrowded and completely unplanned, with innumerable narrow, involved alleyways and courts, and houses containing a great deal of dry old woodwork, the place was peculiarly vulnerable to fire. The great fear was that, when the war emerged from the 'phoney' stage of the first months and hostilities began in earnest for this country, the whole town might all too easily be destroyed by incendiary bombs, with fearful loss of life. As it happened, Cambridge was spared a great deal of possible devastation by something that had originally seemed to many people to be a misfortune, or at least an annoyance – the fact that the railway station and most of the track were sited well away from the centre of the town. Enemy bombers were interested chiefly in putting the transport system out of action and aimed almost solely at the railway. So, although there were actually over 20 raids on Cambridge, surprisingly little damage was done to the town itself. It came to be considered a 'safe' area. The

John Lewis Partnership was quick to take advantage of this; it rented two large store rooms in Cambridge, to house some of the enormous reserves of stock it held – especially of furniture and materials by the yard – which, it was obvious, would in the existing circumstances be more securely laid up here than in London. One of these store rooms was in Albion Row, next to some old schools, off Northampton Street, and the other above a garage in Devonshire Street, between Mill Road and Tenison Road.

Fire-watching was taken very seriously at Robert Sayle, with drills and all necessary instruction, but the watchers seem to have managed to get plenty of fun out of it too. Everyone between the ages of 18 and 60 took turns at it, men and women, hostel residents and others, the General Manager with all the rest, though in fact only men were legally required to do so. At holiday times, such as Christmas and Easter, volunteers were always ready to take on the job, even to cooking for themselves, but of course everything was done to ensure that seasonable cheer was forthcoming in the way of food and that games such as cards and darts were available to while away the hours. A subscription to The Times Book Club gave the watchers 20 books at a time from which to choose, which were later increased to 40. Smoking was allowed only under the supervision of the senior warden. At first the post was manned at all times, but later it was decided that this was not necessary over Sundays, unless there happened to be an 'Alert', in which case two wardens had to go on duty. As part of the safety precautions a tremendous spring-clean was undertaken in mid-February 1940;

no outside help was engaged and the operation was carried out, as Mr Pretty said, by the shop's "small army of porters and men who took upon themselves the responsibility of seeing the job through, by many hours of overtime". One Tuesday evening, early in May that year, a full-dress ARP practice was held after the shop had closed and the duty-warden was able to report proudly that the whole staff got to the basement shelter in under three minutes; "casualties" and "fires" were "discovered" and dealt with; there was no crowding or panic. Altogether a most satisfactory exercise.

Trade at Robert Sayle, and indeed in many of the Partnership's shops, except those in the West End of London, had been picking up astonishingly well in those early months of 1940, with a really noteworthy increase in turnover. A week after the transfer of the SPS group to the Partnership there was a mention in The Gazette that "Mr Pretty... managed a very nice increase of 40 per cent" over the figure for the corresponding week in 1939. Nor was this only a flash in the pan; week by week and month by month during 1940 Robert Sayle was generally able to declare increases that were more than creditably above the figures for the previous two years. These and other items of local news were sent to The Gazette by all branches most weeks and published under the general heading "House Notes". By the end of April and the beginning of May the increases at Robert Sayle were quite startling – 60 per cent, 80 per cent and more. Part of the growth may have been due to "panic buying" of such things as dress materials, shoes, silk stockings, or knitting wools, of which it was rumoured that serious

shortages were imminent, but it is also likely that customers were buying because they found that they were now able to make their choice locally from an excellent assortment of John Lewis stocks, instead of having to make the now possibly dangerous journey to London. In fact, at about this time, John Lewis's accounts department reported that over 200 of their Oxford Street customers had transferred their accounts to Cambridge.

In June 1940 everyone at Robert Sayle heard with real regret that, on doctor's orders, Mr Pretty was obliged to relinquish his post as General Manager. Arrangements were made as quickly as possible to enable him to give up his responsibilities and he was replaced by Mr Leslie J Walsh. Mr Walsh had joined Selfridges as a youth in 1924. In 1931 he had, after a short time as Assistant General Manager at Pratts in Streatham, become General Manager of Blinkhorns, Selfridge's branch in Gloucester, and five years later had been transferred as Assistant General Manager to their much larger branch, Cole Brothers in Sheffield. He took up his new position at Robert Sayle on 1st July 1940. Mr Pretty was appointed Chairman of Robert Sayle & Co Ltd so that his function was thenceforward advisory, while the weight of executive decisions was borne by Mr Walsh. The following month Mr P W Hayes, the recently appointed General Manager of Thomsons in Peterborough, was called up for work of national importance; his place was taken by Miss J E Humphries, as Acting General Manager, on transfer from another position at Peter Jones in London.

Trade for the rest of the year 1940 continued at a very satisfactory level at

Robert Sayle. Weekly takings were still often nearly double, and sometimes more than double, the 1939 figures. By the end of the year, despite an occasional setback, the shop managed to be within a small fraction of 80 per cent above the corresponding cumulative figure for the previous year and just over 128 per cent above the figure for two years earlier. In the week ending 15th December it had been at the top of the weekly list of results for the whole Partnership. In fact, The Gazette remarked that Robert Sayle and Caleys had set up records for the Christmas trade which, but for the prospect of rising prices, would be very hard to beat.

19: Settling down to partnership for all

Thanks to Mr Pretty's remaining to see Robert Sayle through the transfer from Selfridges to the John Lewis Partnership, the upheaval to personnel had been relatively slight, despite the fact that the deal had been kept secret until within two days of its completion, when one of the London newspapers had 'scooped' it. The staff was by now accustomed to working as part of a larger concern; it seemed to be generally agreed that the latest change was accepted with equanimity and that very soon there was reason to believe that most people were pleased with it, though possibly a little bewildered by some of the implications.

The novelty in the situation was the idea that the Partnership system was intended not simply to provide 'a job' but to be in some sense 'a way of life'. The inspiration had come originally from Mr Spedan Lewis's interest in the experiment by the philanthropist Robert Owen (1771-1856) to build a co-operative society in which the workers would share with the owners and managers in the profits of the business. Mr Lewis extended the scheme by making every member of the staff a partner in the business from the day he joined, except anyone who was engaged purely temporarily. He described the chief purpose of the Partnership as the aim "to secure the fairest possible sharing by all the members of all the advantages of ownership – gain, knowledge and power". In order to achieve this aim it was necessary to give Partners freedom to express their thoughts, whether in speech or writing. The Partnership's weekly newspaper, The Gazette, published all relevant information from the management and welcomed letters or articles from any Partner, whether signed or anonymous, friendly or otherwise. "We should err in the direction of being over-candid," Mr Lewis believed, "rather than run the risk of leaving unsaid anything that ought to be said." There were critics who thought that on occasion too much was made public. Partners were given other opportunities of bringing forward suggestions or criticisms and of asking questions, by the institution of councils, whose members were elected by secret ballot throughout the business and who sat with ex-officio councillors, appointed to give technical advice on matters under discussion; these latter, it was ruled, must be outnumbered by elected members in the proportion of roughly two to one.

In the early days, when the Partnership consisted only of Peter Jones, later joined by John Lewis and then successively by four provincial branches, there had been a single council for the whole group, which met in London. Now that the Partnership contained 21 separate shops, which were distributed in many parts of the country, it was felt that, as far as possible, each should have its own local council, though there should still be a central council to which reference could be made if required and at which subjects of importance to the business as a whole would be discussed. All branches would be represented on the Central Council. Not only would money and travelling-time be saved by a system of house councils, but they would also be a convenient method of introducing Partnership ideas to new branches. It was impressed on all council members, local and central, that they were 'representatives' not 'delegates' and should vote according to their own conscience on any and every motion, although this clearly need not prevent their bringing forward any useful ideas suggested by constituents. Some branches which were geographically situated conveniently near to one another were now linked for this or other business matters. On this principle, Robert Sayle was joined with Thomsons, which was renamed Robert Sayle (Peterborough) Ltd, the change of name being registered on 1st March 1940. For internal business purposes and to avoid confusion – especially in the transfer of goods from central offices – Robert Sayle (Peterborough) was known simply as Peterborough Ltd.

Robert Sayle in Cambridge and Peterborough shared one house council at first; later each had it own. The original one was planned in June 1940, to number 14 elected members and eight ex-officio, the latter including Mr J W Pretty, the two general managers, an assistant general manager, the matron and a local merchandise adviser. The first meeting was held in Cambridge on 14th November 1940 in the fashion showroom with Mr Walsh presiding. It was attended by Mr (later Sir) Metford Watkins, the Partnership's Director of Trading, who gave a talk on the Partnership idea and on the functions of the councils. He pointed out that, while most businesses were run for the benefit of owners or shareholders and some, such as the co-operatives, for the benefit of customers, the Partnership businesses were run for the benefit of the staff. Subject to the obvious proviso that proper consideration must be given to the rights of shareholders and customers, all of the true profit in the Partnership was intended for the workers in it. A local council, Mr Watkins explained, was empowered to take responsibility for spending a certain amount of money each year, with which to cover charitable subscriptions outside the Partnership, to give pecuniary help in times of special need to members of the branch and to finance its own social amenities. Furthermore, he continued, the council had the right and the duty to make any suggestions that occurred to its members or their constituents for the more efficient conduct of the business. He then referred briefly to two other elected bodies – the Committee for Communications (later the final 's' was dropped from the title), consisting entirely of rank and file Partners, which could make suggestions upon matters of local administration that came to the notice of its members as a result of their knowledge of the working of their own part of the trade, and the Committee for Claims, which would deal (in absolute confidence) with appeals for help from Partners.

The new ideas were taken up with interest, although at times complaints were heard that there was apathy about the councils and committees among Partners in general. It is, of course, very probable that the mood was not so much one of apathy as a certain hesitation due to inexperience of committee work and to the novelty of the whole Partnership idea. Besides there were other things which were bound to weigh on people's minds in time of war and perhaps make them less receptive to 'internal political' problems. Actually, by early 1943 it was clear that Robert Sayle Partners were showing considerable interest in house affairs with a satisfactory number of candidates standing for election. The council decided, in order to stimulate fuller participation, that an extraordinary meeting should be called at any time if it was felt that the agenda of the Central Council needed discussion or presented obscurities. In February 1944, when Mr Sebastian Earl, who had then become Director of Trading, came to address the first meeting of that year's council, he found a well-filled strangers' gallery to greet him. The minutes of meetings of councils and committees were regularly displayed on the notice board. Later, in 1947, Robert Sayle was one of the first, if not the first, of the branches to have a junior council representing Partners under the age of 18.

Some delays and difficulties were unavoidable before everything could be expected to run smoothly under the new system, and a number of these were concerned with money. Until, for example, arrangements had been concluded with the holders of the old SPS shares, the amount of profits available to the councils at Robert Sayle and other branches in the Suburban and Provincial group could not be assessed exactly and an arbitrary sum, not based precisely on their trading results, had, for the time being, to be allotted for their spending.

A more serious matter to individuals was the question of pay. The Selfridge management had, in October 1939, asked many of its employees to agree to a wage-cut of, in most cases, 10 per cent, but a good deal more in others. The John Lewis Partnership had also appealed to its members after the outbreak of war to accept a deferment of pay in the case of anyone earning more than a certain amount. A week's unpaid holiday in the spring had also been proposed. Deferred pay was to be made up in full as soon as circumstances permitted and its operation could be suspended for a week or more at a time, as in fact it was on several occasions when trading results made it possible. The Partnership intended all its members, new and old, to be treated alike but, since the financial situation of SPS was not yet fully clarified, profit-sharing could not, for the time being, be extended to include the SPS branches. It was, however, felt that these Partners should not, unless they themselves wished it, be asked to take the unpaid spring holiday, at least until their earnings had been brought into line with those in the rest of the Partnership.

In all other respects, such as sick pay and the enjoyment of the Partnership's social amenities, no difference was to be made. In actual fact, until dividends on the John Lewis shares (which had to be deferred for a time during the war) were fully paid up, no bonus distribution could be made to members of the original Partnership either. So, in this way too, all Partners were treated alike, even though for different reasons.

Another point which generated a great deal of discussion was the question of a service subsidy. The Partnership had at first hoped to pay a fixed amount to every Partner called up for war service but, with the great increase in the number of Partners resulting from the absorption of the SPS group, it was – though regretfully – decided to grant the subsidy only in cases where hardship would be caused to Partners or their families by withholding it. The aim was to ensure that no Partner's income should be less than it had been pre-war. No subsidy was to be given to conscientious objectors. After the end of the war accounts showed that about £87,000 had been distributed in subsidies by the Partnership.

Disappointment was caused in the SPS branches by the fact that the Partnership rate of house discount, a penny in the shilling, was brought into operation in this group from 1st June 1940, instead of the Seltridge discount of three halfpence, and while the war lasted there could be small hope of a distribution of profits to compensate for this. Discount remained at the penny rate until the end of the war but soon after that it was graduated up to a maximum of 20 per cent, according to the length of time a Partner, whatever his rank, had worked in the business.

'Membership' in the Suburban and Provincial houses was reckoned from the time a Partner had joined one of these branches, not from the date it had been taken over by John Lewis. However, with trade much more buoyant in Cambridge than it had been for the past years, there was a considerable feeling of animation at Robert Sayle, in spite of the lower discount – and especially since the soaring increases in turnover were published in The Gazette week by week for all to read (and admire!). Trade flourished throughout much of the Partnership for most of the next year too; it was so much better than had been expected that, in September 1941, the central management decided that a great number of the deferments in pay could be rescinded, unless things should get worse again. In any event, no Partner earning less than £500 a year was in future to be asked to agree to any deferment whatsoever.

The Robert Sayle House Council settled down to business during the year 1941, Mr Walsh continuing to act as President. Meetings now took place in the dining room at 9.15 in the morning on the first Tuesday in every month. In those early days the council dealt almost entirely with local matters, often no doubt minor in themselves but concerned with the comfort and welfare of members of the branch: was, for instance, the cleaning and general maintenance of the premises adequate – should smoking be permitted at first party meals – should the electricity continue to be turned off at night in the hostel – should wired glass be put on lights to avoid the danger of splinters in case of an air-raid? And so on. It was obviously helpful to have some definite time and place for airing questions. When things were more organised, such problems were more often settled through the Committee for Communication, if not by immediate reference to the head of branch as they arose.

The amount of money sanctioned for the Robert Sayle council's spending in that first year of its life came to a total of £250, apportioned as to £35 for subscriptions or donations outside the Partnership, £50 for the branch's social amenities, £15 for council expenses, such as fares for representatives to attend Central Council meetings, and finally £150 for grants to Partners needing special help in case of misfortune or 'comforts' in case of illness. A secretary and an almoner were elected to be responsible for the distribution of these last. On one never-to-be-forgotten occasion the council overspent its amenities allowance by £1 – and was severely reprimanded by the Central Council. The money was made the subject of a special grant to Robert Sayle, but with the proviso that such a thing must not occur again. The branch must budget more carefully and, if need arose, ask before spending. Later on subsidised courses were arranged in connection with the university's extramural study department, for Partners who wished to attend them, and occasional visits were organised to concerts or a theatre both in Cambridge and elsewhere as part of the branch's amenities.

There was still quite a number of Partners at Robert Sayle who had spent most of their working lives there and, towards the end of 1942, the council voted gifts of £25 each to two people who had worked in the business for 50

years – Miss A Long, in the fashion workroom since April 1891, and Mr W Rayner, whose term of duty in the maintenance and despatch department had started on 11th October 1892. Both retired on pension in April 1944 but Mr Rayner came back to do part-time work for another year and a half after that. At the end of the first council year, in November 1941, Mr Walsh retired from the acting presidency of the council and, at the first meeting of the following year's council, held on 7th January 1942, Miss W A P Ford, who sat as the member representing the shop's department managers, was elected to take his place. Mrs C M Bull, Assistant to the General Manager, an ex-officio member of the council, became the branch's representative on the Central Council until her retirement in September 1943.

A matter of interest to all Partners was raised in the Central Council at about this time: the question of retirement pensions. The Partnership's plan was on a larger scale than any of the earlier ones and was first discussed in the SPS branches in January 1942. The suggestion was that a pension should be calculated at one-sixtieth of a Partner's pay for each year of membership from a minimum of 15 to a maximum of 30 so that, in retirement, it could be worth annually a quarter to half a Partner's average earnings over those years, proportionately to the number of years he had worked in the business. A pension was to be based on the 30 best years for anyone who had spent more than 30 years with the company. The minimum qualifying period was some years later lowered to 10 years and, still later, the total amount was reckoned according to the average pay in the last three years of service. A man might, but need not, retire at 60; a woman at 55. The ages of retirement were later raised to 65 and 60 respectively. Furthermore, it was proposed that a lump sum or a small annuity should be payable to the dependants of any Partner who died after having spent at least five years with the company. Appreciation of these proposals was expressed in a letter to The Gazette published on 2nd February 1942, in which the writer said that he had been making extensive enquiries and had found that the Partnership's scheme was by far the most generous. The nearest to it that he had heard of was reckoned at one-eightieth of a person's annual income for each year of service and was not payable until the recipient was 65. "Never knowingly undersold!" he quoted, in reference to the Partnership's slogan. The Suburban and Provincial houses were brought into the scheme in June 1942, with a preliminary appropriation of nearly £35,000, and, as it happened, they were the first to benefit under it, because deferred dividends on the John Lewis stock had to be brought up-to-date before increases to the pensions fund and other benefits could be paid to the ('old') John Lewis Partners.

Discussions were also begun about family allowances and the suggestion that a 'dowry' might be given to women Partners who married after having worked for at least five years in the business, this last to be calculated at 5 per cent of their total salary over the period of membership. Mr Spedan Lewis's declared policy was that the Partnership's aim should be to keep on raising the minimum wage, including family allowances and help given to Partners in circumstances of special need. At the same time he emphasised that it was essential to cut one's coat according to the amount of cloth available if one hoped to stay solvent.

20: Real war – the new Suburban & Provincial Stores Ltd

For nearly a year no enemy aircraft had been sighted over England. The Germans were busy overrunning Europe and were saving the British Isles to finish off when the rest had been subdued. Still, fire practice went on here, men were drafted into the forces and sent overseas. In May and June 1940 Holland and Belgium fell, then France, and British units came back via Dunkirk. Refugees poured into England, from France, from Poland, from Norway and elsewhere; some of them were English people who had made their homes on the continent for years, but many more were young continentals who were to continue the fight against their countries' aggressors from these shores. So the 'phoney' war came to an end in the late summer of that year and heavy bombing of this country began in the September.

The John Lewis Partnership suffered an immediate and very serious blow when, in the early hours of Wednesday morning 18th September, an oil bomb, followed almost at once by two high explosives, fell on John Lewis in Oxford Street and gutted the greater part of the older of its two buildings, the West House. A strong westerly wind blew the flames across Holles Street to the newer part, known as the East House and much of this too was burnt out, though the destruction here was not as complete as that of the West House. No insurance had been possible in wartime for the fixtures, fittings and structure of the shop, and the stock could only be insured for what it had cost. The over-all loss was, therefore, colossal, and it was not known what compensation, if any, the government would later allow. In the outcome, the post-war government decided that, as the buildings were old, the value was nil. All stocks in both the East and West Houses were destroyed, except for those in the carpet, linens, and electrical departments, and a certain amount of furniture. Anything that remained saleable was sent to other branches for disposal. By some miracle, not one of the 200 people spending the night in the shop's underground shelter was hurt, though several of the firemen who came to fight the blaze were badly injured. The John Lewis Fire Service and its first aid detachment were warmly commended by the authorities for their bravery and help in this and the general rescue operations that night.

The loss to the Partnership would have been even more crippling but for its acquisition of the 15 shops in the SPS group, which made it possible to keep together a large part of the staff and to preserve good relations with customers and suppliers in a way that could not have been done with only the five remaining shops in the old John Lewis Partnership to call on – that is, Peter Jones in London, Lance & Lance in Weston-Super-Mare, Knight & Lee in Southsea, Tyrrell & Green in Southampton, and Jessops in Nottingham. The grand total of branches provided an excellent buffer against damage from enemy raids. Vacancies in all the 15 new branches, as well as those in the rest of the John Lewis group, were offered in the first instance to staff displaced from John Lewis and fortunately very many were comfortably resettled in this way. Cases of serious hardship, such as when Partners were bombed out of their homes, were dealt with by drawing on a large sum of money (£10,000) which the Partnership had set aside for the purpose at the outbreak of war. Any Partners for whom no alternative positions could be found were given full pay for the week in which the bombing occurred plus another week's pay in lieu of notice – or more if they had been engaged on a longer notice period.

Robert Sayle Partners started a Spitfire Fund at once and kept it going throughout the war, sending subscriptions up to the central fund at intervals. "Quite a lot of Spitfires must have had bits in them paid for by us!" they think.

The monetary loss to the Partnership's trade resulting from the destruction of its largest store was, of course, enormous, and meant that economies of many kinds had to be made, since profits of the whole business were bound to be greatly reduced, apart from the huge capital loss. Dividends on the stock of John Lewis & Co had perforce to be suspended, though repayment in full was promised as soon as circumstances should permit, and, until these had been paid up and until trade recovered, there could be little expectation of profits available for bonus distribution to Partners in the form of what was then called 'Partnership Benefit'. The story of the rehabilitation and partial restoration of the Oxford Street wreck was an epic in itself. Wonders of adaptation and compromise were achieved and it was not many weeks before parts of the East House were reopened for the sale of fabrics, fashions and haberdashery, to the expressed pleasure of many customers, numbers of whom had also written to commiserate with the Partnership over the bombing. London SPS branches came to the rescue by providing some fixtures and their carpenters and polishers came over to help install them and generally sort things out, so as to get the place going again as far as might be.

John Lewis was unfortunately not the only casualty to the Partnership that year. In June 1940 a fire had broken out at Tyrrell & Green, not, however, in consequence of bombing. The fire was fairly quickly brought under control but much of the stock was damaged, not only by the fire itself but also by water and even more by smoke. In the following November the shop was again unlucky and this time it was as a result of enemy action. In one raid on Southampton all its show-windows were shattered, though no further damage was done; a few nights later the branch was bombed out entirely. Fortunately on this occasion too, no member of staff was injured. Two small shops were opened, one in Southampton within a week or two and, a little later, one in Winchester, which carried on the branch's trade until rebuilding could be undertaken after the end of the war.

One more raid on London during that terrible winter was to hit the Partnership badly, when Quin & Axtens, the branch exactly opposite to the Bon Marché, in Brixton, was completely demolished, mercifully again with no staff casualties.

Nor was this the last of the wartime disasters that befell the Partnership – though, as Mr Spedan Lewis said, it was by now fortunately big enough and tough enough to take it. In June 1942, Lance & Lance was almost totally destroyed. Quantities of small incendiary bombs were dropped over Weston-Super-Mare one night and a number of them penetrated Lance & Lance's roof simultaneously; a stiff breeze gave little chance of saving buildings or stock. This time there was one staff casualty, luckily not a fatal one – Mr R C Hurst, the General Manager, got a bomb splinter in his leg. In some ways Weston's 'blitz' must have been even more terrifying than the raids over London, because most people lived within a short distance of their work and the bombs must have seemed appallingly close. Nevertheless, six weeks later, Lance & Lance "proudly presented House Notes once more" to The Gazette. "Down" they might be, they wrote, but by no means "out"! They had got to work with a will and, four weeks after the catastrophe, had started up in a small way as near as possible to the old premises, for the sale of dress materials and accessories, as well as for perfumery and hosiery; preparations were also being made to open departments for china, ironmongery, linens, shoes and millinery in a shop opposite. In spite of the three losses in 1940, the Partnership's trade recovered towards the end of the financial year and The Gazette reported that the SPS group achieved a total far above any known past records.

21: Post-war: Robert Sayle & Co Ltd

After the absorption of the SPS group into the Partnership, and more especially while the war lasted, the history of any one branch was necessarily knit closely with that of the company as a whole; events that took place, good or bad, affected them all in their several ways. Robert Sayle entered briskly into its latest incarnation. Its turnover continued to mount steadily and satisfactorily during 1940/41. Partners themselves evidently enjoyed dealing with the fresh merchandise now coming into all departments and so did customers, one of whom remarked at the time that the price and quality of goods compared very favourably with those of other establishments. The shop's window display was considered to be good and approbation was expressed in The Gazette: "A marked recent improvement," a comment read towards the middle of that year. Mr Spedan Lewis held very definite views in window-dressing as well as on display inside a shop, all of which, he considered, should be of what he called "the dictionary type" rather than the "merely pictorial", if it were to make a real impact. He abhorred a vacuum as much as nature is said to do and he very much disliked seeing space wasted on a wall or in a window that might be used for display purposes.

In one respect the John Lewis Partnership may be said to have followed Robert Sayle's lead: it decided about this time that window-dressing need not necessarily continue to be a male preserve. Robert Sayle had beaten them to it! Its windows had been under female control for a number of years from 1931 (at latest), when Miss M Jelley – a sister of Miss K Jelley, who was for many years a department manager in the shop – was in charge of them until she left to be married. Later on this section at Robert Sayle was looked after most successfully by a mixed party, headed by Mr B E Carroll, who joined the branch as acting manager of display on 30th August 1941, after a number of years' experience in other branches; in fact the whole of his working life had been spent in the Partnership. Mrs Coral Gould – a very talented young actress and singer in her spare time – became his deputy some years later and there were three or four young men and women assistants. One of the notable early successes of Mr Carroll and his team was a special 'Make-do-and-Mend' window in a nationwide competition organised in 1944; there must have been literally hundreds of entries for the competition and, in the final result, Robert Sayle came fifth in the whole country. On 11th May 1946 Mr Carroll was confirmed in his appointment when the previous holder of the post, Mr D Plane, who had been called up for war work, resigned from the Partnership a month or two after demobilisation.

By the middle of 1941 some 46 of Robert Sayle's staff of about 200 were on active war service and those who remained behind, as well as those who took their place in the shop, shared fully in the civilian war effort. They kept in touch by letters and parcels with serving Partners, who often visited the branch when they came home on leave; news of these Partners was published in The Gazette from time to time. Among other war work, Robert Sayle responded nobly to an appeal for 1,000,000 pairs of mittens to be knitted and sent to our Russian allies for the winter – although it was not intended that all of them should be provided by this shop! They were highly successful, too, in raising money for various national projects. They had a splendid record for National Savings, a high spot being touched in 1941 when their total was surpassed by only three of the Partnership's larger branches: John Lewis (in spite of the bombing), Peter Jones, and Holdrons. By Christmas that year nearly £1,000 had been collected and six months later the grand total had risen to more than £2,000. The 'Cambridge Warship' week was also splendidly supported by the branch, something over £600 being garnered. Later on, in 1943, the 'Wings for Victory' week was another triumph. The target for the shop had been fixed at £800 – in the event £1,011.9s.0d was subscribed. "They'll fly 'em if we buy 'em!" Yet again, in May 1944, they showed what could be done in the 'Salute the Soldier' week, exceeding their target of £1,000 by nearly 25 per cent and matching the town's effort, whose target had been set at £1m and who produced £1.25m. At intervals, when blood donors were asked for, a very satisfactory response came from Robert Sayle Partners, who were congratulated on the number of volunteers coming forward. Any parties held at Robert Sayle in war-time included a collection of money to pay for parcels to be sent to serving Partners.

Drama lovers in the branch – the Victoria House Dramatic Society – were busy too and not just for the fun of it. A play was produced every year, generally in the spring, and the resultant profits were sent in the form of an always very useful cheque to some worthwhile cause, usually to either the National or the Cambridge Institute for the Blind. Robert Sayle's Dramatic Society was well known in the

Robert Sayle's 'Make Do and Mend' window, 1944

town for the polished performances it staged. The producer was Mr W W (Beverley) Greenall, the manager of the Men's Wear Department in the shop, who was a keen and experienced amateur. He sometimes acted in a play himself, as well as producing, but as a rule preferred to concentrate on the production. The earliest of 'his' Victoria House shows ('Nothing But The Truth') was given in 1936 and was played on an improvised stage in the yard at the back of the shop. Mr Pretty saw this performance and was so much impressed by the standard of acting and the professional finish of the production that he arranged the hire of the university's Amateur Dramatic Club theatre (the ADC) for the rest of that week, and for the next 13 years or so Robert Sayle's shows were generally given there. In March 1940, the first play presented after Robert Sayle had become a member of the Partnership ('Autumn' by

A performance by the Victoria House Dramatic Society, taken between 1935 and 1955

Ilya Surguchev) was visited by Mrs Spedan Lewis, who was Deputy Chairman of the Partnership, and by Mr Coad Pryor, then General Manager of John Lewis, both of whom thought really highly of it. Theirs was praise worth having, for both visitors were excellent critics and very knowledgeable about matters theatrical. As usual, the society made a good profit, and the proceeds (about £80) were sent to the Cambridge Institute for the Blind. The production was referred to in a local newspaper as "brilliant". Two or three years later, Mr Greenall was made a life member of the Institute by way of acknowledgement of the help given by the Dramatic Society.

In March 1941 a fashion parade was mounted at the branch, which appears from all accounts to have given much pleasure to its audience. In the following month, the sister shop at Peterborough also gave a very successful one. The models in both cases were all members of staff. In those days of austerity, the shows must have provided a very welcome relaxation to producers as well as spectators. After the war, in the early 1950s, similar shows were arranged, with professional models, in the Cambridge shop and, once, at the Guildhall.

Meanwhile, a good deal of internal tidying up was being undertaken at Robert Sayle in Cambridge. The Times Library was refurbished, various sections in the rest of the shop were moved around while painters and decorators were busy and some repairs were done to the roof; so business was carried on under difficulties, with hazards caused by ladders and paint pots in unexpected places and no one quite certain where a department was to be found on any particular day. There was the occasional spot of trouble over blackout when someone omitted to draw a curtain properly after dark, and one thing and another, but these minor storms were weathered and the branch continued to flourish. By Easter 1942 its takings had again doubled in comparison with those in the same period the year before. One afflictive episode occurred when a small delivery of the all-too-scarce silk stockings arrived (nylon was not yet on the market) and Partners were warned that they must leave them for outside customers. The ban held, of course, for all branches, but must have been very hard to bear.

In the early part of 1942 Mr Walsh was called up for service with the Royal Air Force. He was succeeded temporarily by Mrs C M Bull on 11th March. It was not an easy time for anyone to be holding the position. Clothes rationing had been introduced a few months earlier and was just beginning to 'bite'; everyone was waiting anxiously to see how the allowance of coupons would work out. These were issued twice a year and were apt to be spent within the first week or two; after that, one gathers, those in need begged from kind-hearted elders, grandmothers being found particularly vulnerable. It was not too bad during the summer months, when light furnishing materials – which were unrationed – could be bought and turned into very elegant frocks, but the general impact upset the fashion trade for a long time. Takings in many of the Partnership's branches decreased as the year went on and for a time Robert Sayle's name dropped to the bottom of the weekly list in The Gazette. Trade continued 'patchy' throughout – good when there was a new issue of coupons, but falling off in between times, especially of course in any shop whose main turnover was in women's fashions.

Peterborough, however, flourished mightily. This was no doubt due partly to the fact that it had in many departments different and more varied stocks than had come its way in pre-Partnership days and included fairly large items, such as nursery furniture, which had never before been sold in this shop. At Whitsun that year The Gazette's editor wrote: "We are delighted . . . to draw attention to Miss Humphries' achievement in having created, in such an unlikely place as a side-street in Peterborough, such a perfect imitation of a pre-war Peter Jones." Robert Sayle's turnover recovered for a time later in the year. In the early autumn Mrs Bull – to her great relief, so one is told – was

able to give up her position as Acting Manager and become Assistant General Manager to Mr R C Hurst, now happily recovered from the wound in his leg, who occupied the post from 22nd September 1942. Trade took another spurt upwards and The Gazette remarked that "Robert Sayle played up nobly to give its new General Manager a good start and are higher in the table than they have been for a long time... more like old times!"

In May that year a well-known Partnership character had joined Robert Sayle's Furniture Department: Mr Robert Bichan, who had spent more than 20 years previously at Peter Jones, where he had become the outstandingly successful buyer-manager of the Antique Furniture Department. Mr Bichan was tall and elegantly slim and he wore his business dress with the air of a Regency buck. He was immensely popular with his Chelsea customers. Partners no less than customers at Robert Sayle were impressed by his striking appearance and his great knowledge of the trade, but they watched with some anxiety when he decided to make the attempt to master a motor bicycle. He survived – but the internal combustion engine never seemed quite natural to him. (After his retirement he decided on a pedal tricycle.) Unfortunately he was not with the branch for long, as he was obliged, for reasons of health, to retire in April 1949 (he had been on sick leave for some months previously) but he undoubtedly made his mark in Cambridge, as he had done for so many years in Chelsea, and the antique furniture trade at Robert Sayle was said to be "booming" under his auspices. "As an ambassador of goodwill," Mr Walsh remarked, "he was invaluable."

22: Looking ahead

All through the war, the Partnership was looking to future developments. Its planning committee separated the mechanical work to be undertaken into two categories: first, of course, must come the rebuilding of shops that had suffered war-damage; and second – important, though less urgent – were schemes to bring all houses up to the highest possible standard. It was hoped that the various projects would be carried through within two or three years after the end of hostilities. In the event it was found that no extensive rebuilding could be even contemplated before the 1950s, though much long-term planning was accomplished. As regards the secondary operations, preference was given by the government to improving conditions in factories, so as to encourage the export trade, and then to essential services such as hospitals and schools. Hence, licences for the alteration or rebuilding of shops were almost impossible to obtain.

Among improvements to be made to several of the Partnership's branches was included the need to turn to more profitable use those parts of the buildings still occupied as hostels. In Cambridge the subject came under immediate discussion and for a time it was thought that a solution could be found by acquiring premises – a small hotel, perhaps – outside the shop but within easy walking distance, to which hostel residents might move and where they could live in more congenial surroundings than was possible in the present quarters. The House Council came out strongly in favour of the idea at a meeting in July 1943. Negotiations were actually begun that year for a place that seemed suitable but they proved abortive. Cambridge had special difficulties in the matter of accommodation at the time, being an evacuee centre as well as having a considerable number of service personnel billeted in the town, so the plan had not much chance of immediate success. As things turned out, Robert Sayle's was the last of the Partnership hostels to be closed. It was fully occupied for the rest of the war period and for a good many years afterwards. It came to a gradual end within 20 years post-war, when rooms were vacated by departing residents and not re-let; thereafter Partners arranged their own accommodation. For the last few years of its existence the only meals provided in the dining room were the midday dinner and afternoon tea; a kitchenette was furnished on each floor, where residents could cook their own breakfast and supper. The last to leave the hostel was Miss I Lashmar who moved out in December 1964.

Although it did not prove possible to carry through the complete scheme of reorganisation at once, some of the offices were, as the months and years went by, transferred to the residential floors and a few very small cubicles, boxrooms, etc, were turned into stockrooms.

With the Partnership's advent certain other changes had also been made. The large dining room on the first floor, which had heretofore been used only by the senior management, was in 1943 converted into a sitting room for residents and other Partners. The senior management ate in the general dining room, using a small room at the back of the building as a sitting room and later also as dining room. Subsequently a room between these two was assigned to the middle management – that is, department managers and those of equivalent rank –

as a dining and sitting room, because the general dining room became overcrowded when the number of Partners increased. Bedrooms were redecorated and made in various ways more comfortable. All meals were at that time still provided and a matron-housekeeper was in residence.

In the early 1950s some sections of the Counting House were moved up to the second floor and a year or two later also the Registrar's offices, which had until then been on the ground floor close to the General Manager's. In those days the Registry clerks also coped with the shop's correspondence with customers; this duty was taken from them as increased trade made a separate correspondence section necessary. The Staff Trainer was allotted two rooms on the third floor. A number of alterations were required to make accommodation suitable for the new purposes – some walls had to be removed, doors cut between one room and another, and so on.

Some of the shop's stock was still kept in the basement and in premises on the ground floor opening onto the yard. Where possible, goods that were not too unwieldy were now transferred to upper storeys and the rooms so vacated were adapted for use as receiving and despatch docks, with easier access to the main building. The workrooms, especially those which dealt with furnishings, were also due for extension and to be given more convenient communication with the departments which they served. The well-house in the yard was requisitioned as a stockroom for hardware until its demolition in 1964. One of the largest items on the improvements agenda for Robert Sayle was for the utilisation of the area above the carpet showroom. This

A room in the Robert Sayle hostel in the late 1950s

showroom had been constructed in Selfridges' time on the site of the old brew-house. During the clearance and partial demolition in preparation for that rebuilding, the tank above the ceiling, which was known as the water tower and which held 11,800 gallons, had been left in position over the new department. The Partnership's plan included the removal of the tank, so that the whole of the valuable space on the first floor could be converted into a large new showroom for the sale of household linens, soft furnishings off all kinds, blankets, cushions, and so on. (Robert Sayle's water supply, in earlier times dependent on the water tower, had by now been linked with the town mains system.) This plan could not be put into effect until 1954, and the Soft Furnishings Department battled on for all those years in the limited area at the front of the shop now generally occupied by furniture and mirrors and by Christmas decorations and stationery in the proper season. A large extension for furniture at the back of the Carpet Department was also envisaged, but that had to be deferred for lack of planning permission; this particular problem was, of course, to some extent solved when the household linens and soft furnishings were moved to the first floor. In addition, it was proposed that the fashion showrooms should be extended and improved. The Shoe Department was transferred to the ground floor – not altogether conveniently at the time, for it was, and had been since March 1941, under the same management as the Millinery Department, which remained on the first floor.

Efforts were also being made to reorganise the basement. It was desperately crowded, with a rabbit-warren of small cell-like niches in all directions off the two main rooms, which had been transformed into selling areas after the removal of wholesale and other stocks. The surrounding niches then became reserve stockrooms for the departments – Lampshades, China and Glass, Hardware and Electrical – thereafter housed underground. A Polyfoto unit had functioned in the shop since May 1939 and it remained in the basement until the early 1950s. Takings in this section were never large but during the war it was felt to be useful as an amenity department. In fact, in September 1940, the Partnership had authorised the purchase of Polyfoto cameras for four other branches. Pye's had also kept a small radio sub-division at Robert Sayle but this was removed within a few months of the Partnership taking over.

Internal alterations, insofar as they did not affect the building line or anything else in which outside authorities had a say, were made with what speed was possible according to the state of trade and the availability of materials. Lack of governmental or civic planning permission delayed very many of the Partnership's major projects, including the rebuilding of John Lewis in Oxford Street, which was not completed until 1960. Robert Sayle in 1969 still awaited permission to carry out much of the building programme held up

since the war years. Its sales density – that is, the volume of trade recorded per square foot of space – increased out of all recognition, but the crowding, lack of facilities for display of goods and the consequent disruption for both customers and salespeople also increased as the years passed. "When we rebuild ..." became a sick joke in the branch.

Apart from planning alterations to existing shops, the Partnership was also, during the war and soon after, increasing the number of its branches in order to have extra selling space to compensate for what had been lost through the bomb disasters. Several of the new acquisitions were later sold again. In 1944 two small shops were procured in the West End of London – John Pound's premises in Piccadilly and Regent Street, which had previously been known mainly for high class leather goods; they were kept until 1963. A third of these, in the city, was bought with the other two, but resold at once. Another Bon Marché, a delightful little shop under the Pantiles in Tunbridge Wells, was bought early in 1946. Two branches of the Silk Shops Ltd, one in Edinburgh and one in Newcastle, had been acquired at the end of 1943 and, on 2nd December that year, the Lord Provost of Edinburgh wrote a very friendly letter to The Gazette, welcoming the Partnership to that city; a third Silk Shop was taken over in Hull when the proprietor decided to retire in February 1946; it was the smallest of the Partnership's branches, with only an 18 foot front. Blinkhorn's subsidiary in Stroud was first mentioned as a separate branch with its own manager in January 1943 but it had in fact been a member of the old SPS group. Between them all, the Partnership's total sales kept up astonishingly well on the whole, in spite of what must have at first seemed utterly shattering misfortunes. A contributory reason for this was, according to one theory, that enforcedly cheaper holidays left people with money to spend on other things.

On the social side there was further discussion as time went on about such matters as the retirement pensions, about a five-day week (which Mr Spedan Lewis thought must certainly be a possibility before long: it was introduced at Robert Sayle on 26th April 1965); about sick pay and longer holidays; about a minimum wage scale, designed not to level down but to level up, though at the same time the Partnership must not fail to give to those of outstanding ability the extra they deserved. Marriage and family allowances, schemes for further education, for country clubs and other amenities were also on the programme.

The Gazette was, of course, hit by the paper shortage, but quite an amount of its available space was taken up by Mr Lewis's enthusiastic articles on subjects such as the above, though he was always careful to point out that the time was not yet ripe for any great expansion along these lines and that the Partnership must first concentrate on making existing institutions as nearly perfect as possible. His writings were not always easy to follow without a certain amount of what he himself referred to as "the intolerable effort of thinking" and of course readers sometimes failed to understand that he was planning for the future and that, in war-time and the immediate post-war period, circumstances were militating against the possibility that these hopes and aims would be realised at once. Letters to

this effect were from time to time published in The Gazette – and, though Mr Lewis rather welcomed them than otherwise, as showing interest and giving him the opportunity to explain obscure or knotty points, he never minced his words in expressing disappointment if he thought that correspondents had failed to understand his motives. However, as he remarked on one occasion, he felt sure that, as soon as it became possible to distribute the annual Partnership Bonus after the war, it would bring home to the recipients that they really were Partners in more than name.

In those days The Gazette had necessarily to confine itself mainly to serious topics; once or twice a plea was made for some light relief such as a crossword or other form of mild 'escapism', but paper simply could not be afforded for it. In fact, interesting and important articles or memoranda sometimes had to be held over for several weeks on account of lack of space. The size of The Gazette had shrunk from its pre-war 18 to 20 pages to a mere eight. Reports were occasionally published about productions by the Partnership dramatic societies; and Gardening Notes were kept up throughout the war, being an entirely justifiable use of paper from the patriotic angle of encouraging the growing of extra foodstuffs. John Lewis's bombed site was let more than once for "Off the Ration" and similar exhibitions organised by the Ministry of Food to help people who had gardens or smallholdings that would enable them to keep livestock such as hens and rabbits, as well as cultivating vegetables. A small entrance fee was charged, and the proceeds were given to service benevolent funds.

Otherwise the contents of The Gazette were very much what they are in normal times – reviews of trading conditions, lists of appointments, promotions, and transfers from one post to another, reports of council and committee meetings. House notes were published progressively less frequently as the paper famine became more acute; unless anything very startling happened, no branch could expect to see itself in print more often than once in three or four months, in spite of disappointment expressed by local correspondents. Robert Sayle did once at least achieve publication out of turn, when it was reported that a fine healthy roach had been observed swimming down the (then) deep gutter in St Andrew's Street outside the shop; it was not expected, however, that Robert Sayle would apply for fishing rights.

During the first three years of the war, Mr Spedan Lewis also wrote articles for The Gazette evaluating the war news. They were always stimulating; a correspondent once referred to him as Chief Optimist to the Partnership, and immediate petitions for a renewal of the commentaries, sometimes from Partners in the forces, followed upon any occasion when pressure of other work obliged him to miss a week or two. Among plans for the post-war period, Mr Lewis felt particularly strongly that "local Gazettes" should be started with as little delay as possible and as soon as restrictions on paper were lifted. Such a local Gazette need not be as formal in style as the Partnership Gazette but an important point was that any official notice published in it must be considered to be effective for all Partners employed in the branch on the day of publication. In the main, the subject matter was to be concentrated on things of immediate concern to the individual branch and it was hoped that the paper would eventually be enjoyed not only by Partners themselves but also by their families. Although for some reasons local reactions were at first not particularly enthusiastic, it turned out that in many cases Partners' families did become interested and looked forward to the issue each week. Sales of The Chronicle (as the local paper soon came to be called) often exceeded those of The Gazette as time went on.

Among regular contributions to a Chronicle, it was planned, should be full reports of meetings of the house council and committees, which would then no longer appear in The Gazette; there should be a "Notes and News" section with items of local interest and reviews of the local departmental results. When paper supplies permitted, matters in lighter vein might be added. At first it was thought that Partners should have the two publications for the price of one, a Chronicle being printed in the same format as The Gazette. This idea was dropped on account of the expenses of production and the continuing paper shortage. One halfpenny was charged for a Chronicle, The Gazette remaining at a penny; and from 5th May 1950 Chronicles were no longer printed but duplicated locally. They were started in the branches at various times; Robert Sayle's first issue is dated 24th December 1949. A Peterborough supplement was added from 13th February 1954.

As soon as the war came to an end there were some additions to the lighter side of The Gazette. Cricket, football, badminton, table tennis and other games were reported as clubs were resuscitated. The names of Partners returning after demobilisation were published; among them was mentioned on 23rd April 1946 that of Mr Lewis B Smith, who came back to the Partnership as Assistant Buyer of woollen materials, and who some years later became General Manager of Robert Sayle in Cambridge.

Notices of long-membership anniversaries became a regular feature. Mr Lewis made the suggestion at one time that there should be some suitable celebration, when things had recovered enough from the war, to mark the attaining of the status of an 'Ancient Inhabitant of the Partnership'. Robert Sayle would never have had any difficulty in furnishing an impressive quota of such senior citizens. In August 1946, for example, there were – in that month alone – seven Partners who would certainly have qualified, headed by Mr Walter Papworth with 41 years to his credit. He worked for another year before retiring on pension. Some months earlier, in November 1945, Mr William Rayner, of the Despatch Department, had finally retired on pension after having given Robert Sayle 53 years' service. When he first joined Robert Sayle & Co in 1892, he drove a horse and cart, with candle lamps and thought nothing of working till eight or nine o'clock at night.

23: Robert Sayle & Co (Cole Brothers Ltd)

For some years after taking over the Suburban and Provincial Stores, the Partnership was working to rationalise the group's accounts and to bring them into accord with those of the rest of the Partnership. As a step in the scheme for consolidation, the shares in a number of the houses were transferred to Cole Brothers Ltd of Sheffield, one of the largest units in the group. The earliest of these transactions took place in 1941, with the transfer to Cole Brothers of the shares in three of the London branches – Holdrons, Jones Brothers, and John Barnes. Three of the provincial branches – Buckleys of Harrogate, Bulls of Reading, and Caleys of Windsor – were similarly amalgamated with Cole Brothers on 1st February 1944; on 20th July in that year Robert Sayle (Cambridge and Peterborough), together with Blinkhorn's two shops in Gloucester and Stroud, and Trewins of Watford came under the same umbrella. In every case the shops continued to trade under their original names, though no longer 'Limited', since they had ceased to be independent companies. The fact that they were now operating, properly speaking, as subsidiaries of Cole Brothers Ltd made no difference to the lives of Partners working in any of the branches concerned, each place retaining its own individuality and remaining a member of the Partnership; the process was purely one of financial convenience.

1944 was a successful trading year for Robert Sayle, and indeed for many of the provincial branches. The renewal of daylight bombing had given another set-back to the London houses – once again to the advantage of shops in safer areas. In The Gazette's list of branch results, Robert Sayle ended the first half-year in second place from the top, beaten only by its parent company, Cole Brothers. By early September both Cole Brothers and Robert Sayle were reported to be "putting on trade fast"; in fact, these two, with the houses in Liverpool and Reading, were cancelling out the losses on the London branches. Things were looking up in Cambridge in other ways too. War news had become much more cheerful, some of the black-out regulations were relaxed, and home guard and fire-watching duties were eased. All this was stimulating and trade boomed. By Christmas it was said to be "terrific" and the final results "a record".

At the end of July that year Robert Sayle had once again had a new General Manager, when Mr Hurst was posted to George Henry Lee in Liverpool and his place was taken by Mr A Perreur Lloyd. Mr Perreur Lloyd celebrated his transfer to Cambridge by giving a party a few weeks later for the shop's fire-watchers, at which he presented each member of the team with a card on which was stated the length of time the recipient had spent in this service; quite a number could boast of as many as 48 months. At the end of October Mr Pretty finally severed his long connection with Robert Sayle; by then he had been attached to the business for 35 years. To mark his retirement, Mr Spedan Lewis, the Chairman of the Partnership, accompanied a leaving gift with a most appreciative letter, which was also published in The Gazette. Mr Pretty had seen the shop through what must surely have been one of the most socially disturbed and unsettling epochs in the country's history, including as it did the 1914-18 war, the upheavals which followed and then the 1939 war. Since he first joined in 1909, the business itself had gone through important changes of ownership and organisation. It must have given him great pleasure to know that when he said goodbye to Robert Sayle it was flourishing and giving every indication of continuing on a favourable course. At the end of that financial year the shop was congratulated in The Gazette for "showing up as well as ever", having achieved more than 25 per cent increase in turnover above that of 1943.

It was certainly a time when change followed change. In the spring of 1944 yet another fresh idea had been introduced at Robert Sayle – the Registry system. Under this system, which had been long discussed in the Partnership but put into practice only in 1938, a senior Partner was appointed to act as what was in effect a liaison officer between the central management of the company and an individual branch. At first one Registrar was assigned to a group of branches but, with the increase in the number of branches following upon the Partnership's acquisition of the SPS businesses, this was not found to be a satisfactory arrangement and a Registrar was then normally appointed to a single shop, occasionally to two. Tenure of office in any one branch was intended to be for a maximum of from three to five years, after which a transfer to another house was to be expected. A Registrar was officially described as the local representative of the central management of the Partnership. In every case except one the post was held by a woman. Her function was to act as a channel of communication between any section of her branch and the appropriate authority in the central management. She had no executive duties in the branch, except that she was technically in charge of all secretarial work. Her rank was on a level with that of the General Manager, with whom she was expected to work as a team in ensuring that the Partnership's ideas and regulations were faithfully carried into effect. When local Gazettes – later to appear under the new name of Chronicles – came into being, she added editorship to her other roles. A Chief Registrar, who might be a man or a woman, was permanently stationed at headquarters in London.

Robert Sayle's first Registrar was Miss Violet H Hunter, who took up the post in May 1944. She was at first responsible only for the Cambridge branch, but later Peterborough also came under her care for a time, until a separate Registrar was appointed. At the end of the war, when social affairs got under way again, she proved to be a great asset to the Dramatic Society. She was evidently what is known in theatrical circles as a 'quick study', for she first showed her talent by taking on a part, most successfully, at a moment's notice when the original actress fell ill. On another occasion her interpretation of a 'low comedy' character was described by a reporter as "a gem". Miss Hunter remained with Robert Sayle until towards the end of 1949 before moving on to her next assignment. She was followed successively by first one, then another 'caretaker' Registrar, two young women who were marking time before proceeding to other posts in the Partnership, and in 1950 by the present writer, who was allowed to do a double 'stint' in Cambridge, as at the end of her first five years, a new general manager was appointed and it was felt that the two changes at once would cause too great a break in continuity.

24: Into the new peace

By the last week of 1944 an end to the war was beginning to seem a possibility and the Partnership was more than ever occupied with ideas for the future. The plan for the five-day week, in one form or another, was again on the agenda; it might be arranged so that each Partner had two half-days off every week, or one whole day, but for the time being it would not be possible, Mr Spedan Lewis thought, to close the shops for one whole working day, except at the risk of losing all prospect of an immediate distribution of a Partnership bonus. Also among the plans was an extension of the medical service, which had hitherto been introduced in the provincial branches only at Blinkhorns, Cole Brothers and George Henry Lee. Suitable accommodation and equipment were to be provided for a full-time nurse in all houses as soon as possible. Robert Sayle's medical room was sited on the second floor in the hostel and its first occupant was Sister Mason, who started work in the early part of 1947. Her successors in the next few years were Sister Saint-John, Sister Bowerley and Sister Newman, the last of whom joined the branch in December 1953 and retired, to everyone's regret, at the end of April 1968; she was followed by Sister Wake.

Investigations into the possibility of finding accommodation for at least 12 of the hostel residents somewhere outside the shop were intensified but still without success. Two alternative plans were discussed, one of which would leave residents undisturbed, and this one was finally adopted. In principle, however, the Partnership's policy was that, if the space were needed for trading purposes, any or all of its hostels must be closed. It was not very long post-war that Robert Sayle was the only branch whose hostel remained in being.

In March 1945 the Partnership's Secretary for Education visited Robert Sayle and spoke about schemes for enabling Partners of all ages to have the opportunity of attending study courses. Partners on war service were also written to and asked if they had any particular wishes in the matter. Replies included requests for lectures and classes on various social subjects, such as the rights and duties of citizenship, on economics and public speaking, for help in returning to civilian life after the long break, and in getting up-to-date with new ideas in trading and other work connected with shop-keeping. The arts were also asked for, music especially, and a great many people were anxious to learn something about interior decoration. It was also hoped, Partners were told, to supplement

the government's plans for the further education of school-leavers, as was already being done in some other businesses. The Partnership's scheme was to provide four hours' tuition every week for young people up to the age of 18, the classes to include English (spoken and written), with special emphasis on the drafting of letters, short drills in mental arithmetic of a kind likely to be useful to them in their work in the shop, an hour a week on current affairs and a class in some art subject. The school-leaving age at that time was still 14; it was to have been raised to 15 on 1st April 1945 but was postponed to the same date in 1946.

By the early part of 1945 life was really becoming more normal. Robert Sayle's windows were attractively dressed and in former days the usual pre-Easter rush would definitely have been expected. Unfortunately the clothes-rationing system remained in force and would-be purchasers, as well as the shopkeepers, waited with something less than patience for a new issue of coupons. Yet a few weeks earlier, according to official trade returns, Robert Sayle had been cited as one of the six Partnership branches that were doing much better in women's wear sections than most of their competitors. The year before, over 83,000 of the Partnership's crop of 2,000,000 clothing coupons had been handed in by Robert Sayle customers. Things began to brighten up when, in the first week of February, the Mayor of Cambridge opened a 'Children's Welfare' exhibition in Robert Sayle's Baby-linen Department. This was a great success and attracted many customers, so that takings in the shop continued to be satisfactorily above average. The Gazette looked upon Robert

Sayle as "one of the customary leaders" in the trading results. March brought the longed-for new issue of coupons and, in the view of a Partner from another branch writing to The Gazette, crowds were flocking to Robert Sayle's well-stocked departments with clothing ration books at the ready. This Partner even quoted Congreve (more or less), seeing the shop: "With all her bravery on and tackle trim, Sayles filled and streamers waving."

Alas, it was not long before a fresh scarcity of fashion goods brought the figures down, just after Mr Perreur Lloyd had been transferred to Peter Jones and Robert Sayle had welcomed yet another temporary General Manager in the person of Mr J H Spilman, who arrived on 3rd April.

Apart from want of merchandise, salespeople had to contend with the continuing lack of paper supplies, due to import difficulties; they were obliged to persuade customers not to require purchases to be wrapped unless it was absolutely essential. Instead, baskets and string bags became a permanent part of shoppers' normal equipment. The paper shortage went on for some years even after the war was over. Robert Sayle's maintenance team acquired great merit (also bonuses) by saving and baling waste paper, old newspapers and any packaging materials that could be salvaged from stock deliveries, and selling these to local paper manufacturers, who were glad to get them and were ready to pay something like 15 shillings a hundredweight for the bundles.

The end of the war in Europe (VE Day) came on 7th May 1945. The Partnership had arranged that all its branches should be closed on that day, from whatever time the news was published, and on the following day. An additional day's holiday was to be given later, the date to be arranged to suit local wishes. Robert Sayle's Victory Party was held at the end of 1945. Trading figures in VE week made it very clear, as The Gazette remarked, that customers had had more on their minds than mere shopping. In the following week this was even more obvious, when four of the smallest branches alone managed to beat the previous year's figures – Peterborough, the new Silk Shop in Hull, and the two John Pound shops. Robert Sayle was down near the bottom of the list. The silver lining to that cloud was that, in the corresponding week of 1946, Partnership sales were almost exactly double those of the VE week, and Robert Sayle was 101.96 per cent up.

VE Day was unfortunately spoilt for Cambridge because, simultaneously with the news of the German capitulation, information was received that the Cambridgeshires, the county regiment, had been captured at the fall of Singapore. It was not until November, two months after the Japanese collapse, that their friends heard that a considerable number of the men were safe. By the fortnight after VE Day, business throughout the Partnership was back at its highest war-time level, except in some branches which depended for the major part of their trade on piece goods sales, and in one or two places which were feeling the effects of the return of the evacuees to their homes. Robert Sayle was restored to a respectable position half-way up that week's list of results, and for the first four months of the trading year its cumulative position was, more than 'respectably', third from the top among the 25 branches. By the end of that half-year, at 31st July 1945, it had risen over 9.5 per cent above the previous year's figures but at the end of the full trading year six months later it had, regrettably, sunk to a 'minus' position, in common with many of the provincial shops. London branches were coming into their own again.

Meanwhile Robert Sayle Partners were returning from war service, and life began to feel real once more. Robert Sayle's fashion windows were dressed with special reference to demobilised service-women – and how delightful the 'New Look' clothes seemed after five and a half years of austerity, though Cambridge customers seem to have been somewhat hesitant in adopting them. Later in that year two members of the United States forces spent several weeks in the branch, to help them catch up with the progress of trade since they had been in the service, and others came for shorter periods to study the Partnership's methods. Some of them wrote afterwards to say how much they had been interested in the Partnership's ideas; they had been particularly impressed with the central and house councils and committees, and with the general feeling that the atmosphere was, as one of them put it, like that of a huge friendly club. On 2nd August that year the freedom of the borough of Cambridge was granted to the 8th United States Air Force.

25: This and that

It was hardly possible in those days to speak of 'returning to a normal way of life' because things had changed so much during the war – far more than during the 1914 war – and working in the Partnership was in many ways very different from what Robert Sayle had been accustomed to in former times. While the war lasted, conditions were bound to be rigorous, however much the Partnership might try to temper the winds of austerity for its members. Food rationing continued for six or seven years after the end of the war and the (then) ten-minute morning break, as well as the afternoon tea-time, were on occasions complicated by the delicate question whether those who did not live in the hostel should be allowed sugar in their drinks. It was even discussed in the House Council.

However, things were not all on a contentious level. At the end of 1945 the last arrears of interest on John Lewis preference stock were paid off, so in 1946 the 'old' Partnership branches could be included in the pension fund. Better still, especially for the Suburban & Provincial branches, to whom it was quite new, was the announcement that distribution of Partnership Benefit (soon to be renamed Partnership Bonus) could once more be expected, if not immediately, at least by 1947. It was pointed out that this would have to be started in a small way, because the back-log of building and maintenance which had piled up during the war must be cleared off before profits would be available for the purpose; but it was thought that for the first year 5 per cent of the payroll should be a possibility – about two-and-a-half weeks' extra pay.

In the following year, it was hoped, the allocation would be larger, though probably still under 10 per cent. But in the future, so Mr Spedan Lewis believed, the average should be about 12.5 per cent, say six weeks' pay every year. It was something to look forward to, something that would be worth saving, either to supplement an eventual pension or for some other useful purpose. Trading conditions being still very abnormal, it was not really possible to judge how good results were likely to be but, during the summer of 1946, the performance throughout the Partnership was fairly consistently satisfactory, Robert Sayle being mentioned as among the best, although at one time earlier in the year it had gone down to the bottom of the list – fortunately not for long. On 11th June 1946 the shop had been happy to welcome back Mr L J Walsh, upon demobilisation from the Royal Air Force, to his former position as General Manager – though Partners were also sorry to say goodbye to Mr Spilman, who was transferred as General Manager to Trewins at Watford; he was always a welcome visitor to the branch in after years.

The Partnership Education Committee was now busy implementing some of the many plans which had been under consideration. Lectures and discussions were arranged in the branches; for the time being most of these were in London but they were later extended to the provinces. The variety was enormous. Among others, Mr E F M Durbin MP gave

a series of addresses on subjects of current interest, such as the United Nations Organisation, as compared with the old League of Nations. Other titles were: 'Does Democracy Matter?' and 'Do we need a Party System?'; 'The Economic Future of Britain' and 'Need we be poor after the war?' At Peter Jones, Dr C E M Joad gave a talk on 'What is Philosophy?', and Dr J C Flugel countered with 'What is Psychology?' at John Lewis. John Barnes enjoyed one of several series on music, with gramophone illustrations; the first was on Tchaikowski and others were on the art of conducting and on American orchestras. Particularly popular and well-attended was a talk given in the canteen at Clearings, Chelsea, one evening by Jimmy Wilde, the ex-fly-weight boxing champion of the world. Naturally an enthusiast for the sport, he said it was one of the finest of all forms of exercise but, he warned, anyone who wanted to take up the game must be strict with himself and give up "the fag and the glass".

Classes in public speaking were also organised, and a Partnership Brains Trust, at one of which the question was asked: "Can the Brains Trust define what, in their view, is a successful Partner?" There was no real disagreement about the answer; perhaps the neatest was given by Mr

The Partnership College at Cookham, 1946-7

(now Sir) Bernard Miller, who has since become the Partnership's Chairman. His definition was: "One who enjoys the Partnership and makes the Partnership enjoy having him." The Partnership College, a project for further education at all levels, which had been seriously discussed for some years, was finally opened at The Grange, Cookham, on 25th March 1946, rather later than had been hoped, and not, it was regretted, quite fully equipped, as there had been incessant delays in obtaining necessary materials – owing, as Mr Spedan Lewis remarked, to the difficulty of getting any ministry to believe anything to be essential, even for the promotion of a worthwhile educational scheme. The declared object of the college was to try to analyse and understand the problems which civilisation creates: How best to run the affairs of a community? How to reconcile a man's personal interests with those of the community in which he lives? It was not expected, said Mr R I James, the warden of the college, that these problems would be solved at Cookham, but students would at least have the stimulus of recognising the existence of problems which must be solved if the human race could hope to progress. There were to be three terms, each of six weeks' duration, for each set of students, some for seniors, some for juniors; and two such courses would be organised every year. Applications for admission to the college must be made by candidates themselves; those accepted would, in the year in which they attended a course, be expected to give up all but the one week of their holiday which must statutorily be taken in the summer. Later on some shorter courses

were instituted, lasting for a week or a week-end each, which did not affect the holiday entitlement of participants. The college was residential. By 1948 the college, though functioning most successfully from the students' point of view, was running into difficulties. The warden was finding the work heavier than he had expected and felt that he must resign, though he very generously offered to carry through a course which had already been planned. The Partnership also was finding that, until deficits from past losses had been made good, economies would be essential while trading conditions remained as unsettled as they were proving to be. It was therefore decided that for the time being the college must be closed, though it was hoped that this would be only a temporary measure. As things turned out, the college was not re-opened and further education for Partners was carried on by subsidising external courses when required.

The Partnership was not concentrating wholly on the more serious aspects of life. Classes in other forms of art appreciation besides music were arranged, including visits to exhibitions and galleries, and tuition was made available for ballroom and stage dancing enthusiasts. Drama was particularly encouraged. Several members of the central management were interested in this and a number of branches had flourishing dramatic societies. To give the added attraction of competition, the Partnership planned one-act play festivals, for which a challenge cup was presented by Mrs Spedan Lewis. The first festival was held in London on 18th January 1946. Six branches entered, Robert Sayle being among them with its presentation of 'The Distant Drum', by Philip Johnson – a play, as the adjudicator said, which needed suspense, and got it from this company. Among the actors were Mr Beverley Greenall, who was also producing; Mr J H Spilman, the General Manager at the time; and the Registrar, Miss Violet Hunter. All acquitted themselves well and, in the adjudicator's opinion, the cast "made a good effort at a difficult play", but Robert Sayle was not among the winners at this time. One of the troubles seems to have been that they found the stage uncomfortably larger than the one on which they had been accustomed to rehearse. At the AGM of the Partnership Dramatic Society in May that year it was decided that the competition should in future be held in the autumn, preferably in October or November, and that at least one team should be entered for the British Drama League Festival each year; also that a professional adjudicator should be invited to judge the finals of the Partnership's contestants. The heats were arranged

regionally and, on 30th October 1946, Robert Sayle played off the first heat at Nottingham against a team from Cole Brothers and two teams entered by Jessop & Son; the winner this time was one of Jessop's teams, but Mr W Deacon, a member of the Robert Sayle cast, was judged to be the evening's most finished actor.

The Partnership's trading year 1946/47 ended on a pleasurable note. On 4th January 1947 the first item in The Gazette was a congratulatory paragraph, signed with Mr Spedan Lewis's initials:

"The Partnership will, I am sure, wish to join me in offering to the Chancellor of our Exchequer respectful and affectionate congratulations upon a knighthood richly earned by his services to our country in peace and war." J S L

The editor of The Gazette echoed the congratulations "to Mr M Watkins, the Partnership's Financial Adviser and Director of Financial Operations and President of the Central Council, on receiving a Knighthood in the New Year Honours List".

26: The Cambridge Experiment

The Partnership's post-war plans included, as has been said, a great expansion of its social life. Mr Spedan Lewis had always hoped to make it possible for Partners to enjoy pleasures previously available only to the rich, such as country clubs, yachting, good seats at theatres and concerts and so forth; as well as to provide wider opportunities for the cultivation of the arts and other intellectual pursuits through social organisations both centrally and in

the individual branches. For a number of years the Partnership had an arrangement with the Boyd Neel Orchestra, whereby concerts were given in connection with the branches and to which both Partners and customers were invited, not only in London but also in the provinces. Robert Sayle had its first concert under this scheme on Tuesday evening, 12th February 1952. It was an enormous success, and was followed in future years by other

The Masonic Hall, Corn Exchange Street, Cambridge. The Robert Sayle Club was upstairs. This building was demolished in 1968

concerts from artists of similar first-class standing, sometimes orchestras, sometimes chamber music, sometimes soloists.

Robert Sayle's Social Club had been formed towards the end of 1946, and was inaugurated by a highly successful staff party just before Christmas. Its constitution was a natural development in the shop's long history of out-of-business activities. In the old days it had competed against the town's organisations at rowing, cricket or football. Later it became well-known through the Victoria House Dramatic Society, as producing excellent shows. It had always been fortunate in the encouragement given by its owners and managers. In the John Lewis Partnership even more opportunities for leisure occupation presented themselves. The war had made things difficult at first, of course, but once that was over and

service Partners returned, old clubs and societies were revived and new ones were formed, and it was decided at Robert Sayle to bring them all within a single, though many-sided, framework, which came to be known as the Cambridge Experiment. The moving spirits in the plan were at first three young women Partners – the Staff Trainer, Miss C Buckland (who, on 29th November 1949, became Mrs King), Mrs M A Martin, a saleswoman in the Gown Department, and Miss M Peachey, the General Manager's secretary. Their membership cards in the combined Social Club were, respectively, numbered 1, 2, and 3. A subscription of fourpence a week (twopence for young people under 18) was levied later, to amplify funds available through the branch council's amenities allocation.

Classes and clubs now included among others such a diversity of subjects as current affairs, squash, and the French language. There was ballroom dancing, tap dancing, Greek dancing, and old time dancing, the last of these taught by Mrs Martin, whose pupils were several times winners in competitions. Instruction in fencing was given by a Cambridge teacher, Madame Perigal, whose training enabled her students to give an impressive display at an end-of-season party in April 1949. Riding could be enjoyed at one of the local equestrian academies. A Choral and Operatic Society was formed in 1948, with Mr Ludovic D Stewart as its most helpful and gifted conductor; Mr Stewart was no newcomer to the Partnership, for he had, before he came to live in Cambridge, also given valuable coaching to the Partnership Opera Group when that was started in

London in 1946. In October 1949 Robert Sayle's Choral Society won first prize, with the finale of Act I of Mozart's 'Cosi Fan Tutte', in a competition run by the Cambridge Education Committee. The Dramatic Society continued on its path of glory and, not to be outdone by the singers, won the Partnership's One-Act Play competition in the same year. A carol service was held each Christmas, the first one in 1948, with special renderings of carols by the Choral Society as well as congregational singing. The services were very popular and were always attended by Partners and their families, as they have continued to be ever since. They have been held in alternate years at the churches of St Edward and St Andrew the Great and have been most kindly encouraged by the incumbents of these parishes.

Sports and games, such as tennis, cricket, football, and athletics, featured largely in the Social Club's programme, as did also sketching and other forms of artistic endeavour. The first Robert Sayle Sketching Club was started by one of the salesmen in the Furniture Department, Mr D G Manning, and his wife who, before her marriage, had been a member of the shop's Display Department. The club was taken up with great enthusiasm, especially by younger Partners. Chess, darts, table-tennis and badminton were played; the only former club not revived was the Victoria House Rowing Club, though two punts were bought for the pleasure of Social Club members; several people also availed themselves of the opportunity to go sailing in the Partnership's ocean-going yachts when these came on the scene in the 1950s. In 1964 the purchase of a sailing dinghy

was authorised by the Partnership Sailing Club, and so Robert Sayle once more became a member of the Cam Sailing Club. Some of the activities did not have a very long life but many continued as permanent features in the branch's pursuits and participants entered into competition with other institutions in Cambridge as well as with clubs in the Partnership. Some Partnership events became annual fixtures, such as the Swimming Gala in London, generally held in late September, and the Rag Regatta on the Thames at Cookham during the summer. Robert Sayle sends up teams for all such contests, and has also two or three times organised its own Rag Regatta on the Cam. For some reason, Robert Sayle never had a Rifle Club, although several of its Partners were good shots and Mr Walsh, the General Manager, was a particularly fine marksman. He was chairman of the Gogs Rifle Club, and an honorary member of the Cambridge University Small Bore Rifle Club, where at one time he acted as coach.

For some years Robert Sayle's social functions were held in various, not always convenient, places available for renting, but in January 1950 it succeeded, at the end of two-year-long efforts by Mr Walsh, in obtaining the lease of a splendid club-room of its own, in the old Masonic Hall in Corn Exchange Street. This consisted of a large hall, where about 120 people could be seated, with a stage – the best amateur stage in Cambridge after the ADC – and all back-stage facilities, together with a utility room where small catering operations could be carried out. Later on, too, a bar was installed. When not in use as a theatre, there was space in the hall for two simultaneous games of table-tennis and it was frequently occupied in this way during lunch-hours. Parties and dances, whist drives and other entertainments, all of them well-attended by Partners and their guests, were organised in the evenings and on special occasions. Probably many Partners' children have happy memories of Christmas parties, complete with Father Christmas, coming down a chimney on the stage, and a big Christmas tree holding the presents he was about to bestow on the lucky recipients.

Of all Robert Sayle's out-of-business activities the most notably successful was always the Dramatic Society. In common with other branches it gave up the old name – Victoria House – when it was affiliated to the John Lewis Partnership Dramatic Society, and was thenceforward known as the Robert Sayle Dramatic Society. It was extremely fortunate in its producer, Mr Beverley Greenall, who acted in this capacity not only while he was manager of the Men's Wear Department in the shop, but also after he retired. Moreover, after 1951, the branch was proved to have manifested inspired foresight in choosing Mr Philip Lloyd as manager of its Furniture Department: it thereby acquired a playwright and musician of no mean calibre. Mr Lloyd is not only a first-rate pianist but he has an enviable gift for original melody and has planned, composed and written revues and pantomimes for the branch, himself acting as producer, accompanist and conductor. He has spent a great deal of time on it and has given a great deal of pleasure to a great many people. Long may he continue to do so!

It was a sad day when 'the old Masonic'

had to be given up in 1968 and the whole building was demolished. There was a feeling as though the old homestead were being abandoned when the curtain fell for the last time, with dramatic slowness, on an Old Time Music Hall, nostalgically entitled 'Ring Down the Curtain'. The hall had in its day been the premises of the university's Footlights Club, which accounted for its good stage potentialities. Robert Sayle's electricians and other enthusiasts did wonders in the way of stage lighting and 'effects'; a beautiful curtain was made, hung, and kept in repair by the branch's clever needlewomen (including wives of Partners); scenery was brilliantly designed and built by members of the branch, outstanding among them being Mr D G Manning and some members of the display section; and stage discipline was controlled kindly but firmly and efficiently, by the branch's Display Manager, Mr Basil E Carroll. Decorations and general maintenance of the hall were looked after by volunteers in their spare time; everyone took a pride in keeping the place up to scratch as well as in arranging suitable decor for special occasions. Other branches may well have envied Robert Sayle's good fortune in enjoying the use of such a place for close on 20 years. It may also have helped to win the branch its successes in competitions – although it was, in fact, before the hall was hired that The Gazette once remarked that "to many of us Robert Sayle is the branch that wins the One-Act Play Festival when Peter Jones doesn't!"

During the 1950s, again as a result of Mr Walsh's negotiations, the branch's Social Club also rented the university's hockey ground, in Newnham village, as a playing field for the summer months. It was a good-sized field, attached to which were a dressing-room and a club house where light refreshments could be served. The ground was used mainly by the Robert Sayle cricket club; attempts were made to adapt parts of it for lawn tennis, but not with much success, and the tennis players then rented courts elsewhere, as had been done in earlier years. The most popular event on the ground was the annual sports day, a very pleasant occasion, on which even the over-60s were given a chance to show what they could do. It was regretfully decided after a few years, however, that the expense of hiring the field was not justified by the amount of use made of it and it was given up. The climate of Cambridge does not, unfortunately, afford enough fine, warm days when Partners might have enjoyed simply relaxing there in the sunshine during leisure hours. The sports day did, nevertheless, continue to be a summer function, in which other branches were also invited to join, for several years after the hockey ground had been relinquished, different fields being rented for the occasion, but changing tastes eventually led to its lapsing, and other interests took its place.

The Cambridge Experiment was a fine, healthy growth in its young days, and it will no doubt continue to produce good fruit as it matures still further.

27: 'Near peace' and reorganisation

The end of the 1940s and the 1950s saw the Partnership shaking down with the rest of the world into what might be called 'near-peace'. Trade continued to be difficult, because the government was doing all it could to discourage private spending and to limit profits, especially in retail business, by rationing and savage taxation. It was hoped thereby to prevent the employment of people in non-productive, distributive trades, and to force them into factories working for export. The Partnership reckoned that, as a result, something like 7 per cent of Partnership Benefit was lost to its members; besides which, it was almost impossible to increase pay rates as had been hoped, although they had been raised to some extent from 1941 onwards and, since the middle of 1946, marriage and family allowances had been in full swing. All these factors obliged the Partnership to consider some modification of its structure. In buying the SPS group it had acquired a mixed collection of businesses, with differing trading potential, not all of which fitted into its system. The Central Board was faced with the prospect of rebuilding its bombed shops which, with essential maintenance and repairs needed on all the others, was going to involve enormously heavy expenses – particularly since the government was refusing all compensation for the destruction of John Lewis in Oxford Street. If, as seemed not improbable, a satisfactory price were to be obtained for the sites, premises and goodwill of certain units in the group, the money would make the improvement of the remaining branches possible.

The first to be offered for sale was H Holdron Ltd of Peckham. The decision to sell was taken in the latter part of 1946, and a purchaser soon appeared; £400,000 was received for the business. The sale was concluded on 4th January 1949 and the shop ceased to trade under the Partnership after 29th January. No further branches were sold for some years but, in 1948, a long-planned expansion of the Partnership had been carried out by the opening of a branch in Cape Town, South Africa, which was later followed by a second in Port Elizabeth and a third in Johannesburg. Mr Lewis B Smith was given charge of these branches and remained there until they were closed down in 1954. On 29th January 1951 a 'satellite' for George Henry Lee, the Partnership's branch in Liverpool, was opened in Chester, to sell dress and furnishing materials, under the managership of Mr M W Goss, who had been Merchandise Secretary at Robert Sayle since April 1950, after having been a section manager in piece goods departments at John Lewis. The Chester shop remained with the Partnership until 1965. In 1953 a series of fluctuations took place in the number of Partnership branches. The first to be sold this time was W J Buckley, in Harrogate, which went in July that year. At the end of August, the Tunbridge Wells Bon Marché and the Hull Silk Shop left the Partnership, and in September Blinkhorns, in Gloucester and Stroud, followed suit, as did also Vinalls of Eastbourne. As far as possible, all workers who wished to remain with the Partnership from shops which were sold were offered alternative positions in other branches, or were paid generous compensation if this proved impossible.

In the same year two large new branches were bought – Bainbridge in Newcastle, and Heelas of Reading. A H Bull, the Partnership's older branch in Reading, was incorporated with Heelas, the new name being kept for the amalgamated businesses; Bull's premises, which were on the opposite side of the road, were sold. After the sale of Blinkhorns, the only branch remaining to the Partnership in the West Country was Lance & Lance in Weston-super-Mare. This shop had made a wonderful recovery after the bombing, despite the difficulty of obtaining a licence to rebuild. By the middle of May 1948 a single-storey structure had been put up on the old site, where most kinds of household goods were sold, and a few months later a fashion showroom and workrooms were also contrived. Conditions being what they were, the shop made an astonishingly good come-back but, by 1955, it was decided that its position was too isolated geographically from the rest of the Partnership for it to be carried on satisfactorily and it was disposed of in February 1956. This, for the nonce, ended the programme of reorganisation.

Robert Sayle was, meanwhile, bringing itself up to standard. In 1948 the shop front had had a thorough clean-up ("a good scrubbing", someone called it), to remove as far as possible the traces of unavoidable war-time neglect, and in the spring of 1949, for the first time, flowering plants were ranged in window-boxes along the top of the arcade show-windows, with hanging baskets at intervals. The effect was fresh and charming, everyone agreed. During the summer of that year it was at last found possible to improve conditions for the Receiving and Despatch Department of the shop, by moving them from very cramped quarters into what had previously been the 'cloth room' on the north side of the yard. Up till then it had been necessary to unload incoming goods in the yard itself, with no cover at all. Now a corrugated iron roof, high enough not to interfere with lorries, was erected immediately outside the new offices and, though not ideal, it at least provided shelter from the worst of the weather. Swifts and other birds also found this to be a desirable residential area – but, probably because of the noise and other disturbances, they abandoned it after a year or two, to the relief of the maintenance staff, who had found themselves acting as refuse collectors to the colony.

Trade in those days was fairly satisfactory in Cambridge and the branch's position rose in the weekly tables of results. While this was in itself gratifying, it meant of course that it was taking more money than some of the larger branches, which were therefore not trading to capacity, and the Partnership as a whole was rather in the doldrums. Clothing coupons were abolished in 1949, but at Robert Sayle it was half suspected that customers were afraid of a re-imposition of rationing and that much of the increase might be attributed to 'panic buying'. Fashion stocks were difficult to get and money was tight throughout the Partnership. By 1952 it was unfortunately found necessary once again to ask Partners earning more than a certain figure to allow part of their pay to be deferred. The cut lasted from 1st August 1952 to 21st January 1953 and

the temporary decreases were all refunded in the week ending 28th November 1953, together with a bonus of 5 per cent. No Partnership Benefit had been possible for the years 1948 to 1952 inclusive, although 6 per cent had been distributed in each of the years 1946 and 1947 and a 'holiday bonus', of one day's pay for every year of service up to six, had been given in 1951 because of an unexpected increase in sales. The regular flow of Partnership Benefit was resumed in 1953, at 4 per cent, since when there has been no interruption and a steady increase in the percentage.

Trade was not helped in the early 1950s by power and fuel cuts which occurred from time to time. Workroom Partners had every now and then to be stood off in winter because of coal shortage and, but for kind friends who lent hand- or treadle-machines, work might have been held up even more frequently when power cuts prevented the use of electrically operated sewing machines and other tools of the trades. The Partnership did its best to help people through the difficult times by offering to reckon some of the enforced days off as part of the paid holiday entitlement, with the exception of the single week that must statutorily be taken in the summer, and everyone was expected to apply for national unemployment benefit as applicable. Power cuts affected even the publication of The Gazette, which once or twice could issue no more than a single broadsheet of information and encouragement during those dark ages.

In February 1951, Robert Sayle had the pleasure of hearing that Mr Walsh, its General Manager, had been promoted to

**Robert Sayle
Peterborough
on fire,
August 1956**

awaited building licence for alterations to the first floor above the Carpet Department at Robert Sayle, when the splendid new showroom was built, giving an extra 3,800 square feet of selling space for the Soft Furnishings and Bedding Departments. It was opened in the spring of 1955. A new staircase was made at the western end, connecting the ground floor with the first floor – a particularly comfortably negotiable flight of stairs, with a convenient landing half-way up, most useful for display purposes. For a time part of the new showroom at the top of these stairs was let to Poly Tours travel bureau, who celebrated their opening here with a cocktail party which was attended by numbers of Cambridge notabilities. The bureau was successful in this position, but trade in the Soft Furnishings Department increased to such an extent that it became impossible for the two to co-exist and the bureau moved out after a year or two. Early in 1955, a customer wrote to congratulate the shop on the new department: "There isn't a dark corner anywhere, and yet no glare", she said, and added that she was sure there was no shop in London which was better arranged.

the rank of Managing Director and in October of the following year, further reorganisation in the Partnership made him Managing Director also of Peterborough, Mr A G Hurrell remaining there as local General Manager, a position which he had held for the past three years. In February 1956 Mr Hurrell transferred to another post in the Partnership and his place at Peterborough was taken by Mr Derek G Birch, who had been Staff Assistant and then Assistant to the Managing Director in Cambridge since 1951. In 1953 some of the senior Partners at Robert Sayle attended a course in civil defence organised by the Cambridge authorities, and in 1954 they passed on what they had learnt in a series of talks to other members of the branch, with help also from some civil defence officers. But thereafter the technicalities of destruction progressed so rapidly that it was felt that civil defence must remain an expert's job and the Robert Sayle contingent retired from the attempt to keep up with it.

1953/54 saw the granting of the long-

The story of the Peterborough branch came to a sad end in August 1956. A fire broke out not long after the shop had been closed for business one evening and the flames spread with incredible rapidity. After less than three hours hardly more than a shell was left, despite the efforts of the fire brigade. The cause of the fire was never determined. Mr Walsh, who was enjoying a fishing holiday in Hampshire, was told of the news by telephone as soon as the fire was discovered. He rushed up to Peterborough in his car at once, covering the 150 miles in about two hours, but there was nothing he could do – the place was a heap of smoking rubble.

Relations between the Cambridge and Peterborough branches had been very cordial. They were guests at each other's council dinners and other festivities; Peterborough hired a coach once a year to bring a large party over to Cambridge for the Dramatic Society's production and individuals often came at other times; their Chronicle was shared at first, until the regular Peterborough supplement was added in February 1954, so they knew all about each other's doings. The destruction of the branch was felt in Cambridge as a quite personal loss. The shop was not rebuilt by the Partnership and the site was sold, to the regret of many Peterborough residents, one of whom wrote to Mr Walsh and said she thought it was the worst thing that had happened to the town since the dissolution of the monasteries in the sixteenth century. Some of the Peterborough Partners were welcomed to posts at Robert Sayle in Cambridge but

most of them left again after a short spell to find work nearer home. Those to whom no alternative posts could be offered were given up to four weeks' compensatory pay. Mr Birch went on to another appointment in the Partnership but left finally in January 1960.

Other changes were pending for Robert Sayle. Miss M W Middleham retired from the managing directorship of Cole Brothers in Sheffield and Mr Walsh was asked to take over that shop. After some hesitation he agreed to leave Cambridge, where he had many ties, and went up north at the end of 1957, followed by very warm wishes from all his friends in the branch and in the town. He died there, very suddenly, on 1st December 1965. A number of Partners from Robert Sayle went up to Sheffield for the memorial service. His successor in Cambridge was Mr Lewis B Smith, whose career in the Partnership had been very varied since he joined in 1934. His first appointment had been that of Assistant to the General Manager at Lance & Lance. From there he moved to London and worked for a time in the John Lewis buying office for woollen

The members of the Waterloo Club at its first meeting, at The Red Lion, Trumpington, in June 1958

117

materials. In 1936 he became a General Manager at John Lewis, first in the West House and then in the East House, and in 1938 he was promoted to General Manager at Tyrrell & Green. He was called up at the outbreak of war and served in the King's Own Scottish Borderers and the Gordon Highlanders; he was demobilised with the rank of major in December 1945 and returned to the Partnership early in 1946. After another brief spell on the buying side, he went out as manager of the South African branches and, during his time there, he and his wife entertained Mr and Mrs Spedan Lewis when they spent a winter in that country. On his return to England at the closure of the South African Company in 1954, Mr Smith became General Manager of the Bon Marché, in Brixton, where he remained until he moved to Cambridge in 1957, to inaugurate another very happy and successful era in that branch.

Mr Smith has encouraged sport – witness the Lewis Smith cup for darts – and he has done much to bring older Partners, including pensioners, into the branch's life. A particularly enjoyable innovation has been the formation of the Waterloo Club, so called because the annual luncheon party, known as the Founder's Feast by permission of Mr Spedan Lewis as founder of the Partnership, was first held on the date of the Battle of Waterloo, 18th June, and has been held as nearly as possible to that date ever since. The members of the club are men and women at Robert Sayle who have spent 25 or more years in the Partnership. The first gathering took place in a private room at the Red Lion Hotel in Trumpington on 18th June 1958. Twenty-one Partners were present, including three pensioners. Subsequent reunions were arranged at Mr and Mrs Lewis Smith's own house, where the delightful surroundings and a lovely garden added even more to everyone's enjoyment – on only one occasion has the weather been less than kind. By 1968 the number of Partners qualifying for membership of the club was 31, of whom 18 were pensioners. Some of the older ones had in the intervening years dropped off but each summer one or two more people reach the 25-year target, so the numbers are kept up. Old friends are remembered, newcomers are welcomed.

28: Envoi

Robert Sayle's is a success story and fortunately one of which the end is not in sight. The business was started as a small general shop some 130 years ago. Nobody knows what its turnover was in 1840, nor the number of assistants employed, but it is fair to guess that the takings amounted to a very few thousands during the first years and the number of employees is likely to have been not more than ten. When young Mr Sayle opened his shop, conditions of life were so different from what they are now that it seems as though the story were set in an imaginary world. Values of all kinds – not only monetary – have changed beyond anything that could have been seriously supposed likely; in many ways for the better, in some possibly not.

The nineteenth century saw the beginning of the urbanisation of England. In 1840 the population was still to a great extent agricultural and illiterate and the industrial age was in its infancy. Overseas there were chances for expansion – Asia, Africa, Australia and much of America were largely unknown territory; the world seemed spacious and ripe for exploration, its mysteries asking to be solved. Extended opportunities for education, new ideas and scientific discoveries, new sciences and peoples, new sorts of goods, were enlarging everyone's experience. Possibilities of trade were increasing in every direction, at home and abroad. Robert Sayle was one of those who realised and made the most of the potentialities. Wars there were but most of them were relatively small and local; insofar as they concerned England, they were carried on in far corners of the earth and as a rule casualties were comparatively slight, as also were the repercussions upon most people at home. It was taken for granted that England won its wars and that they were justifiable.

The twentieth century had barely begun before the most deadly, destructive and widespread war of any known age broke out; and within 20 years of its ending, a second, at least as widespread and in material ways even more destructive, burst upon a world which had by now shrunk to a fraction of its former size through the ease of all forms of communication, making it vulnerable

to a degree yet undreamt of. The reverberations have not yet faded.

Against this restless background, the erstwhile tiny shop in Cambridge survived, grew and prospered. It passed through successive phases in its evolution from a one-man business to being a limited company and then part of a group and, finally, in 1940, just 100 years after its foundation, it became a member of the John Lewis Partnership, to join in what has been called an "experiment in industrial democracy". The winds of prosperity did not always blow favourably but the main trend has been good and even when, from a financial angle, the little argosy might have seemed to be in danger of foundering, that state never lasted for long and somehow it got back onto an even keel. From all accounts, it has always been a loyal and happy shop. In 1955 a customer wrote to the Managing Director saying: "So many young people nowadays are bored in their work – but not at Messrs Sayle's. It is always the greatest pleasure to shop there."

The first £1m of turnover in a single year was achieved in 1960; £1.5m in the year ending 31st January 1965. The number of workers was by then little short of 450 – management and salespeople, fashions and furnishings, factories and finance, correspondence and catering, transport, maintenance and other service sections – they all contributed to the results. The future cannot be foreseen but, now that it has well passed its first century, it may not be over-optimistic to express to Robert Sayle, with the rest of the John Lewis Partnership, the wish for "Good fortune and good trading in the next 100 years".

Appendix A: Proprietors & managers of the Robert Sayle business

21st March 1840	Shop opened at Victoria House, St. Andrew's Street, Cambridge. Sole proprietor Mr Robert Sayle.
5th October 1883	Death of Mr Sayle.
October 1883/ August 1884	Business in charge of trustees.
7th August 1884	Business transferred to new joint owners, Messrs J Clark, A E Chaplin and H W Porter. Now trading as Robert Sayle & Co. (Sale backdated to 19th January 1884.)
27th April 1898	Death of Mr Porter; the other two owners continue in partnership.
1902/03	Mr Chaplin's elder son, A Hugh B Chaplin, taken into partnership.
14th August 1911	Death of Mr Clark, leaving Mr Chaplin and 'Mr Hugh' as proprietors.
21st May 1917	'Mr Hugh' dies of wounds received on active service in France.
1st August 1919	Business turned into a private company, Robert Sayle & Co Ltd; Mr Chaplin Governing Director.
17th August 1934	Death of Mr Chaplin, aged 90. Mr J W Pretty, a Director, acts as Manager.
29th November 1934	Business sold to Selfridge Provincial Stores (SPS). Mr Pretty remains as Manager of the shop.
1st February 1940	SPS group sold to John Lewis Partnership; Mr Pretty remains as General Manager.
1st July 1940	Mr Pretty obliged, on health grounds, to resign; replaced as General Manager by Mr L J Walsh.
11th March 1942	Mr Walsh called up for service with the RAF; his place taken by Mrs C M Bull.
22nd September 1942	Mr R C Hurst replaces Mrs Bull.
31st July 1944	Mr A Perreur Lloyd replaces Mr Hurst.
3rd April 1945	Mr J H Spilman replaces Mr Perreur Lloyd.
11th June 1946	Mr Walsh returns from war service.
February 1961	Mr Walsh, Managing Director, Robert Sayle, Cambridge and Peterborough.
22nd August 1956	Peterborough shop burnt down, and the site sold.
1st January 1957	Mr Lewis B Smith replaces Mr Walsh as General Manager.
29th March 1969	Retirement of Mr Smith.
31st March 1969	Mr G P K Miller becomes General Manager.

Appendix B: Robert Sayle Dramatic Society productions

1936-1951, known as Victoria House Dramatic Society; performances at ADC Theatre.

1936	Nothing but the Truth	James Montgomery
1937	Under Cover	Roi Mogrue
1938	Interference	R Pertwee and H Dearden
1939	The Happy Ending	Ian Hay
1940	Autumn	Ilya Surguchev
1941	Quiet Wedding	Esther McCracken
1942	Marry at Leisure	Frank Vosper
1943	Interference	R Pertwee and H Dearden
1944	Square Pegs	Lionel Brown
1945	April Clouds	P Barwell and M Malleson
1946	To Kill a Cat	R Pertwee and H Dearden
1947	Give Me Yesterday	E Percy and R Denham
1948	Young Mrs Barrington	W Chetham Strode
1949	The Shop at Sly Corner	Edward Perch
1950	The Sacred Flame	W Somerset Maugham
1951	Power Without Glory	M C Hutton

1952-1968, affiliated to the John Lewis Partnership Dramatic Society, and known as the Robert Sayle Dramatic Society; performances at the Social Club Theatre in the old Masonic Hall, Corn Exchange Street.

1952	Setting Sayle (Revue)	Philip Lloyd
	Family Drama	W Dinner and W Morum
	The Tinder Box (Pantomime)	Philip Lloyd
1953	See How They Run	Philip King
	Gaiety Nights (Music Hall)	Arranged by Philip Lloyd
1954	One Wild Oat	V Sylvaine
	Cinderella (Pantomime)	Produced by Philip Lloyd
1955	The Giaconda Smile	Aldous Huxley
	Carnival Nights (Variety)	Arranged by Philip Lloyd
1956	Love in a Mist	M Boileau and J Erle
	Jack and the Beanstalk	P Lloyd and E E Greenhalgh
1957	Old Man's Castle	L S Howarth
1958	Victoriana (Music Hall)	Arranged by Philip Lloyd
1959	Vogues and Rogues (Revue)	Arranged by Philip Lloyd
	Aladdin (Pantomime)	Produced by Philip Lloyd
1961	See How They Run	Philip King
1962	Jonellmania	Junior Revue
1963	Sailor Beware	Philip King and F Carey

1964	Dangerous Corner	J B Priestley
	Sinbad the Sailor (Pantomime)	Produced by Philip Lloyd
1965	The Tinder Box	Philip Lloyd
1966	Fly Away Peter	A P Dearsley
1967	No Time for Love	James Liggatt
1968	Ring Down the Curtain (Music Hall)	Arranged by Philip Lloyd

Entries for the Partnership One-Act Play Festival

1946	(January) The Distant Drum	Philip Johnson
	(October) The Dressing Gown	E Percy and R Denham
1947*	Interference	E Pertwee and R Dearden
1948	The Dressing Gown	E Percy and R Denham
1949*	The Friends of Valerie Lane	Dollond Parsons
1950	Familiar Strangers	Nora Radcliff
1952	The Drummer of Shawm	Violet Rutter
1953	The Shining Hour	Keith Winter
1954	The Heiress	Mary Seymour
1958	Home is the Hunter	R F Delderfield
1960	Ride a Tiger	Anthony Booth
1961	Familiar Strangers	Nora Radcliff

(* Robert Sayle won the Partnership Challenge Cup)

Note: Pantomime and Revues were arranged by Philip Lloyd, who also composed much of the music. Other plays produced by Beverley Greenall.

Appendix C: Partnership Bonus

The John Lewis Partnership was first started at Peter Jones, Chelsea, in 1914, shortly before the outbreak of the first World War. Peter Jones was then a derelict shop running at a loss and no profits became available for distribution until 1919, when a bonus of 15 per cent of the payroll was given in cash. With some gaps, the bonus – generally in 'share promises' or shares – was kept up until just before the outbreak of the second World War.

Robert Sayle, with the rest of the SPS group, joined the Partnership on 1st February 1940 and from then until 1945 inclusive no bonus was possible. In the succeeding years, distributions have been as follows:-

1946	6%	1960	14% in shares
1947	6%	1961	12% in shares
1948-50	None	1962	11% in shares
1951	Holiday bonus of one	1963	12% in shares
	day's extra pay up to a	1964	13% in shares
	maximum of six	1965	15% in shares
1952	None	1966	12% in shares
1953	4% in shares	1967	18%, of which 12% in
1954-56	8% in shares		shares and 6% in cash
1957	9% in shares	1968	18%, of which 10% in
1958	7% in shares		shares and 8% in cash
1959	13% in shares	1969	12%, all in cash

Appendix D: The Robert Sayle Trade Mark (made for overseas branches)

At some time between 1935 and 1940, while Robert Sayle & Co was a member of the Selfridge Provincial Stores group, the scroll displaying the Robert Sayle trade mark was discovered in a stock room by Mr T E Potter, then a young sales assistant. It had been rolled up and stored in one of a number of large Chinese vases, having presumably been sent home near the beginning of the century, when Sayle's oriental trade was brought to an end. In due course the scroll came to Mr L J Walsh, when he was appointed General Manager after Mr Pretty had retired, and the business had passed to the John Lewis Partnership. Mr Walsh had the scroll framed and hung in his office in St Andrew's Street, where it has remained ever since.

The trade mark is largely symbolic. At the very bottom of the picture is a sinuous blue band, signifying the River Cam (as in the Cambridgeshire Arms), the business having been founded in Cambridge. The black bar above this would denote the ocean ('the black water') that must be crossed between Europe and Asia. Above are three Coats of Arms: at the top the Royal Arms of Great Britain, to show that trade was carried on with places that came under the Crown (Hongkong and Shanghai, in this instance); below these Mr Robert Sayle's own bearings, to which have been added some Chinese characters that are transliterations, reading round the pictured shield from left to right, of the sounds we hear as "Sayle, Hongkong", "Company", and "Sayle, Shanghai". The third Coat of Arms is that of the City of London, because the company's wholesale and overseas business was routed through the metropolis. Mr Sayle was not a liveryman of any of the

Mr Robert Sayle's scroll, 19th century

city's great companies, however, nor, it has been ascertained, was he a freeman of the city of London.

The Sayle Arms are, rather mysteriously, flanked by a pair of handsome tigers, for which no definite reason has been found, except that there is an old-established factory, sited in Hongkong, that produces a very strong, very popular local medicament known as Tiger Balm. This, though originally designed specifically for chest complaints, has come to be used more or less as a cure-all – so the tigers might be intended as a general symbol of good fortune. But this is mere conjecture and it is not known whether Robert Sayle ever dealt in the balm.

The painting, done on linen or cotton cloth, was – to judge by the workmanship – probably executed in the Far East by one of the many commercial artists who do this type of work for foreign residents and visitors.

The whole design is embellished by decorative patterns and floral tracery, among which may be seen the long twining stalks and mulberry-like fruits of hop plants – surely an allusion to the fact that for many years beer was brewed in the Cambridge shop for export as well as for home consumption? And might not the other flowers be stylised references to various sections of the firm's main stock-in-trade, such as cotton or flax?

Robert Sayle's personal Arms (pictured opposite), granted in 1874, appear to derive from the ancient Arms of three North-Country families: Scales, Seale, and Sale – which may indeed have been some of the many variants of the same name. The scallop shells in the crest come from Scales: the animal heads in crest and shield from Seale and Sale. (Purely as a matter of coincidence, it is perhaps interesting to note that the buyer of the Silk Department at Robert Sayle & Co in the 1930s was named Scales.) In the 1899 edition of Fox-Davies' Armorial Bearings, at which date the Sayle Arms were borne by Mr Robert Sayle's fifth son Charles Edward, these are described as follows:-

Arms: Argent on a fesse cotised engrailed azure between three wolves' heads erased sable, as many griffins' heads erased or.

Crest: on a wreath of the colours (blue and white) in front of a wolf's head erased sable gorged with a collar gemelle or, three escallops gold.

Motto: Who most has served is greatest.

Glossary:-

Argent   - white, silver
Azure   - blue
Cotised   - edged with a series of
           short lines
Engrailed   - indented edges
Erased   - jagged edges
Escallop   - scallop shell
Fesse   - a horizontal band across
           the middle of a shield
Gemelle   - twin (double)
Gorged   - wearing a collar
Or   - gold
Sable   - black

**The derivation
of the Sayle
family arms**

Postscript: 1969-71

Since this history of Robert Sayle was completed in 1969 there have been considerable changes. Mr Lewis Smith, who had been General Manager at Robert Sayle for the last 12 years of his 36 years with the Partnership, retired in March 1969 and was succeeded by Mr G P K Miller.

During 1969 and 1970 the old arcade with its island windows and three entrances was replaced with the present, modernised frontage, with one large central window run and smaller windows beside each of the two entrances. This change provided an extra 1,400 square feet of much needed selling space on the ground floor. A 'Miss Cambridge'

department, selling young fashions, was opened in 1969 and, in August 1970, a Silverware Department was opened on the ground floor. This was the return of an old favourite which was in being until just after the last war. The Hairdressing Department and Garden Furniture and Whitewood Furniture sections were closed in 1969/70, to make way for the better presentation of the remaining ranges of merchandise.

The Magnet Service Building in Mill Road was acquired in 1971 and opened in June of that year. The need for additional storage space outside the city centre had resulted from the city council's

opportunity was taken to incorporate some of the space, previously not being fully used on the ground floor, into the shop and to extend the fashion floor above it. The most recent developments are the extension of the furnishing textiles selling area at first floor level, by building out over the yard – some 1,500 square feet – for which completion is expected towards the end of 1974 and an increase of some 40 per cent in the basement from digging out further selling and stockroom space. In all, there will have been an increase of 24 per cent in selling area during this period.

LMS

Robert Sayle in 1969. The 'arcaded' shopfront was replaced with flat display windows during the following year redevelopment of the Lion Yard car park which resulted in the loss of some 11,500 square feet of outbuildings at the rear of the shop from Christmas 1970 onwards. The rebuilding necessary to rehouse the Soft Furnishing Workrooms and forward stockrooms was completed progressively up to 1973 and the

Robert Sayle's family tree

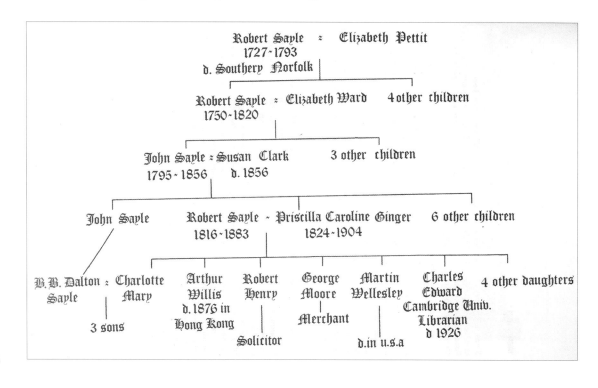

126

Some references and sources

Sayle family papers.
Cambridge electoral rolls and street directories.
Church records.
Cambridge local papers, daily and weekly.
Scrap book on the Gas Question; October 1867 to January 1869. (A collection of newspaper cuttings held in the Cambridge public library.)
'The Pontefract Advertiser', 2nd February 1886.
The Gazette of the John Lewis Partnership.
'Victoria History of the County of Cambridgeshire'.
'Victoria History of the County of Yorkshire'.
Cambridge County Handbook, 1949.
Butler's 'Lives of the Saints'.
'Diary of Josiah Chater', edited by Enid Porter.
Richard Holmes, 'The Book of Entries' 1653-1726.

Florence Ada Keynes, 'Byways of Cambridge History'.
C F Mather, 'Chartism'.
The Reverend James Morgan, 'A Short History of the Church and Parish of St Andrew the Great'.
Gwen Raveret, 'Period Piece'.
Frank Tice, 'A History of Methodism in Cambridge'.

'A Portfolio of Twelve Maps Illustrating the Changing Plan of Cambridge from the Sixteenth to the Twentieth Century', edited by Tony Baggs and Peter Bryan and published in 2002 by the Cambridgeshire Record Society, contains maps which show well the changes to the street layout around Robert Sayle. It is available from the Cambridgeshire Collection in the Cambridge Central Library.

Photographs and illustrations

The Cambridgeshire Collection: pp8, 20, 24, 25, 27, 29, 36, 93, 110
The Leys School: p26

Jenny Josselyn: pp34, 56
John Lewis Partnership Archive: pp39, 52, 60, 64, 65, 70, 94, 97, 107, 116, 126

A History of Robert Sayle

Part 2
1969-2004

by
Jenifer Gooch

29: The changing face of retailing

During the last 30 years of the 20th century, retailing saw many significant changes – in the way shops displayed and marketed their goods; in the service they offered; in the location of shops themselves; in customer expectations and shopping habits. In effect, the face of retailing altered beyond recognition.

In 1970 the traditional shopping areas in towns and cities were the high streets. Most larger shops clustered around the historic centres, often near the market places which could trace their existence back over many centuries. They were literally central to where people lived and easily accessible in the days before motorised transport. However, this whole concept was about to be turned upside down and, in many towns, the character of the high street was to be transformed.

What brought this about was the development of the undercover shopping mall and the out-of-town shopping centre. In some places the mall was built in or near the traditional centre but out-of-town centres were often sited some distance from residential areas, frequently on undeveloped land in the countryside. They varied in size but by the 1980s bigger and bigger centres were appearing. Milton Keynes was the largest shopping centre in the country when it opened in 1979, but the trend culminated in Bluewater, the largest undercover regional centre in Europe, on the site of an old cement quarry in Kent a few miles from the Dartford crossing. The feature common to all the out-of-town centres was that they catered primarily for the car-borne shopper. However, in the early 1990s another policy shift started to take shape. The impact of these malls on town centres and the increase in traffic had become obvious.

There has been a move away from out-of-town centres on the Bluewater model and, for the foreseeable future, shopping centres will be built in existing towns, not away from them. Traffic congestion, access and parking availability are still problems in many urban areas but government policy and local councils are now beginning to address them by expanding park-and-ride schemes and encouraging people back onto public transport.

Another factor that has contributed to the changing face of retail is the diminishing number of independent shops in town centres. Retail companies have grown, smaller ones have been taken over and well-known names have merged. The buying power of the multiple chains has brought about keen price competition; smaller independent shops have not always been able to absorb the rise in overheads like rent and rates and to stay competitive. The multiple chains now have branches everywhere and have squeezed out some smaller competitors, although speciality shops can usually find a niche in the market.

The extension of trading hours is also having a noticeable effect. At the beginning of the 1970s most shops opened for five or five- and-a-half days a week. Most provincial towns had a half-day closing. Six-day trading was not widespread outside London except in the two weeks before Christmas. It is very different now. In the space of a relatively short time, six- and seven-day trading throughout the whole year has become accepted by many retailers and customers alike.

These issues have all influenced the way the John Lewis Partnership operates. It has had to adapt its trading patterns to meet the changing demands of customers.

30: Robert Sayle – the search for larger premises

It can take a very long time to bring a department store development to a satisfactory conclusion. Harry Legg, Director of Research and Expansion, made that point in 1976 when referring to the recent opening of John Lewis Brent Cross. Nineteen years had elapsed since the initial moves to develop the shopping centre and the Partnership had been closely involved for 10 of those years. In another example, regional planners identified Cribbs Causeway as a site for a substantial and viable out-of-town shopping centre as early as 1973 but it did not open until 1998.

For Cambridge the timescale has been even longer. The Partnership was actively looking to redevelop, expand or relocate Robert Sayle more than 30 years ago, not only to take the business forward beyond 2015, when the leases on the present site expire, but also to offer its customers in this region the full John Lewis assortment, something not possible in the existing premises. Only now is the end tantalisingly within sight. Hopes have been raised and dashed on numerous occasions. Many different schemes have been initiated and planned, only to be rejected or abandoned as unsatisfactory. Some schemes have involved rebuilding Robert Sayle on its present site or extending onto adjacent land; others have been more ambitious and have involved complete relocation. As Mr Legg also said in 1976, what the Partnership wanted for its department stores was well-located, full-scale efficient buildings, pleasant to shop and work in, and with good road access, parking and other transport services. That was to prove exceptionally challenging and elusive in Cambridge.

Retail development in the city had been the subject of debate and discussion from 1949 when the first plan was published. From then on, through to the end of the century, the city sought to find new sites for shops or develop existing ones, but a series of appeals and public enquiries followed scheme after scheme. Miss Sieveking wrote in 1969 that Robert Sayle was still awaiting permission to carry out much of the building programme held up since the war. The sales density, the crowding, the lack of facilities for display all pointed to the need for expansion. She says that the phrase "when we rebuild...." had become a joke in the branch. That refrain, or one very similar, was to echo through the years right up to 2000. It was heard not only in the branch but at the Partnership's central offices also. In 1972 the General Inspector wrote that "our many attempts to expand this branch have so far met with frustration". At that time the branch's trading densities were second only to John Lewis Oxford Street.

Lion Yard was the first area in the city to be extensively developed. The earliest proposals were put forward in 1952 but it was not until the early 1970s that these began to come to fruition and plans were at last put in hand to rebuild the car park, followed by new shops nearby and a new central library. Several old streets disappeared and Petty Cury was rebuilt and pedestrianised. The scheme for the car park meant that land to the rear of Robert Sayle was the subject of a compulsory purchase order, depriving the shop of workrooms and storage space so a certain amount of rebuilding was imperative. The Partnership had looked for suitable premises in the development around Petty Cury, but none was satisfactory.

In another initiative around the same time, the city council started discussions about plans to develop the area around Burleigh Street. The network of small narrow streets was known as the Kite. A new shopping complex was proposed and the Partnership expressed its interest, becoming involved from the early stages of substantive planning. The Partnership was not only interested in a department store but also in a supermarket: the desire to bring Waitrose to Cambridge was as long-standing as the desire to expand Robert Sayle. Initial plans showed a main covered shopping mall following the line of Fitzroy Street, and parking for 2,500 cars – more than the total provided by all the existing official car parks in the city centre. In a memorandum to the Branch Council in February 1973, Mr Legg confirmed the Partnership's interest in the development. He said that Robert Sayle could add only about 10,000 sq ft to its existing premises and such an addition would be disruptive and exceedingly costly. There was no other Cambridge site suitable for the rebuilding and, although the proposed centre was a much less attractive location than St Andrew's Street, it was prudent for the Partnership to keep its options open on a development opportunity that could provide, if all went according to plan, a full-scale unit in Cambridge along the lines of its newest department stores and, moreover, one with good car-parking facilities.

In that same year informal enquiries about the redevelopment of the St Andrew's Street site were put to the city planners. These incorporated plans for shops on the ground floor and in the basement facing the street, with three floors of offices above and five floors of office accommodation to the rear. The planning committee agreed in principle because they viewed the transfer of Robert Sayle to the Fitzroy/Burleigh Street development as having a "beneficial effect" on the proposed shopping scheme. Two years later the city council had still not taken a firm decision about development of the Kite area and it appeared that, if it did go ahead, it might be in a piecemeal fashion, rather than as a large compact scheme. In November that year Mr Legg addressed the Branch Council. He outlined the history and current prospects for development and explained the benefits and difficulties attached to the existing site, as well as those resulting from a move to the projected shopping complex. He said some progress had been made: following a public enquiry the government had given approval for the scheme and outline planning permission had been granted. However, financial considerations could hamper progress and the city council might defer development. Even if all went ahead, detailed planning would take time and ideas on the sequence of building meant that a department store at the far end of the mall would not be open for another 10 years.

At this early stage, plans included a new bus station: this would move from Drummer Street to a site underneath the new branch. Car parking would be above the shops. A Waitrose site was provisionally included. The proposed new Robert Sayle would have as many departments as John Lewis Brent Cross and be three times the size of the current department store.

Not everyone was in favour of the scheme. Some customers reportedly asked why Robert Sayle wanted to move out of Cambridge's 'shopping centre' and Kite residents were dismayed at the thought of being uprooted. When questioned by a Branch Councillor about the wisdom of moving out of the traditional centre, Mr Legg cited the example of Cole Brothers, whose move within Sheffield had been so successful that other shops had followed suit and a thriving centre had been established. The same could happen in Cambridge.

In 1977 Mr Legg reported the Partnership's withdrawal from the development. The subject of a continuing campaign against its size and cost to ratepayers, the development had been scaled down to the point where it would no longer house a Partnership department store. The Kite was eventually developed and the Grafton Centre opened in 1983. A car park was built on top of the centre but the bus station stayed in Drummer Street and Robert Sayle remained in St Andrew's Street.

The Partnership looked again at a possible expansion of Robert Sayle's city-centre site. The city council had agreed that a development of the shop would be appropriate for the southern end of Lion Yard and would make use of an empty, untidy piece of land currently used for car parking. Plans for an extension to the rear of the shop were reported to include parking for up to 250 (half for Robert Sayle's customers and half for public use) as well as offices and student flats. Objections surfaced on the grounds that more cars would be encouraged into the city, lessening the likelihood of a proposed cycle lane to run east to west

along Downing Street. Discussions continued. In February 1979 the city council was split along party lines: the Conservative ruling group thought that expansion would improve city shopping facilities; the Labour opposition thought it would create more traffic problems. The latter also claimed that plans were being rushed through without full public consultation, even though they had been in the public domain for two years. Outline planning permission was granted but the plans were never implemented, although they remained an option for several years and the permission was renewed in 1982. Meanwhile, Robert Sayle acquired the premises at 25 St Andrew's Street in 1979 and this enabled the business to open new departments for radio and television and sports.

The expansion of the Partnership was the subject of a Branch Council discussion topic in January 1981. Councillors noted that Waitrose branches had increased from 57 to 71 over the previous five years. Three department stores had closed, including John Barnes, but John Lewis Milton Keynes had opened and further shops at Bristol, Peterborough and Kingston were already on the drawing board; later that year the Partnership was also to acquire Bonds of Norwich. There was some comment as to whether the Partnership was expanding too quickly at a time of economic uncertainty; questions were asked about Peterborough and its proximity to Cambridge as it was thought that this could have an adverse effect on Robert Sayle's results. Councillors were also concerned that plans for the expansion of Robert Sayle seemed to have gone into abeyance at a time when Marks & Spencer and Eaden Lilley were both undergoing expansion and refurbishment. The Managing Director, Peter O'Ryan, said that growth and development were necessary in order to prosper; nothing remained static. With regard to the expansion of Robert Sayle, the Partnership was biding its time until everyone involved was in agreement.

In 1983 the city council drew up further plans to extend Lion Yard car park and there was mention in the local press that Robert Sayle was considering linking its shop with a bridgewalk to a new building put up over the extended car-parking area. However, some members of the city council remained set against any major rebuilding or expansion to Robert Sayle. In July that year the Managing Director, Chris Mitchell, gave the Branch Council detailed information about the proposed development and the reasons behind the apparent lack of progress. He said that negotiations had been going on for many years with the colleges and the city council to provide sufficient security of tenure and additional land on which to expand. The Partnership had pursued various possibilities. The preference had been to buy the freehold of the site but the colleges would not sell. An alternative, to substitute new leases for the existing ones and to take a lease from the city for the land on either side of St Tibbs Row had proved unviable. The colleges had sought an unacceptably higher percentage of sales than the Partnership had paid in better locations elsewhere, as well as an escalating base rent inconsistent with a percentual arrangement. Furthermore, they had not been prepared to recognise the residual value of the existing leases. The city council had been more flexible and

helpful and, while not abandoning hope of a compromise with the colleges, the Partnership had examined the possibility of a development farther along St Andrew's Street, with an extension across St Tibbs Row on several levels above a car park. Moves had been made to secure additional properties, such as 24 St Andrew's Street. The Partnership had also co-operated with the city council to produce the design for the car park and had suggested a contribution of £1 million towards the costs to secure a five-year option to undertake its own development.

Despite these negotiations the city council appeared to change course. The following year the talk in Cambridge was of a hotel and cinema complex on the site in St Tibbs Row, with student flats and a shopping arcade included, as well as an extension to the car park. There was general agreement that the area was an eyesore. In November an exhibition at the Guildhall sought public reaction to plans for a hotel. The Partnership was no longer pursuing the site. It had been unable to reach a commercially viable agreement, and a satisfactory connection to an extension across the road had proved too difficult to achieve. In 1988 the site was still undeveloped and queries arose as to whether a hotel would actually go ahead: problems existed with funding the project. In this year Robert Sayle obtained the lease on 18/19 St Andrew's Street, a former chemist's shop, and art needlework and knitting wools moved there, releasing selling space in the main shop. The site across St Tibbs Row was eventually developed as a hotel, with a car park underneath, and completed in 1990.

Towards the end of 1989 a completely

new plan was unveiled: the wholesale relocation of Robert Sayle to a proposed out-of-town complex at Duxford near the M11. The latest Cambridgeshire Structure Plan had laid great stress on removing excess development pressure from the historic core of Cambridge and had indicated that an out-of-town shopping centre would be acceptable. Duxford was one of four proposals emerging at the time for consideration as a new sub-regional centre in South Cambridgeshire: two of the others were at Bar Hill, north of Cambridge; and the fourth was at Four Wentways near Abington to the south-east. The Duxford plan was spearheaded by Grosvenor Developments, at an estimated cost of £100 million. In total the centre would offer shopping space not far short of that at Brent Cross, with a Tesco superstore at one end. A planning application was submitted in November 1989. For the Partnership a move out of the city would overcome the increasing problems of car parking and access which existed in Cambridge. A new store by the M11 would also serve a widely dispersed catchment population of customers. Public transport links would be put in place for the development which would also provide Robert Sayle with an on-site warehouse. The scheme aroused fierce controversy among local residents and city councillors expressed fears that any move by Robert Sayle out of Cambridge would create a commercial vacuum in the main shopping centre there. However, in a statement to the local press Stuart Hampson (now Sir Stuart), at that time Director of Research and Expansion, said that the Partnership had considered all the various proposals and was convinced that Duxford offered

the ideal location. The development would produce the kind of high-quality shopping centre in which the Partnership would be happy to invest.

In 1990 Mr Hampson again set out the position very clearly. He said: "Robert Sayle has been in Cambridge for 150 years, for the last 50 years as a branch of John Lewis. We would have liked to have stayed there and we have a whole cabinet of plans for the redevelopment of the store. The real problem has always been that it is a very complex site and one would really have to have a different lease structure. Our present leases have 25 years left to run. For a new department store, costing more than £25 million, that is nothing at all; the payback period is very slow. The other problem is that more and more of our customers want to come in by car. There is a conflict between the customer draw of the store and the conservation objectives of the city. We are convinced that Duxford is the right place to create a new Robert Sayle department store. We shall be able to show the full John Lewis assortment, which we are unable to do in the cramped conditions of St Andrew's Street, and our customers will be able to reach us and park their cars easily and free of charge. We are confident that Grosvenor are intent on providing very high- quality retailing". He added that neither of the Bar Hill proposals would suit John Lewis because "if you are going to go out of town it must be easy to reach. In our view there is too much congestion on the A604 [now the A14] for a site there to be satisfactory."

A public enquiry into the four competing schemes started in November 1991, with a welter of technical information about transport, road systems, the environment and architectural considerations being presented before two Department of the Environment Inspectors. They in turn put their recommendations to the Secretary of State for the final decision to be made. There was no news for some time. Mr Hampson said in 1991 that it was frequently the nature of property developments to have long gaps when nothing appeared to happen. In 1993 the Duxford site was still a field; development remained a long way off, even if it were given the go-ahead. However, by this time the climate of opinion towards out-of-town shopping centres was changing. New planning guidelines were issued for town centres and retail development. Two of the four proposals, those at Four Wentways and at Slate Hall near Bar Hill, were refused. John Gummer, Secretary of State for the Environment, then announced that he was minded to refuse permission for Duxford, despite the recommendation of the Planning Inspector that it should be approved. He gave all parties 12 weeks to make further representations. At the beginning of 1994 he gave his final answer: he would not allow the development to go ahead in the light of the government's revised guidelines and on the grounds that it would adversely affect the vitality and viability of Cambridge city centre. By then Luke Mayhew had become Director of Research and Expansion, and he expressed the Partnership's frustration and disappointment. He said: "It has always been our ambition in the long term to find a new site for Robert Sayle where we could provide our Cambridge customers with a full-scale modern department store. That ambition has not changed

although clearly it has been delayed."

Meanwhile, schemes and ideas for retail development in Cambridge were springing up regularly. Everyone acknowledged the need to provide additional retail capacity but they could not agree on where this should be. The emphasis was moving towards sites within the city boundaries or on its edges. In 1991 there was talk of the Homerton College site becoming available and of it being of interest to the Partnership for a Waitrose food store. However, nothing happened and the college remained where it was. In 1992 plans were put forward to relocate the Arts Cinema and create a small new shopping mall in Market Passage based on the old Joshua Taylor premises. Satisfactory agreement could not be reached and another plan failed. Joshua Taylor, an old family firm of outfitters, had been sold to a retail development company in 1988; it was one of many familiar names which were disappearing from the city. Laurie McConnal's department store had vacated Fitzroy Street several years earlier and Waring and Gillow, the furnishers, no longer traded in Sidney Street. Eventually Eaden Lilley, another long-established family-owned department store, closed its doors. It had undergone a substantial refurbishment and change of emphasis in 1993 when it lost several departments, including furniture, kitchenware and electrical, to concentrate on fashions. It ceased trading altogether on its Market Street site in 1999. The one development that did go ahead was a £19 million, 100,000 sq ft extension to the Grafton Centre; this opened at Easter 1995 and included a cinema complex and food hall.

Following the failure of Duxford to win planning permission the Partnership announced an alternative proposal in July 1994: a department store and a Waitrose supermarket on the same site to the south-west of the city, beyond Trumpington, near junction 11 of the M11. Mr Mayhew told the Branch Council that finding a solution for Robert Sayle remained a top priority for the Partnership. The prospect of combining the two shops was very appealing and the project was planned as a stand-alone development by the Partnership. It represented a potential major investment of £40 million. The land was owned by the Pemberton Trust and the proposal, for which no formal planning application had yet been submitted, offered a park-and-ride facility, a visitor centre and a coach park. Free parking was to be provided for 2,000 cars. Drawings showed a low-level, stone-faced building with a basement floor. The site was to be landscaped and a broad belt of land to the north was designated as a nature reserve, to be planted with mature indigenous trees. It was hoped that these features would make the development attractive and address some of the objections raised against Duxford. However, the site was on green belt land, which gave rise to controversy. A public exhibition at St Columba's Hall in Downing Place explained the proposal to customers and residents.

Strategic issues about retail development and transport management came to the fore when the Structure Plan Review for the Cambridge area began its Examination in Public in September that year. A report commissioned by the city council and the South Cambridgeshire District Council stated that, even with the extension to the Grafton Centre, Cambridge still needed a further 500,000 sq ft of shopping space. Peter Studdart, the city's Director of Planning, acknowledged that decisions had to be made. Several schemes were on the drawing board in addition to the Partnership's plan for the M11/Trumpington site. Sainsbury's was seeking approval for development of the Arbury Camp site off Histon Road. This would include a 200,000 sq ft department store, two variety stores and its own supermarket. Chesterton Sidings, which had surfaced as a possible site a few years earlier, was still in the frame, despite its proximity to sewage works. Finally, Anstey Hall at Trumpington was being promoted as a possible site for a supermarket. The Partnership's proposal failed to win a place in the revised structure plan and the independent inspector into the city council's local plan rejected the development because it was on green belt land.

Government policy was by now advising local authorities to look closely at town-centre developments before considering those on the fringes or outside. To this end a feasibility study was commissioned in 1994 by three colleges – Jesus, Emmanuel and Christ's – and the city council. The study, by London architect James Duffy, envisaged development behind the existing Robert Sayle frontage in St Andrew's Street. The site would accommodate a new department store and an arcade of shops behind the Post Office, linking up with Lion Yard. Mr Studdart is quoted as saying: "At present the back area behind Robert Sayle is a hotch-potch of temporary car parks and building extensions. The study suggests creating a galleria-style set of shops there, making a new pedestrian route to Lion Yard. A new store could be established where Robert Sayle now is, keeping the frontage. There would be around 200,000 sq ft of retail space." Mr Studdart saw this scheme as complementary to, and not instead of, an edge-of-town development, and said it could be implemented whether Robert Sayle moved out or remained.

In 1997 another study was published. This one had been commissioned by the three local councils – city, district and county. It was drawn up in response to projections showing growing demand for shopping facilities in the 21st century. This newest study recommended that all the options for expanding retailing within the city centre should be pursued strenuously before any consideration was given to development on the fringes. Until this time it was widely believed in Cambridge that planners favoured the northern fringe proposal promoted by Sainsbury's. The other contender still being considered was Chesterton Sidings. However, this new study, supported by key businesses, proposed that a large department store could be built on Robert Sayle's present premises, with other shops adjacent to it. Development could take place while the existing shop carried on trading. Question marks about the project remained, not least the traffic implications created by additional shops, but the Partnership described the study as "both practical and potentially attractive" and was invited to apply for planning permission. The plan was to be aired at the public enquiry into all the competing proposals scheduled to begin in June that year. The Partnership remained cautious

because of the difficulties of car parking and access, but one element of the proposal was a new park-and-ride scheme at Trumpington. Improved transport was seen as the key to developing the city centre. Simon Fowler, the Managing Director, informed the Branch Council of the latest developments in May that year. He said that businesses involved with the northern fringe scheme were forcing the pace but another developer, the Shearer Group, had produced a city-centre plan. This plan would create 'The Grand Arcade' in St Andrew's Street. It would be on four levels with space for a large department store. Guy Shearer, of Shearer Property Group, described the scheme as a "grand traditional arcade, reminiscent of period shopping arcades in Central London, with a dramatic entrance from St Andrew's Street".

At an extraordinary meeting in August, Mr Mayhew brought branch councillors up to date with the situation. He said that the Partnership was very interested in the potential offered by 'The Grand Arcade'. The scheme took a completely new view of how the Partnership could approach retailing in Cambridge. It allowed for a large site stretching as far as Downing Street and using St Tibbs Row as part of a shopping mall leading into Lion Yard. The department store would have a sales floor nearly as big as that at John Lewis Cheadle. Lateral thinking added the important extra dimension: a customer collection facility based next to a park-and-ride site on the edge of the city. Although it would be complicated and challenging, Mr Mayhew was confident that the existing shop would be able to trade during rebuilding. The Partnership was still seeking certain assurances critical to the proposal's viability: an effective park-and-ride scheme was an essential prerequisite, as was an assurance that a shopping complex would not be allowed at Arbury Park.

In May 1998 a draft planning brief was on display in the Guildhall and residents were invited to give their views in advance of a full planning application being submitted. At last it seemed that Cambridge had found a scheme that city councillors would support. Mr Studdart said that the development was expected to enhance the vitality and viability of the city centre; at the same time it would respect its character and distinctiveness. In April 2000 the city council's planning committee finally approved the proposal.

Hand in hand with the approval for the building of a department store was the need to obtain a new service building for Robert Sayle, which needed to be up and running in advance of the new shop. Plans for a service building at Trumpington received approval in December 2000 and work started on the site in 2003. It opened in March 2004.

The future – The Grand Arcade
The final scheme for The Grand Arcade, to be completed in 2007, is a partnership with joint venture partners Universities Superannuation Scheme Limited (USS) and Grosvenor Developments, together with Cambridge City Council and Cambridgeshire County Council. Although initially it was envisaged that Robert Sayle would continue to trade on its city-centre site while redevelopment took place around it, a more satisfactory alternative presented itself in due course – the temporary removal of the entire shop to Burleigh Street, to a site where the Co-op

once traded. "It was getting the Burleigh Street site that made the whole equation work," said Graham Clark, Senior Project Manager, in 2003. "Really everything hinged on finding a suitable site for a temporary shop. We were finally able to do this through Grosvenor... They are building the shell for our shop and we will be kitting it out... it is only for three years but it must provide the quality shopping experience our customers expect." This final plan means that, while Robert Sayle is occupying the premises in Burleigh Street, the work in the city centre can go ahead without disruption. When Robert Sayle returns to The Grand Arcade, the building in Burleigh Street will be converted to a mixture of retail, office and residential space with garden terraces.

The vision for The Grand Arcade is of a comprehensive shopping complex that will prevent the city becoming simply a tourist centre and offer the country a powerful model of sustainable development in an historic centre. It will have around 450,000 sq ft of retail space. In addition to a 250,000 sq ft John Lewis department store, there will be 50 other shops, restaurants and cafe-bar facilities. The development will adjoin the existing but totally refurbished Lion Yard shopping centre and link Petty Cury to Downing Street. The siting of the department store is in the most environmentally sensitive part of the site and the architects have found an excellent solution to retaining historic buildings of importance along the frontage, part of which is Grade II listed. The front of No. 25, for example, is described in these listings as a "three storey modern shop front, with a parapet of hipped slate roof not visible from the street. It dates from the late 18th century".

Hence, the facade of the old buildings along St. Andrew's Street, including that of the existing Robert Sayle, will be retained, while the frontage of the new building will use patinated bronze and local Cambridge stone.

The new John Lewis shop has been designed by Sir Colin Standfield Smith CBE, until recently Professor of Architectural Design at Portsmouth University, and his design has been developed by architects Chapman Taylor. "The whole aim of the design is not to overpower the surrounding buildings but at the same time it had to be something that could house a modern shopping development," said Chris Coombs from CODA, a team of architects working for the Partnership. The shop will be positioned on the corner of St Andrew's Street and Downing Street, a little to the left of its present position, and will carry the full John Lewis assortment. There will be a licensed restaurant, with views of the ancient college buildings, and easy access for disabled people.

The shop will have two parts or 'selling boxes': the main box will contain the majority of the selling floors, with five levels including the basement; the second, smaller, selling box will be located on the corner of Downing Street and St Andrew's Street and will be on four levels to help it blend in with the style and size of the existing buildings. The two boxes will be linked by two bridges at different levels.

No additional car parking will be provided but the old concrete car park will be partially demolished and completely remodelled to provide 950 spaces. However, a first-class integrated park-and-ride service is already running successfully in Cambridge, from five edge-of-city sites. The most recent site, which is integral to Robert Sayle's plans, was opened at Trumpington and is next to the new warehouse. A pick-up point for the service will be outside the new shop in Downing Street and will take customers directly to the car park at Trumpington. As Kirsteen Roberts,

The Grand Arcade: an artist's impression of the planned development for St Andrew's Street, to include a brand-new John Lewis shop

Manager, Retail Projects (DS), said in the Gazette in 2003: "This is one reason why Trumpington, with its easy access to the M11, is such an important part of the jigsaw. It will have a customer collection area close to the park-and-ride site and the main road to Cambridge, but will also offer additional services – which include customers being able to go online and shop with John Lewis Direct, or book appointments with the furnishing advisor, without going into the city centre."

The proposal for The Grand Arcade has come up after years of debate about the location and nature of retailing in the region. Plans for the future of Robert Sayle have come full circle: city-centre development, out-of-town development and back to the city centre. Proposals have been promoted, pursued and abandoned. Finally, at the turn of the century, a potentially viable scheme surfaced, one in which the Partnership has decided to make the substantial investment necessary for the development of Robert Sayle.

Everyone can now look forward to the opening of a new shop very close to the site where Mr Robert Sayle first opened his drapery shop in 1840. In addition, the Partnership has built a large, successful Waitrose food store, which opened at Trumpington in October 2000, on a site adjacent to the park-and-ride.

31: Keeping up appearances while bursting at the seams

"It's a funny old shop, with lots of nooks and crannies, but well laid out just the same," said a customer in 1978. More than 20 years later the same is still true; lots of nooks and crannies remain, even though considerable imagination and ingenuity has gone into enlarging them and straightening some of them out. Although the hope has been ever present that new premises would be found or a major rebuilding project become feasible, the business has had to maintain a fresh, up-to-date appearance and offer as wide a range of the Partnership's assortment as possible in its "funny old shop". Furthermore, had any of the planning proposals or initiatives – Fitzroy/Burleigh Street, Duxford, the M11 – been successful, Robert Sayle would still have needed to trade in its existing premises until they came to fruition.

The story of the shop from 1969 to 2004 is primarily one of trying to squeeze a gallon into a pint pot and turning as much space as possible over to selling. Projects to improve the selling floor, stockrooms, offices and Partners' amenities have been a continuous part of the history of those years. The lack of space has been an ever increasing challenge as the volume of trade has grown alongside the growth in the assortment of merchandise offered to customers. Robert Sayle has addressed the problem by using every last little bit of room on the premises and by leasing units nearby. Each time more space has been found there has been an announcement that this was positively the last time....until the next time. In 1974, when almost 1,600 square feet was gained on the first floor, Peter Miller, the General Manager, described the area as "the last piece of space we can obtain without too much inconvenience on our present site". Yet two years later another 900 square feet was found, again on the first floor. The 1976 improvements meant that in seven years the branch had increased its selling space by about one third. Chris Mitchell, the Managing Director in 1990, said "there is no doubt we have now used every inch of space we can". Yet even more room has been found since then. So it has gone on, with the shop becoming extremely adept at utilising the most unpromising and inconspicuous corners.

As Miss Sieveking noted at the end of her history, during 1969 and 1970 the old arcade that fronted the shop, with its island windows and three entrances, was replaced with one large central window run and two other windows, one beside each of the two entrances. A report in the local press commented that the modernisation and expansion would "further remove the front from its appearance when the business started last century". The change to the front of the shop alone provided an extra 1,400 square feet of selling space on the ground floor. Since then, apart from improvements to the canopy, the St Andrew's Street facade has stayed very much the same.

As time went on some departments closed and others opened. By the middle of 1970 garden furniture, whitewood furniture, a beauty salon, hairdressing and toys had all disappeared, although some of these reappeared in later years. A new department in 1970 was silverware. It was sited on the ground floor near to one of the entrances, close to where it remains today, and offered customers stainless-steel cutlery, clocks and barometers. Another comparatively new department, opened the previous year, was 'Miss Cambridge' which sold young fashions.

Robert Sayle was an old building: old buildings have their special problems. As the result of a cloudburst in June 1970, the basement and part of the ground floor flooded, to a depth of four inches in places. Customers had to be asked to leave the basement and baling out began. However, it was reported that one customer pleaded to be allowed into the basement to buy a wedding present from the hardware department where the till was still working. She was escorted down, paddled through the water, bought the present and left the shop satisfied!

Considerable refurbishment began inside the shop in 1971. A new stockroom was created for the china and glass department in the basement and a scissor lift was installed alongside one of the walls at the back of the shop. A hole was dug from the ground to basement level and the excavation was then extended sideways. This meant that goods no longer had to be carried through the shop as the lift could be loaded at ground-floor level and lowered to serve the stockroom. Extra room was also gained for display. Some of the spaces used for storage in the basement had been coal holes, no longer needed after the branch changed to oil-fired

heating. The ceiling 'underground' was very low. This was a particular problem in the lighting department. The Gazette noted that "a tall Partner could find himself up for sale as a standard lamp"! The ceiling was also festooned with pipes. These had been tidied up to a certain extent but could not be hidden completely or moved. The pipes carried water and electricity, the source of some of the branch's constant problems. The electricity system, with its old cables, was prone to become overloaded at busy times, resulting in the loss of a phase. It was not unknown for the lights to fuse on Saturdays when all the tills were active. As part of the refurbishment in the basement some reorganisation of the electrical and household assortment took place; large equipment was moved to a position along one of the walls in hardware and it became possible to demonstrate washing machines to interested customers.

On the ground floor changes were made to the display of fashion accessories. In a fairly revolutionary

move for the time, handbags and gloves parted company. It had been traditional to match them but gloves had become less of an impulse buy. The stocking section became more compact, with greater emphasis on self-selection, and scarves were positioned so that their bright colours drew the eye of the customer. Still on the ground floor, the shoe department, which had always suffered from overheating, had a cooling unit installed in the stockroom, with vents through to the department, and stockholding was increased by the introduction of mobile racking. An awkward little corner near the gift department was turned to great advantage by the clever hanging of mirrors; mirrors had previously been in the area now given over to silverware. 1971 also saw the modernisation of the school uniform department where new fittings replaced old brown shelving. These changes gave the shop an impression of being more light and airy. Further refurbishment took place on the first floor where furnishing fabrics and

144

linens had a face lift. Stock was displayed more effectively and lights were fixed behind draped nets to give an attractive appearance. The removal of the slats covering the unsightly skylights enabled more light to reach the whole area and the windows were tidied up, although these were still not things of beauty. The intention was to draw customers' attention to the stylish displays rather than upwards to the windows!

The following year work started on rebuilding at the rear of the premises. Land in that area had been the subject of compulsory purchase by the city council as part of the redevelopment of Lion Yard. Robert Sayle lost 11,500 square feet of stockrooms and workrooms. The St Tibbs building, which included a rest room and the security box disappeared, as did the soft furnishing workroom. Space was needed to rehouse all these facilities. Conditions were very cramped and temporary accommodation had to be found while a new steel-framed building was erected to house the workrooms on the first floor and provide a rest room and

a small stockroom area. Between its old premises being demolished and its new ones built, the furnishing workroom found a home in the old YMCA building, off St Tibbs Row, which was itself knocked down the day after the workroom vacated it. On the ground floor, stockrooms were created for gifts, haberdashery and menswear; in the meantime, they too spent months camping out in a boy scout hut in the yard! During the building work Partners had to run the gauntlet of bulldozers, cement mixers and dust which turned to sticky clay in wet weather, as well as cross a wooden bridge to reach their entrance, but they coped as they always had done. As work progressed into the autumn of 1972 the yard appeared to be filled with huts, building materials, rubble, ladders and wheelbarrows and the link vans from the Magnet service building had to manoeuvre in and out with great care to reach the receiving dock. While demolition work was in progress customers could not use the rear entrance of the shop and Partners were

A view over the rooftops before 1970. The top floor of the buildings in the middle of the background housed the old hostel. St Andrew's Street is on their far side. The area in the middle of the picture with the short flight of steps was filled in during the rebuilding work and became the new sunroof. The door gave access to the Registry corridor

145

not allowed into areas that had been handed over to the builders unless it was absolutely necessary to reach stock, then very precise instructions were given as to the route to be taken. Once the demolition was finished and the new workroom built, work then started to create a link across the back of the shop in order to help customer flow. On the first floor a bridge was built over the three small roofs adjoining the cloakroom and toilet area which comprised the end of the 'T' of the old hostel building. This was designed to connect nursery furniture and schoolwear with soft furnishings and linens, by means of the link staircase. It did away with the horseshoe-shaped selling floor, enabled customers to reach different departments without retracing their steps and greatly improved circulation. On the ground floor a second rear entrance to the shop made it more accessible from Lion Yard car park. To complete the project the new stockrooms were connected to the shop, the area behind menswear tidied up and the existing domestic boiler replaced with a new boiler house in St Tibbs Row. The city council's work in Lion Yard included changes to St Tibbs Row, which in turn created a new service road behind Robert Sayle, thus providing better access to the yard.

Inside the shop reorganisation brought about an improvement to the layout of departments. The accounts desk moved upstairs, into space made available by contracting millinery; this enabled menswear to expand on the ground floor. Prior to this time all shoes were together in one department sited next to fashion accessories but, after the building work, children's shoes relocated upstairs to the children's wear department. An archway was made in the wall between the main shoe department and dress fabrics. With space at a premium every effort was made to take administrative functions off the shop floor and clerks were tucked away behind fixtures or "exotically hidden behind bead curtains", according to the Gazette.

Partners' amenities suffered from lack of space just as much as the selling floor. The main dining room was still in the same position as it had been for many years; it was too small for the 450 Partners and an extension was planned. Rest-room facilities were also insufficient as two small rest rooms had been lost as

a result of the compulsory purchase. One of these seems to have been used exclusively by male Partners, as in October 1972 they asked the General Manager if another room could be found for them. They had used the sun lounge during the summer but were concerned about the lack of an alternative facility during the winter months. A larger rest room was included in the new building but work on it was held up by a builders' strike. As a stopgap measure Mr Miller suggested that a room might be found on the second or third floor of the hostel. In the event, even after the new rest room was completed, lack of space in the yard meant that the room was used for storage for some considerable time. However, a roof garden was created, with access from the Registry corridor, and the Gardening Society looked forward to using its talents to provide pots and tubs.

This rebuilding and refurbishment all took time. It was 1973 before the ground-floor departments were able to take up their new positions. Boys' wear and travel goods found a home in the extended area, along with the new customer entrance onto St Tibbs Row; haberdashery moved towards the rear of the shop to make more room for dress fabrics. At the front, toiletries, silverware and gifts were reformed. On the fashion floor work continued for some time longer while the dividing wall between underwear and the new area at the back of the shop was removed. The new link bridge was opened in time for Clearance in July 1973. Later that year the extension to the Partners' dining room was completed, together with new toilets and a staff entrance. Other projects involved creating stockrooms for soft furnishings and linens in the area previously occupied by builders' huts and an extension onto the roof area to accommodate counting house machinery and sales ledgers, releasing their existing room for clerical work. Building materials were increasingly difficult to obtain during 1973 and this caused some delays on completion dates. However, eventually work was carried out on the second-floor hostel offices where the contracts office, registry, the Chronicle office and duplicating room were situated. New offices were also created for the Service Manager and the Carpet Workroom Manager. A secondary staircase leading to the third floor was removed to improve access.

Burrowing in the basement provided the next addition to the selling space. In the summer of 1973 someone wondered what was on the other side of a wall in the lighting department. Surveys showed that it was mainly earth and investigative work began to remove it. A small area was cleared first, with such success that it was decided to continue. Eventually 3,000 square feet was cleared and transformed. All the excavated earth had to travel up a conveyor belt and through a hole in the building at ground level. From there it was pushed in a wheelbarrow to skips in the yard and taken away. The new area opened as selling space in June 1974. Lighting and electrical appliances expanded and gained new stockrooms. A small room next to the kitchen became a rest room for catering Partners. In the lighting and china department woodblock flooring was taken up and waterproofing carried out to the sub-floor. The work involved noise and dirt, things by no means unknown at Robert Sayle where it seemed that an endless progression of building work, alterations and improvements were taking place.

The basement plans had included a unit to provide additional fresh air. A cooling unit costing £3,500 had been put into the soft furnishings department in 1972 and a quote of £2,000 was obtained for a similar unit for separates and Miss Cambridge. Roller blinds for the long skylight in linens were also under consideration. During the hottest weather it was planned to use temporary fans to keep the air circulating, something that still happens 30 years later. Full air-conditioning has never been a truly feasible option for an old building like Robert Sayle.

In 1975 a small extension to the rear of the ground floor allowed the furniture department to move back towards the rear of the shop and so give extra space to the departments at the front. However, alongside any improvements maintenance work still had to be fitted in and it was not always plain sailing. The basement flooded that summer; the problem was traced back to broken supply pipes beneath the yard which had to be partially dug up to allow for repairs. Nevertheless, a major improvement to Partners' amenities appeared on the drawing board that year. A reduction in the number of Partners in the fashion workroom meant that they could move to smaller quarters in what had been the dissections office (later called stock accounting) at the far end of the management office corridor on the second floor. Work then began to convert the old fashion workroom into a social club room, an amenity Partners had not enjoyed since the time they had leased the old Masonic hall before it was demolished. The new facility opened at the end of 1976.

Ingenious efforts to increase space and convert nooks, crannies and cubby holes into useful selling areas were never far away. A varied selection of opportunities presented themselves. An old wooden display staircase, situated between gifts and furniture and leading down to the basement, was dispensed with and the area over the top made into an office for the Display Manager. Some years later this little office became a beauty room and is still used as such by the perfumery department. In 1976 the business was able to acquire the lease of a small nearby warehouse behind the Wine Market (now Threshers) with 600 square feet of storage space. This meant it was possible to move display fittings and the tradesmen's workshop, both of which had been situated behind children's wear on the first floor. Children's wear and nursery furniture benefited from this move, gaining the space at the bottom of the small flight of stairs, and there was a knock-on effect for separates and Miss Cambridge. A new name added to the fashion floor that year was Country Casuals; initially Robert Sayle was one of only five branches to have this range. For children's wear the move meant that the shop offered a wider assortment of children's merchandise all in one area than any other branch. It became a very successful department, giving particularly good service in prams and babywear. Also in 1976, a first-floor building adjacent to soft furnishings was brought into service to create a small extension to the selling area and additional stockroom for both furnishings and linens. It had previously been used as an overflow storage area by one of the colleges. Nets moved into the new selling space and the additional stockrooms meant that Partners saved time and leg work as they no longer had to travel between the department and the third floor to fetch stock. The room was 22 feet wide and 32 feet deep with an emergency fire exit at the rear. The ceiling was eight feet high. A 14-feet-wide opening was made between it and the shop. For several

months Ted Grover, the Service Manager, had been promising his Partners that a quieter time lay ahead but he had to admit at the end of the year that his forecasting had gone astray!

Further changes took place in the shop. Wigs disappeared and chrome floor-to-ceiling poles with hanging arms were introduced to display hats instead of the standard drawers. Evidently this change received a mixed reaction from Partners but was welcomed by customers. Alterations to fixturing were made in haberdashery and fashion accessories. Stockholding in children's wear was improved with the installation of mobile racking. A new venture in 1977 was the opening of an export desk on the ground floor. It was sited between furniture and gifts. The Partners manning the desk advised overseas customers on export procedures and directed them to the departments they needed. Mr Miller said the shop had been concerned for some time that they were not making the most of the potential export trade. The previous week a bureau de change had opened on the second floor. Its service was limited to the exchange of foreign currency into sterling but Cambridge was an historic university town and hosted many foreign visitors and students. Ladies' shoes moved upstairs to the first floor in 1978.

1978 also saw the introduction of RSS – Retail Stores System. For the first time Robert Sayle's accounting system – including cash and customer account takings, invoice and credit control – was linked to the main Partnership computer. Electrical trunking was installed around the shop, going in and out of many nooks and crannies, and a new room

was carried out in record time by contractors and the branch's own service team. No 25 added about 10 per cent to the shop's selling area. An enlarged toy department – previously the shop had sold just nursery toys – and new radio/television and sports departments moved into

**Nos 24 and 25
St Andrew's Street**

was created on the third floor to house the necessary equipment – a controller, VDUs, a ticket machine, a printer and some cash registers. There followed a period of several months during which all Partners were trained on the new technology and electronic registers replaced the old tills. Over the next two years more systems were introduced and in 1980 RSS was updated to PSS, Programmable Store System. This allowed for future adaptations and modifications to meet the specific needs of the business. Technological change was starting to move very rapidly.

The shop acquired its first 'satellite', 25 St Andrew's Street, in 1979. It was separated from the main shop by five other business premises. No 25, as Partners soon began to call it, was formerly a china shop but it had been empty for two years. It was in very poor condition; there were holes in the floor and it even had shrubs growing out of its walls! The long, thin building ran from St Andrew's Street back to St Tibbs Row. Some people remarked that it looked like a garden shed or a barn from the rear, with nothing much to commend it except space and proximity to the shop. Considerable work was needed to transform this dilapidated building but it

two parallel rectangular rooms decorated in cheerful shades of green, orange and yellow. Two rather old-fashioned windows flanked the entrance from St Andrew's Street; this led into the radio and television department which had a large audio room at the far end. Toys and sports shared the other room and had an exit into St Tibbs Row. Robert Sayle opened the door of No 25 on 10 April to begin trading. The television department offered a display of nearly 50 different models and behind those were radios and music centres. In toys, large outdoor equipment was on sale, together with old favourites. The premises at No 25 had a small rest room, ample stock room and, on the first floor, new quarters for the display department. The old display area in the basement of the main shop was used for electrical appliances and kitchen planning. Next to the rest room was a small patio garden which Partners tended; they planted flowers and there was a trellis up which greenery could trail. In its early days the unit at No 25 was self-contained, having its own float and two ex-Waitrose safes.

One facility lost in 1979 was Partners' hairdressing. This had operated in the shop since the closure of the customer hairdressing department ten years earlier.

150

The intention had been that it should be self-financing. However, its premises were cramped and only a limited number of Partners patronised it, at an increasing cost to the business. In the financial year 1978/79 the amenity showed a loss of £881 on a turnover of £3,458. Regular customers numbered 32 working Partners and 12 pensioners. There was much discussion by the Branch Council as to whether refurbishment would encourage greater use by Partners but a survey threw up little extra potential custom and the decision was taken to close it down and to utilise the space for the shop.

For a short while things were fairly quiet but this did not last long. Inventive ways of using the shop's odd corners and cubby holes were constantly being explored, even though it was not an easy task to achieve some of the ideas thrown up. Major structural alterations were not involved. The configuration of the building was far from ideal but, as the Service Manager said, to start moving exterior walls under the existing circumstances would have been a risky business. Nonetheless, what was loosely termed "a hole in the wall", seven feet high by eight feet wide, opened up between children's wear and furnishing fabrics to improve customer flow without the need to use the link stairs; this was a great help to customers with pushchairs. Adaptations to the existing children's wear hoist also allowed beds to be brought up to the first floor more easily. At the end of 1980 it became possible to create a new stockroom in the area behind children's wear: non-selling activities were then moved backwards and extra space given to the selling floor. Adjustments to the selling areas of

adjacent departments and a considerable amount of re-fixturing followed. This all helped to create a more streamlined look on the fashion floor.

A few changes took place to the assortment, including the addition of a new section for gardening supplies, introduced at No 25 in 1980. Garden furniture remained in the main shop for a few more years but from 1983 it was displayed in a more appropriate setting when the area to the rear of No 25 was paved. In 1982 the removal of a 20-feet-long wall in No 25 meant that a new layout for radio and television was achieved and computers joined the assortment. In the main shop a new section of home assembly furniture was introduced and cane furniture was extended. This coincided with the opening of John Lewis Peterborough. Service department Partners were never able to rest on their laurels for long, however, and they were kept busy ensuring that other departments around the shop benefited from refixturing and improvements to their layout.

The following year a pilot scheme for CMO – Central Marking Off – was introduced, initially for radio and television, hardware and haberdashery. It was later extended to include sports and toys. At the same time some stockholding transferred to the Magnet. Once more the branch was able to increase selling space by utilising former non-selling areas. There were other ways in which the shop took on a sharper definition. The green lino that covered the floor at the front of the shop disappeared, to be replaced by new carpet. Not only did this reduce noise but it also gave a more spacious impression. Towards the end of 1984, No 25 was

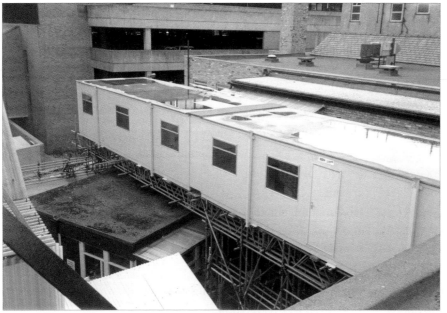

Temporary storage: Portakabins on the roof in the yard, 1988

able to extend into the adjacent premises at No 24 and expand its computer and electronic goods assortment. An archway was created to link the two areas.

In 1985 several major changes took place, both at the shop and at the Magnet. The soft furnishing workroom moved to the service building and improvements were made to the amenities there. Thirty Partners were involved in the move. At the shop a lift was installed just outside the door to the menswear department. It was not possible to extend the lift down to the basement but it served the first floor and the roof where a new social club room took shape. The room was made available during the daytime as a rest room, replacing in part the old St Tibbs rest room which was converted into stockrooms. The former social club room became a marking-off area for fashions. Additional stockroom space meant that once again extra selling space could be achieved. The sports department transferred from No 25 to the main shop and took up its new home in a further extension behind the haberdashery and boys' wear departments. A new customer entrance was built facing Lion Yard car park and this improved customer flow. Overall a better grouping of the ground-floor departments was achieved.

As if to demonstrate once again that it was never easy to turn an old building into a modern one, the excavations for the lift ran into problems. Whenever digging took place any pipes and drains that were found had to be checked carefully before further progress could be made. In this case further investigations showed that the geology of the ground meant a satisfactory drilling could not be guaranteed. Originally the lift was to have had a ram underneath, accommodated in a 40 ft vertical borehole, but this had to be replaced with side rams.

In July 1985 Chris Mitchell, the Managing Director, announced the closure of the fitted kitchen department to the Branch Council. The department was no longer generating sufficient sales to support the costs involved in planning, ordering and administration. The space occupied by the department was insufficiently large to produce a reasonable level of profit, and it could not show the full range of kitchens. For once the walls in the basement could not be pushed back any further and the hardware department, at that time the smallest in the Partnership, was able to use the area much more effectively. During the next year the fashion floor was reorganised so that the area 'read' more sensibly and the assortment was extended. The fitting rooms moved at the same time and the fixturing was upgraded. Christmas stationery, which had usually been accommodated on the ground floor next to furniture, moved upstairs near lingerie. In 1988 cameras were added to the assortment in No 25.

Robert Sayle acquired another satellite that year. No 19 was a former chemist's shop and was adjacent to the main shop, although it did not link easily with it. Art needlework and knitting wools relocated there, enabling menswear and boyswear to expand. Central clerking moved to one of the upper floors of No 19. For Partners the connection to the new shop was via the second floor, through the former central clerking department, which was now a stockroom, and across a metal bridge. Stockroom space was always at a premium and Portakabins, hired on a two-year lease, were erected in the yard. No 19 eventually offered an extra amenity for Partners in the shape of a non-smoking rest room on the second floor looking out onto St Andrew's Street. A further improvement to amenities was achieved by refurbishing the dining room and introducing a new layout for the servery.

One enormous improvement at around the same time was the installation of a new telephone exchange. The old system was unable to handle demand at peak times and it was replaced with a new one. This was not the most recent type but it did offer more sophisticated facilities so that outgoing calls no longer needed to go via the operator and it linked Robert Sayle directly to all the other Partnership branches, including central offices and buying offices. New registers arrived in 1990. These could read account cards, and the old imprinters, by then almost obsolete, disappeared. A few months later the shop started to accept Switch cards. Initially these had been accepted at seven of the Partnership's department stores before the system was extended to include all the other stores.

1990 was a year of celebration, marking the 150th anniversary of the founding of the shop as well as the 50th anniversary of Robert Sayle joining the Partnership. A party to celebrate both these events was held at the Duxford Officers' Mess.

Robert Sayle has found additional space in the most unlikely of places but one facility must be really unique. The shop acquired a small storage facility known as the blue bus. It was neither blue nor a bus, but a room in a corner of Lion Yard car park, opposite the rear entrance to the sports department. In the 1980s there was a real blue bus. It was a double decker parked on the piece of ground in St Tibbs Row where there is now a hotel. At that time discussions were still taking place about the future of the site. The old bus arrived and opened as a shelter for some of the homeless people in Cambridge, somewhere they could go during the day for a cup of tea, warmth and company. When planning approval for the hotel was finally granted, together with an extension to the car park, it was expected that the bus would disappear and with it the people who congregated there. What happened instead was that the city council provided a room in the car park for the people from the bus; it retained the same name – the blue bus. The

The 'blue bus' storage facility

Refurbishing the canopy at the front of the shop...

siting of it was a deliberate policy by the city council which acknowledged that homelessness was becoming an increasingly pressing problem in Cambridge. The blue bus was in the centre of town but not close to any residential buildings; it drew people away from congregating near the shops in Lion Yard but was within easy reach of all the social security services. In 1994 a permanent facility was found for the customers of the blue bus when the charity Wintercomfort acquired premises elsewhere in the city. Robert Sayle negotiated the lease on the room in the car park and took it over the following year. The services department and later the display department stored equipment there. It continued to be used for general storage up until 2004 and was still called the blue bus. In one of the frequent 'knock-on' effects, the acquisition of this additional storage facility meant that space elsewhere could be released and used for keeping stock.

The ever-increasing amount of merchandise passing through the shop has put continual pressure on space in the yard. Link vans from the Magnet have to be unloaded and cages moved out of the way as quickly as possible. The presence of the customer collection point in the yard has added to the pressure. Stock for toys and gardening is unloaded at the rear of No 25, to be transferred to the stockroom at the back of the building or to the garages that are used for larger items. Merchandise for the audio and television department is unloaded in St Andrew's Street. This can be a difficult operation, firstly because of the busy traffic and constant flow of people up and down the pavement, and secondly because the stockrooms are located on several floors, with access via small staircases.

Until 1993 the yard at the rear of the shop was open to the elements. That year the branch applied for planning permission to erect a canopy. The initial application was turned down but permission was later granted and a canopy put up. However, the passageway from the yard along by the dining room remained uncovered and was often awash with water in wet weather. Stock for the basement was stored in this area and it eventually proved possible to achieve some protection for it. This was not an easy task: there were a number of technical problems to overcome and a great deal of ducting and pipe work to accommodate. Partners using the passageway still continue to get wet! The canopy at the front of the shop was replaced in 1994, together with the signs and illuminated lettering along the St Andrew's Street frontage. The whole process took nearly two months. Once the old fascia had been removed, strengthened supports were added to the steel structure underneath to protect the

... and putting it
to good use at
Christmas time

canopy from high winds. The project involved five different firms of contractors including a structural engineer and laboratory analyst. The canopy has provided a suitable place for Christmas trees each year.

Barely a year has gone by without refurbishment or refixturing in one part of the shop or another. It has always been regarded as essential to keep the public face as up-to-the-minute as possible, notwithstanding the problems thrown up by the physical restrictions of the various buildings in which Robert Sayle trades. Furniture acquired a new look in 1994 and kitchenware had a make-over in 1996. The original idea and first layout plans for the kitchenware department were designed in-house, then more detailed plans drawn up after consultation with the Interior Design department and the Development Manager (DS). Only one of the new fixtures had to be brought in from outside; everything else was made in the branch's own workshops. In order to create the new look some interior walls were demolished and the department's office was reshaped. A light-coloured floor, new lighting and coloured panels added the finishing touches.

Furnishing fabrics was the next department to undergo refitting. New technology in the 1990s has meant that initial plans and ideas can be fine-tuned on the computer and a realistic idea of what a finished project will look like can be obtained. Sales in textiles have been moving towards ready-mades and made-to-measure furnishings, although the department still runs a wide range of metreage fabrics. As part of the refurbishment two fabric-cutting benches were removed to make way for a wider range of samples, as well as a display of workroom expertise. The walkway from the lift to the main cash desk, a major thoroughfare in the shop, was widened. In 1996 the bureau de change opened in the cash desk and offered a wide range of facilities: foreign currency exchange, travellers' cheques, cash advances on credit cards and Western Union money transfer service – a far cry from 20 years previously when the only service available was changing foreign currency into sterling. The bureau traded successfully for several years, until the acceptance of third-party credit cards and the introduction of the euro diminished its usefulness; it closed in 2002.

More holes appeared in walls in 1997, followed by extensive trunking and large quantities of wiring. The Selling Branch Computer Infrastructure was about to arrive. The system to upgrade computer processes was installed throughout the Partnership. At Robert Sayle five new distribution wiring cabinets were linked to the computer controller room. These were designed to serve all the branch's communication needs. The technology involved the use of fibre-optic cables from the controller room to the

155

**A crane outside
the front of
the shop in St
Andrew's Street...**

**...delivering new
equipment over
the roof**

branch. Further improvements in the following two to three years included a new point-of-sale system to provide a better service for customers at the tills.

Keeping the building warm in winter and cool in summer has always been a challenge, not least because conditions vary considerably around the shop. The first floor was always particularly difficult. Full air-conditioning has never been practical but individual units have been installed into certain areas or sections. In 1998 three units, each weighing a quarter of a ton, were lifted onto the roof with the aid of a huge crane; these greatly improved conditions in the linens and ladies' shoes departments. Building refurbishment work was also carried out in non-selling areas. Financial accounting's premises on the third floor were refurbished and altered in 1999. Several small rooms, relics of the hostel days, were knocked into one. This work necessitated reinforced steel joists being put in the roof. Purpose-built benching was made in the workshop. Stock accounting moved to an adjacent office, bequeathing their former room to branch systems.

cabinets and special copper cabling from the cabinets to the various outlets. Among other benefits register alterations became much easier. Further system changes followed over the next three years. PLU – Price Look Up – was introduced, initially into a handful of departments, the new Meridian telephone system went live in 1999 and PCs became commonplace across the

A regular part of any major planning application, such as that proposed for The Grand Arcade, is an archaeological dig, and such a dig took place at the back of the toy department at the end of 1999. The paved display area for garden furniture was dug up. The small paving blocks were removed and a mini-digger made a hole 1.2 metres deep. The search unearthed some brick

footings, probably part of the old back wall of the building, which had been shortened 30 years earlier when all the demolition work in St Tibbs Row had been carried out. Underneath this was some fine-quality garden soil, then some gravel into which was cut a ditch or a pit. After the dig everything was replaced, leaving no trace.

Behind the scenes, Robert Sayle's expertise in using all sorts of apparently unpromising nooks and crannies has resulted in the provision of offices that can only be described as 'compact' or 'cosy' – as many a department manager will relate. In 1999 the manager of the electrical department moved from one end of the main office into a cubby hole previously used to house a VDU screen. Branch audit found their new home in an office cleverly created in a corner of the schoolwear stockroom. On the other hand, a make-over for the audio and television department office resulted in a more spacious and re-designed reception area with seating for customers, a far cry from the original tiny office created when No 25 first opened.

In the summer of 2000 a major move and transformation took place when the majority of selling-support offices vacated the main shop and took up residence on the top floor of St Andrew's House across the road. The whole floor was converted and services, financial accounting, management offices, registry, the Chronicle, staff office and staff training all relocated there over a ten-week period. The new offices were unlike anything Robert Sayle had been able to achieve

before. They were spacious, light and airy; several sections were open plan. For some selling-support Partners the change could not have been more marked. Attic offices, with evidence of their previous history as part of the hostel, became a thing of the past. The new offices were linked to the main shop by an 'umbilical cord' – a catenary link. This was a steel wire, stretched taut across the road at a high level, onto which cables were attached to feed all the PCs, VDUs, training registers and telephones in the new offices.

The offices vacated in the shop were turned into stockrooms for linens and children's wear, haberdashery, fashion accessories and furnishing fabrics. Branch systems took over the third floor and some operations were centralised. The selling floor was able to grow yet again. On the first floor beds and furnishing fabrics expanded, as did stationery on the ground floor. The ability to make the best use possible of what is there continued. The racking needed for the new stockrooms came from John Lewis Oxford Street, some of the storage furniture came from central offices at Victoria and some from Tyrrell & Green when it moved and became John Lewis Southampton.

When the branch moves to its temporary premises in Burleigh Street,

John Brown at work in the Audio & TV department in 'No 25', 1999

Gifts in 2000

The toy department in 2000

it will relinquish St Andrew's House. Some of the departments currently there will relocate to the service building at Trumpington and others will go with the shop, although space in Burleigh Street is very limited: that's nothing new – the branch has been squeezing itself into small spaces for much of the past 30 years!

Furthermore, despite the plans for rebuilding finally becoming a reality, efforts to improve the present premises

have continued: it has always been important to give the shop an as up-to-the-minute feel as possible. In recent years, telesales, especially in the electrical department, have become increasingly important and the Partners involved moved from their cramped quarters in the basement to a dedicated office on the top floor of the shop.

In 2001 children's wear took over schoolwear from the menswear department, which necessitated a rearrangement of both areas. The fashion floor had a makeover so the individual sections could be grouped together in a more defining way. Also in 2001, No 19 became The Gallery, a showcase for pictures and sculptures, as well as frames, prints and mirrors. Art needlework returned to the haberdashery department in the main shop. In October 2002 the perfumery department expanded to take in a new house, Origins, which was located beside the stairs up to ladies' fashions. In turn, the quality soaps fixture moved to the other end of the department, to create a 'grotto' of gifts, and several other small changes have taken place behind the scenes to streamline the whole operation of selling and meeting customer expectations. Flooring, too, has kept up with the times, perfumery having a brighter new look with mock marble in 2000 and furniture with wood in 2002.

32: From bowling alley to service building – The Magnet

Today a service building is a vital part of a branch, receiving large quantities of merchandise from central warehouses and suppliers then channelling goods through to the shop or delivering them directly to customers. Before 1970 Robert Sayle did not have a service building. Stock was received and held at the back of the shop. Even then the yard was far too small for the amount of traffic flowing through it. Evidently the entrance was so narrow that on occasions suppliers had to bend their wing mirrors back in order to squeeze their vans through the gate. The delivery bay was also inadequate for the demands made on it and was open to all weathers. As an additional facility an old school building in Albion Road, near Castle Hill, was sometimes pressed into use for storing certain merchandise.

At the same time as this chronic shortage of space was dictating the need to find premises for a service building, the land to the rear of Robert Sayle was subject to the compulsory purchase order which was a result of the city council's decision to redevelop Lion Yard car park. The shop lost around 11,500 square feet of stockroom and workroom space and it was therefore essential to obtain good alternative accommodation. Several premises were considered, including a one-and-a-half-acre site at the Trinity Hall Farm industrial estate where there was planning permission for a 22,000 square feet building. However, no building yet existed on the site whereas there was suitable space immediately available at the old Magnet Bowling Alley in Mill Road, about two miles distant from Robert Sayle's shop in St Andrew's Street. The bowling alley closed in 1968 but

there are still several Partners who remember going there in the early 1960s when bowling was the current craze. Before that the site had been a wood yard and a CMO Partner recalls seeing trees laid out ready to go into the saw mill when she passed that way en route to school. The Magnet, as it soon became known by everyone, was leased by the Partnership in 1971. Initially it was seen as a short-term solution to the need for a service building but it has continued to provide warehouse facilities throughout the 30 years since it was first acquired.

Once the lease had been signed it was necessary to obtain planning consent to use the building as a 'retail outlet servicing store'. Work then began straight away to convert the bowling alley so that it met the needs of storing and receiving goods. The new premises offered around 19,000 square feet of space but, initially, only the actual bowling lanes were used; these took up about two-thirds of the building and consisted of fairly clear floor space. The floor was sealed, the fluorescent lighting was modified and racking was installed to a height of six feet. The only real structural alteration that was immediately essential was the construction of five loading bays at the back of the building, two for receiving and three for despatch. A wall was demolished to accommodate the loading dock, five steel shutters were erected and a ten-feet canopy constructed over the entrance. An office was also created for the loading bank officer. The remaining area, old offices, cloakrooms and bar, stayed as they were for the time being.

A link van operated between the Magnet and the shop. The main merchandise

The Magnet service building in June 1974

stored there in the beginning was furniture, bedding, electrical appliances, kitchen and nursery furniture and gifts. Carpets were stacked in large tubes at the end of each row of racking. The construction of the racking was a lesson in economy: some of it came from the old stock rooms and some from Stevenage; the rest was constructed on site with wood taken from the false floor of the Albion Road building. Two weeks after the alteration work began the Magnet was able to function as a service building and stock was moved to Mill Road from the shop. Partners who worked there from the first day recall that the building still looked like a bowling alley as the lanes and numbers remained visible. Other reorganisation and alteration projects were carried out as they became necessary. In 1972 the heating system was improved and space at the building was found for an upholstery workroom. At that time Robert Sayle's upholstery workroom was the only one remaining in the Partnership. It had started after the war with one man. John Lewis Oxford Street had also had a flourishing furniture upholstery trade but that had since closed. In 1974 there were four Partners in Robert Sayle's workroom. The upholsterers, helped by a cabinet maker and a French polisher, dealt with a steady flow of chairs, sofas and stools for repair or renovation. They stuck firmly to the rule that a piece of furniture had to be re-upholstered in the kind of materials used in the original. As a result they kept a permanent stock of different types of springs and old-fashioned forms of binding, hessian, webbing and horsehair. Evidently horsehair was not easy to work with. It was also difficult to obtain and had to be ordered from a firm in Belgium. The oldest piece of furniture sent to the workroom for re-upholstering was made during the reign of Charles II (1660-85). The upholstery workroom eventually closed when it was no longer easy to recruit Partners with the necessary skills.

The five loading bays at the Magnet very soon proved insufficient for the volume of traffic. In 1973 another bay was built at the front and was used for loading the van for city deliveries. The receiving area was very small and incoming goods had to be cleared quickly before the building became congested. When the daily Stevenage van arrived at 7.30am some of the load was put straight on the link van to go to the shop. The rest was dealt with during the morning before the second link van left at 11am. That year the service building reached a peak of 3,000 lots in one week, while deliveries reached 1,200 a week. The three delivery vans covered a radius of 30 miles from Cambridge on a regular basis but they also went farther afield to places such as Northampton and Peterborough when necessary. Robert Sayle had taken over deliveries to the Peterborough area when fire destroyed the branch there in 1956 and this service continued. Once every four to six weeks van loads went to destinations across East Anglia – King's Lynn, Hunstanton, Norwich and Ipswich. In an average month in 1974 the three furniture vans and one parcel van travelled a total of about 6,000 miles.

Later that same year the Magnet tried out a new parcel delivery service, on contract with the Post Office. Parcels were sent from the shop to the Magnet from where they were collected by the Post Office each morning. This worked out to be less expensive than running the branch's own parcel van and provided a quicker service for customers. People in outlying areas sometimes had to wait up to two weeks for a van delivery; by post they received their goods within two days. The trial proved successful: productivity improved, the scheme became a permanent arrangement and the business was able to reduce its van fleet by two vehicles.

Despite the acquisition of a service building, space continued to be at a premium. When building work was carried out at the shop, stock was moved to the Magnet for storage. The quantity of merchandise there was so great that it started spreading out into the gangways,

every bit of space possible was pressed into service, including the old bowling alley cloakrooms which had previously been left unused. Moving stock around the building was not easy either. There was no mechanical order picking equipment in use at that time. Heavy merchandise was stacked only to the level of the first shelf and was managed with trolleys, fork lifts and pallet trucks. Peter Miller, the General Manager (head of the branch at the time), said that this equipment mirrored what was available at Clearings which, although much larger, was a similar warehouse to Robert Sayle's. Other aids were brought into use as appropriate: these included platforms on wheels for the movement of furniture such as wardrobes, various types of sack barrows and a carpet dolly. Although carpets were stored at the Magnet, initially there was no designated carpet workroom. Any seaming required was carried out by the two carpet fitters on what was left of the bowling alley stage.

Twenty-eight Partners worked at the Magnet in 1974. There was a small rest room and a kitchen/dining room where refreshments were provided in the

A Partner at the Magnet service building in the 1980s

Inside the Magnet service building in the 1980s

mornings and the afternoons, and "a very good meal" at lunchtime for the standard price of 15p. At teatime a teapot stood in the middle of a wooden table and Partners helped themselves. The Magnet was one of the few branch service buildings that was not purpose built but it was proving adequate and workable: it was a question of making the best and most appropriate use of the space available.

There was always the possibility that Robert Sayle might acquire new premises for the shop, in which case it would also require a new service building. According to Mr Miller, "this would be designed to the most modern specification as to storage and handling methods", but in the meantime work continued at the Magnet to increase its storage capacity. Some additional racking costing £1,500 was added in 1975 and the Central Board sanctioned greater expenditure the next year. The work involved removing two-thirds of the false ceiling left over from bowling alley days and installing 13 lines of racking, each 14 feet high and 100 feet long. New carpet rollers were also installed capable of storing over 350 large carpets and enabling their removal by the tug of just one arm. The bays themselves were enlarged slightly and the floor area, as well as the floor of the warehouse aisles, was given a new smooth surface,

banishing for ever any remaining evidence of bowling lanes! For the first time it became possible to separate the incoming flow of goods from the outgoing flow and it was easier to ensure that no goods were put away without being carded. The following year a specially developed order picker was purchased to improve the goods handling facilities even further, making the merchandise in the higher levels of racking as accessible as that lower down. The order picker was a large cage, battery driven and operated by two men.

Statistics throw an interesting light on the Magnet's workload. In 1979 deliveries were made to 17,875 customers and the vans travelled 61,384 miles. This mileage rose to 70,665 in 1983. The comparable figure for 2000 was 90,396 miles.

In 1981 plans were mooted to move the office at the Magnet from one side of the building to the other; this would have enabled the Partners working in the office to keep an eye on goods. However, this alteration, together with a proposal to extend the canopy, was one of several projects under consideration by the shop at the time; they all had to compete for funding and the Magnet was not deemed a priority. Four years later a more major project to improve facilities at the Magnet was undertaken. The soft furnishing workroom was relocated to the warehouse from the shop and 30 Partners moved with it. The purpose behind this was to give as much space as possible at the shop for selling rather than for ancillary work. In the warehouse a mezzanine floor was put in along the left-hand side of the main part of the service building

where there was considerable height. The Partnership had not previously installed a mezzanine floor of this type. On the ground floor the office space was rearranged and a soft furnishing workroom was created which combined with the upholstery workroom in the same area. Two lifts were installed to take stock up to the next floor. Also on the first floor, cloakrooms, a dining room, kitchen and a rest room were created. Some Partners involved in the move from the shop did not welcome the change, having doubts about transport, car parking and shopping time. In the same year Robert Sayle obtained a long-term lease on the premises which secured occupancy into the foreseeable future. The Partnership had made enquiries into the purchase of the site but it had not proved to be financially or commercially sensible.

Two years later proposals were drawn up to extend the Magnet. Planning permission was initially refused: the people occupying the adjacent premises had lodged objections because they were concerned about the appearance of the building and the effect it might have on light reaching their properties. Robert Sayle appealed against this decision. The General Manager held an evening session to address the concerns of the nearby residents, some amendments were made to the plans and the appeal was successful. Some Partners suggested that it might have been better to have had a purpose-built warehouse on one of the new industrial sites around the city edge

but the Magnet suited the business well and the recent improvement constituted a major investment that Robert Sayle would not have wanted to lose. In 1988 the Central Board approved expenditure on a new separate carpet store to one side of the Magnet. This had a knock-on effect on the storage and handling of other stock. By moving the carpet office and cutting area more space was found for marking-off larger items and for assembling cages. The next project was to move some sheds in the yard and replace the oldest of them. The Magnet duly acquired the Addlestone shed, so called because it came from Addlestone when Taylor & Penton moved their premises from there to Brooklands. This shed was sited in the corner of the yard, adding extensively to stock-holding space. The yard itself was resurfaced and a pathway laid to allow for easier movement of cages from CMO. Room was also found for another delivery van as trade had reached the point where it made economic sense for Robert Sayle to have another van of its own rather than hiring one when necessary.

Warehouses converted from bowling alleys can sometimes throw up their own particular problems. In 1990 investigations were made to see if the

The Addlestone shed at the Magnet service building, acquired in 1988

**The front of the
Magnet service
building on Mill
Road – after
losing its canopy**

canopy could be extended, a plan first
put forward nine years earlier.

A survey showed that the structure of
the building was insufficiently strong to
support an extension without a significant
amount of rebuilding to the whole of the
back. An alternative type of canopy was
eventually constructed, with a heavy-duty
flexible plastic curtain.

Further improvements to the Magnet
took place in 1996 when extra racking
was put into the Addlestone shed to
make better use of the vertical space.
The racking in the receiving area was
improved at the same time, to ease some
congestion. As trade at the shop grew so
did the amount of merchandise passing
through the Magnet. Lorries and vans
arrived so frequently that there was not
always sufficient space in the yard to
accommodate them. From 1995 a limit
was imposed over the movement of
vehicles in the yard and they had to wait
outside if the yard was full. A sign alerted
drivers to the situation, although
customers arriving to collect goods from
the warehouse could still do so.

The service building was not without
mishap. One Monday evening in
December 1997 an unidentified lorry

(not a Partnership one) drove into the
front of the building and knocked down
the canopy. Windows in the soft
furnishing workroom and the smoking
rest room were also smashed. A local
builder was called in to clear up the mess
and board up the front of the building.
By Wednesday the Magnet was back to
business as usual. The mezzanine floor –
that Partnership 'first' – operated
successfully for years but in 2000 its
layout was improved. Some of the
walkways were very narrow and space
was wasted elsewhere. Two Partners
planned the reorganisation of the area: by
adding extra shelving above existing
fixtures they were able to lose a complete
run of racking. This meant that cages
could be manoeuvred more easily, saving
time and effort. They also reorganised the
way merchandise was stored, making
items more accessible and easier to find.
The 'rifle racks' where blinds were stored
were redesigned using string rather than
solid bars to divide them: a simple but
effective change that allowed more blinds
to be stored in the same amount of space.

In its final years as a service building
only vestigial traces remained of the
Magnet's former life as an entertainment

venue, but the old bowling alley served the branch well. It held stock for call-off (a facility that provided early morning stock replenishment), stored goods in its high bay and carpet warehouse, handled customer collections and co-ordinated customer deliveries. On occasions the building also provided a venue for branch parties.

During its lifetime the furnishing workroom offered a professional measuring and estimating service for bespoke curtains, drapery, loose covers, upholstery and blinds and carried out the fitting of these items, although, from February 2004, the making-up and machining of curtains will be completed by contractors. The new service building at Trumpington, on what was once a muddy field, will now offer all the support necessary for a modern shop. The warehouse is adjacent to the park-and-ride site and has an easily accessible customer collection facility. After 30 years of service to the business the Magnet has closed its shutters for the last time. Wood yard, bowling alley, service building. Who knows what next?

33: Sundays, Mondays – hours and hours

In 1970 shops were required to trade within the hours set down in the 1950 Shops Act. This act also regulated Sunday trading by specifying in detail the items that could be sold legitimately on Sundays; it was illegal to sell anything else. Department stores and food supermarkets did not open.

The Branch Council discussed Sunday trading as early as 1971, following a report in the local press that some shops in Cambridge thought there was tourist trade to be had. Councillors were firmly against any suggestion that the Partnership should follow suit if this were ever to happen. Peter Miller, the General Manager, said that it was much more important to concentrate on obtaining a high calibre of staff, paying the highest possible rates and increasing sales density than to open for longer hours.

No move was made on trading hours for some considerable time but by the early 1980s some retailers were starting to press for the abolition of the Shops Act in order to allow unrestricted Sunday trading. The law was widely acknowledged to be unsatisfactory, full of anomalies and confusion. However, feelings were very sharply divided on the issue and an attempt by the government to change the law was abandoned in 1986 in the face of widespread opposition in the country.

Discussions on how to resolve the matter continued. A compromise was sought that would allow traders more freedom while preserving the traditional character of Sundays. One option was to have some relaxation of the law that fell short of complete deregulation. In 1988 the government was presented with a set of proposals for consideration, based on the key idea that, instead of having a list of exempt goods that could be sold, the law should allow only certain classes of shops to open: these would include restaurants, garden centres, petrol stations. The Partnership maintained a firm stance against Sunday trading and gave its support to the 'Keep Sunday Special' campaign, which opposed full or partial deregulation of Sunday trading. The campaign was backed by many other household names. Their opposition was not 'Sunday observance' but the protection of family and community relationships, a commercial desire to keep costs down and concern for the social environment. However, in December 1990 some larger shops began blatantly to flout the law and open for trade in the run-up to Christmas. The Partnership's Chairman, Peter Lewis, writing in the Gazette, said that the Partnership had several reasons for not jumping to follow suit, including the fact that it was plainly illegal. However, he warned that if deregulation were to come about in a lawful, proper manner then the Partnership might have no option other than to open on Sundays.

The following year Tesco and various other stores openly announced their intention to trade illegally at Christmas. Mr Lewis engaged in correspondence with the Home Secretary, stating that the current position whereby the law was being openly flouted was a disgrace. A great deal of heated debate on the subject took place throughout the country. The Partnership held on to its view that Sunday trading laws should be settled by Parliament in the interests of the whole community. The government finally resolved the issue in 1994, allowing all shops to trade on Sundays, although those over a certain size were restricted to a six-hour formula. Meanwhile, in January 1994 the Central Council was asked to agree to the principle of Sunday trading. As the Chairman, Stuart Hampson, said, the Partnership was not an advocate of Sunday trading but the competitive forces in retailing made it impossible for an individual retailer to stand completely apart when other shops in the area selling similar goods and offering similar services decided to open. It would be "commercially unsound for the Partnership to turn its back".

Initially Sunday trading was limited to the pre-Christmas period, but the years since then have seen a complete change in shopping habits. Although traditional city centres do not open universally on Sundays throughout the year, the large undercover centres do, and Sundays often come second only to Saturdays in terms of trade. Some of the newest John Lewis department stores, such as Cribbs Causeway, have traded on Sundays since opening. However, the Partnership first experimented with Sunday trading in 1995, opening 16 of its branches for between two and four Sundays in December. Robert Sayle was not one of the 16, although many other shops in Cambridge opened; for some of them it was their second year of doing so. Robert Sayle first traded on Sundays in December 1996, opening for four hours on three Sundays. Since then Sunday trading in December has become the accepted norm; in December 2000 the branch opened for five hours on four Sundays, and the hours were then increased to six in the following years, the maximum permitted.

Other changes at Robert Sayle took

place in the years after 1969. In 1970, outside of London, a five-or-five-and-a-half-day trading week was usual in most towns and cities. In London some of the large multiples had moved towards six day trading but John Lewis Oxford Street and Peter Jones maintained a half-day closing on Saturdays until 1985. As with the rest of the Partnership's established provincial department stores, Robert Sayle opened on Mondays only in the pre-Christmas period. The Tuesday to Saturday formula throughout the rest of the year enabled the shop to match trading hours to Partners' working hours, creating a full-time, experienced staff, but, as the new century began, a different picture emerged. Customers' shopping habits altered substantially, and not just with regard to Sundays. Shops started to trade for longer and longer hours and the seven-day trading week arrived for many retailers. The Partnership again had to move to meet customers' expectations. In March 2001 John Lewis Brent Cross became the first of the Partnership's department stores to agree to open every day. The five-day trading week in other branches soon became a thing of the past. During 2000 every branch started a review of its trading hours to see how they fitted in with the locality in which it operated. Branch councils discussed all the issues raised and by March 2003 eight of the Partnership's department stores had moved to seven-day trading. At Robert Sayle a focus group was established to examine all the options. It concluded that the shop should consider year-round Monday opening and the Branch Council discussed a proposal to do just that in 2001. Six-day trading arrived and was then followed within

a short period by discussions to consider seven-day trading. In 2003 the decision was taken to open the shop every day when it relocates to Burleigh Street in the autumn of 2004. These changes have brought about significant changes for the business in terms of staffing.

The contrast between 1970 and 2004 is striking. In 1970 Robert Sayle traded for a five-day week. That Christmas it experimented with extending its trading hours to 6pm for two weeks before Christmas. The following year the shop continued the experiment and also opened on one Monday in December, for the first time. There was little change to these arrangements for many years. In 1973 the branch closed for Christmas on Saturday 22 December and reopened on the following Friday, with Clearance starting the next day. Until 1977 Christmas arrangements covering all the branches were presented to the Central Council by the Director of Trading (DS). They appeared as proposals to each individual branch council for the first time in 1977. In 1984 the branch was still opening on only two Mondays, and Wednesday late nights were extended to 8pm for three weeks. The fall of the calendar brought about some surprising arrangements. Christmas Eve fell on a Monday again that year, as it had done in 1973, but the branch stayed closed as it was not felt that there would be many customers about! After a three-day Christmas break in 1985 the shop opened on Saturday 28 December, then closed until the following Tuesday when Clearance started. After that the situation started to change. The extent of additional trading hours in December was widened; more Mondays were included and the additional half-hours to 6pm started earlier. In the late 1990s the extra hours tended towards the same pattern: to include all the Mondays in December and for the shop to remain open until 6pm for the four weeks before Christmas. In 2002 the hours were further extended and the shop opened until 7pm on certain weekdays in the final run-up to the holiday. Sundays have been part of the picture since 1996 and, from 1999 onwards, the shop has closed for only two days at Christmas, although, where possible, Partners have had a three-day break, either at Christmas or New Year. In 2002 the start of Clearance was brought forward: preparations for it were made once the shop had closed on Christmas Eve and Clearance itself started on the day after Boxing Day: the 'fallow day' had disappeared.

One further issue about trading hours concerns late-night shopping, a practice pioneered by the Partnership in the 1960s. Robert Sayle has operated this on Wednesdays until 7.30pm. Around 1980 the shop was the only one in Cambridge to have a late night. Other shops gradually began to experiment, particularly in the run-up to Christmas, and some actually extended their late nights in December to 9pm. This was something Robert Sayle did not countenance at that time. In 1985 and again in 1988 the Branch Council debated proposals to extend the late night to 8pm throughout the year but on both occasions the proposal was defeated, even though some other Partnership branches traded until that time and several have more than one late night. However, in 2004 an extension to late-night trading to 9pm on Wednesdays became part of the Christmas trading hours package.

Significant changes in the future are likely. Shopping is now seen as a leisure pursuit and customers demand an ever wider choice of facilities. One of the options that has gathered pace since the end of the twentieth century is e-commerce. As Luke Mayhew, now Managing Director, John Lewis, said in 1999, "e-commerce is a growing part of the way people shop". Within the first few years of the new century John Lewis Direct has established itself and its share of the online market is increasing.

34: Up and up, rarely down

Robert Sayle, though a small shop in 1970, was a successful one with a high sales density. The story of the next 30 years was one of continuing success, notwithstanding the ups and downs of the national economy which were to be a feature of those years. The business marked a succession of turnover milestones at the beginning of the 1970s. These were usually celebrated with a party. In 1970 the £2 million party was held on the fashion floor; three years later the £3 million party was held at the Guildhall. Decimalisation was introduced in 1971 and in that year the Partnership announced profits of £8 million. Turnover had risen by £13 million to £116 million. The next year it climbed to £140 million and trading profit exceeded £10 million for the first time. Robert Sayle made an important contribution to those results. However, despite the strong rise in sales during the early 1970s, expenses also rose steeply and new costs, such as the acquisition of the Magnet, had to be absorbed. Nevertheless, when reviewing the branch's performance for 1972/73, the General Manager remarked that Robert Sayle had achieved nearly 4 per cent better sales than the Partnership average, despite the fact that the shop had neither radio and television nor DIY and offered only half the full electrical assortment, all of which produced a good turnover across the rest of the Partnership. Robert Sayle's strength at that time lay in linens and fabrics, as it had done for many years. In 1973, the year VAT was introduced, Robert Sayle topped the average performance of the 16 department stores for the third year running, sales having risen strongly in advance of the imposition of the tax.

There was considerable industrial unrest in the country by the end of 1973. The miners were on strike and the country as a whole suffered widespread disruption of power supplies. This necessitated the branch trading under very difficult circumstances. The government introduced a rota of power cuts during what became known as the 'winter of discontent'. Power shortages affected everyone. At the Magnet, where they relied entirely on artificial light, it was reported that on Mondays and Thursdays, their allotted days for power cuts, Partners worked through their lunch hour in order to get goods moving before

the power went off. The power crisis ended in March 1974 but the economy still faced a challenging time as inflation continued to gather pace. As Mr Miller pointed out at the branch's AGM, of the 22 per cent increase in sales probably over half was due to an increase in prices. Nevertheless, this 22 per cent represented the largest percentage increase of any of the department stores, with the exception of Jessops which had had the benefit of a new shop. The budget that year was a tough one. The government imposed new and substantial cost increases and sought to control inflation by restricting the earnings of the retail trade. These measures were viewed with disquiet in the Partnership. The Chairman, Peter Lewis, estimated that any restraint on profit could cost the Partnership £4 million during a full trading year. He went on record to say that any government-imposed reduction on the real profits of retailers would prevent businesses from earning enough money to support improvement and future development. In the Partnership economies would have to be made in the running of the branches. As he put it, "the same cannot be had for less".

Despite this difficult background Robert Sayle continued to perform consistently well. In 1975 its average percentage sales increase was the fourth highest in the Partnership and its branch trading profit the fifth highest. The following year another turnover milestone was reached. The celebratory party was combined with one to celebrate the 25th anniversary of the branch's social club. However, the general outlook was still not promising. The government had yet to get inflation under control. There were gloomy warnings about a financial crisis and economic disaster, and unemployment was on an upward curve. In retailing, costs continued to rise rapidly, whereas the real purchasing power of many of its customers did not. Profits were being squeezed but for Robert Sayle the 1975/76 trading year was the best for a decade. The branch was benefiting from additional space and, for the first time, sales overtook Jones Brothers whose turnover in 1940 had been two and a half times higher.

The economic turmoil quietened down over the following two to three years. A new head of branch arrived at Robert Sayle towards the end of 1977. Mr Miller left to become the Partnership's Director of Management Services and Peter O'Ryan succeeded him in Cambridge. Mr O'Ryan had previously been General Manager at Bainbridge. As far as trade was concerned the branch continued to flourish. Its progress was recognised in 1979 when the title of head of branch at Robert Sayle was changed from General Manager to Managing Director. 1979 also saw an increase in VAT from 8 per cent to 15 per cent; this triggered a customer spending spree in advance of the imposition of the higher rate. The week before it was introduced sales in the branch rose by 116 per cent, resulting in a level of turnover not previously encountered, although it was exceeded the following Christmas.

In 1980 the mood at the AGM was one of quiet satisfaction and caution. It reflected a successful year. The economy had picked up and the pound was strong, although the tourist boom of recent years had faded. For the 10th year running Robert Sayle had beaten the Partnership

average. The 10 per cent additional space created by the opening of No 25 St Andrew's Street had contributed significantly to the strong upward movement of the sales graph and the branch had achieved another turnover milestone. The Guildhall was again the venue for the celebration.

Unfortunately things never stay the same for long! Another difficult time for retailing was around the corner. The economic climate was again showing signs of strain and prices were not rising at the same rate as inflation. Giving a brief resumé of the previous decade at the AGM in 1981, Mr O'Ryan pointed out that between 1971 and 1981 pay in the United Kingdom had increased by 329 per cent but productivity by only 1 per cent. However, Robert Sayle continued to compare well with the rest of the Partnership and had one of the highest profitability records. At the end of December 1981 Chris Mitchell became Managing Director and Mr O'Ryan moved to Peterborough to become Managing Director of the new Partnership branch that was about to open there. Like Mr O'Ryan before him, Mr Mitchell had previously been General Manager at Bainbridge. The shop remained in good health. At the AGM in 1983 Mr Mitchell said that the branch's percentage increase had been beaten only by Brent Cross, Milton Keynes and Bristol. That year the Partnership saw its trading profit pass the £50 million mark. There had been a period of expansion in the department store division but for Robert Sayle that meant it became more of a challenge for the branch to match the average increase. The competition in Cambridge also increased that year, with the opening of the Grafton Centre but, as Mr Mitchell said, "the bringing of other well-known retailers into the city will have the effect of creating more interest for customers". The conclusion a year later was that this additional competition was more in line with what Robert Sayle had projected than with what some people feared and by 1985 it had been satisfactorily beaten off. The market generally was more fiercely competitive than it had been ten years previously but Robert Sayle's results still compared favourably with other established branches.

The late 1980s saw a retail boom and Cambridge was particularly well placed to take advantage of this. Another milestone was reached in 1989 and, as an experiment, the party was combined with the AGM. However, once again a turndown was on the horizon and recession loomed. At the 1990 AGM Partners were informed of a fall in volume sales, an event not seen for many years. The economic climate was deteriorating again and the competition was getting harder and fiercer. Robert Sayle weathered the storm more easily than some other Partnership branches. Cambridge had become known as 'silicon fen' and new high-tech businesses were attracted to the region. After 11 years as head of branch, Mr Mitchell left Robert Sayle in 1992 to become Managing Director at John Lewis Brent Cross. He was succeeded by James Furse, who joined the branch from John Lewis Peterborough where he had been General Manager. As the country came out of recession, sales picked up further momentum and continued to grow at a satisfactory pace, although it was possible that the change in Sunday trading laws

had some effect in the mid-1990s.

Another change of Managing Director took place in 1995. Mr Furse moved to Jessops as Managing Director and his place was taken by Simon Fowler. Mr Fowler was already at Robert Sayle, having been appointed General Manager in 1994. The upward trend in sales continued and 1997 saw the largest percentage increase for seven years. Despite its relatively small selling area the branch held on to a very respectable house position. AGMs were by now enjoying the benefits of modern technology in the form of informative graphics and visual aids, making Partners very aware of the progress of their business. The 20th century ended with Robert Sayle holding on to its position as one of the most successful of the Partnership's established branches and achieving another turnover milestone. On this occasion the celebration was held at the Magnet. The party served a dual purpose. As well as marking the trading success it was also an opportunity to wish Mr Fowler farewell and good luck as he left Robert Sayle to become Managing Director at Jessops (now John Lewis Nottingham). His place in the branch was taken by Jenny Tomley, previously General Manager at Knight & Lee.

The start of the 21st century witnessed a downturn in the economy and a fall in the stock market. The increases in turnover and profit previously enjoyed by Robert Sayle have not been sustained over the past two years, although the economy in general is now beginning to look more promising. However, the profile of the branch remains high, and the need to attract and retain customers has seen the introduction of customer events: these are usually held in the branch but, in 2002, a fashion show was held at the Imperial War Museum, Duxford. The Cambridge YMCA, whose links with the branch stretch back to 1852 and to Mr Robert Sayle himself, joined in this latter event, to mark their 150th anniversary. Half the price of each ticket was donated to the charity.

35: Sharing power

Branch councils had their beginning in the council that the Founder, John Spedan Lewis, started at Peter Jones in 1919. He was president from that year until 1928 although meetings were generally chaired by the director in charge of staff affairs. The functions of the clerk were undertaken as a part-time activity by various management nominees. After John Lewis Oxford Street 'joined' Peter Jones Mr Lewis intended that it should have its own council but this actually met on only one occasion before it was combined with that of Peter Jones to form a single staff council, the forerunner of the Central Council. When Tyrrell & Green, Jessops, Lance and Lance (not rebuilt after the war) and Knight & Lee were acquired during the 1930s there was no provision for them to have their own councils, but they did have their own committees for communication. With the acquisition of Selfridge Provincial Stores in 1940, of which Robert Sayle was one, branch councils and a new central council were established almost immediately. Robert Sayle held the first meeting of its 'House Council' in December 1940. Spedan Lewis had seen the function of branch councils as reflecting public opinion in the branches on matters brought before them. In 'Fairer Shares' he wrote: "The branches have councils of

their own for their local affairs. The relation of the two [Central Council to Branch Council] is roughly comparable to that of the country's Parliament and local authorities. These bodies play ... a very great part in the formation and expression of opinion. They enquire, discuss and recommend but they also have executive powers and these may perhaps grow far."

The early councils had their own funds out of which they could finance social activities, make grants to local charities and help Partners through their elected committees for claims. Branch councils met regularly and discussed issues as wide ranging as they do today. However, by 1970 there was a feeling across the Partnership, and particularly at Central Council, that the branch councils were not as effective in their contribution to Partnership affairs as they ought to be. This led the Central Council to appoint a special committee to undertake a complete reappraisal of the functions of branch councils. The committee's terms of reference were to consider what role the councils ought to play in the future development of the Partnership, the methods by which that role could be made effective, the scope of their business, their relationship with the Central Council and with central and branch management, the position and responsibilities of the president and the clerk, and the provision of services, including training, to help the councils in their work. The subsequent 'Blue Report', issued in 1972, examined current opinion on branch councils and reasons for dissatisfaction, then put forward a blueprint for the future, a framework within which branch councils were to operate for the next three decades. The report concluded that there was little wrong with the general concept of the councils, but where they failed was in not making full use of the opportunities available to them. They were "prone to sit back and complain that they had no part in management". However, they were never intended to run the day-to-day business of the Partnership; their purpose was to bring public opinion effectively to bear on management and in that way establish their value to the Partnership and its particular way of life. Among the report's detailed recommendations was a requirement for heads of branch to report annually to the councils on the profit and loss account and to review pay and staffing each year. The report also encouraged greater use of oral question sessions at council meetings and advised that constituency meetings should be held before each branch council meeting. This was not something that had been routine. At Robert Sayle, constituency meetings were initially held on the morning of the council meeting but in 1979 they were moved to the previous Thursday so that councillors had more time in which to pursue issues raised by constituents. In all, the role of councillors was given greater significance after 1972. As the Partnership's Chairman, Sir

Bernard Miller, said, the branch council should be the channel by which each Partner in a branch could ensure that his voice was heard, and heard effectively.

In its very early days Robert Sayle's branch council met on the premises but by 1970 it was using the rather austere surroundings of a committee room at the Guildhall, as there was no room large enough in the branch to accommodate a meeting of the size to which it had grown. The layout of the tables and chairs was formal and oval in shape. After the building work at the shop was completed in the early 1970s the council was able to use the new rest room in the branch, where the surroundings were more relaxed. From 1969 meetings were held on Thursdays. Originally they were held wholly in non-working hours, starting at 5.45pm, but this changed to 5pm, then 4.30pm and by 1980 meetings were starting at 3.30pm. In more recent years this became 3.15pm when there was a particularly long agenda. A more radical change was introduced in 2000 when the council agreed, as an experiment, to hold meetings in the morning. The General Purposes Committee initiated this move in an attempt to foster greater interest in council meetings and to enable councillors to report back to their constituents immediately after a meeting, rather than waiting until the following day. Even so, this was not such an original idea as it might seem; the council had discussed holding morning meetings as early as 1973 but had rejected the proposal. The trial in 2000 proved successful and meetings continue to be held in the mornings, except when the council meets at the service building. The practice of holding one meeting a year at the Magnet was established in 1989. Other recent innovations include the setting up of a video link from the council meeting to the adjacent non-smoking rest room, so that Partners who might not wish to visit the strangers' gallery can nonetheless see what is happening as it happens, and the introduction of the Branch Council Forum meetings, designed to enable councillors to go into topics in more depth than is possible at regular branch council meetings.

Training for branch councillors was not universal in the Partnership before the Blue Report but it subsequently become the norm. In 1971 Robert Sayle organised training for councillors spread over three days; the venue was the Guildhall. Since then training for new councillors has been held each autumn after the elections, and sessions cover the history of the councils and the Partnership, as well as more practical help in how to run constituency meetings and how to present an argument at a branch council meeting. A mock branch council meeting usually concludes the training.

Until the early 1970s the officers of the council were Partners with full-time positions elsewhere in the business. They were nominated or elected and were paid a specific fee for their council work. However, after the publication of the Blue Report there was a move throughout the Partnership towards the appointment of 'professional' part-time officers to the posts of Clerk to the Branch Council, Retirement Secretary, Secretary to the Committee for Claims and Social Secretary (this title was changed to Social Events Organiser in 2000). These posts are combined in a number of ways in

different branches, depending on local circumstances. At Robert Sayle the position of Retirement Secretary became a permanent part-time post in 1977, followed shortly afterwards by Clerk to the Branch Council. A Social Secretary was appointed in 1980 but Secretary to the Committee for Claims remained an elected office until 1989 when it was combined with the post of Clerk.

Originally charitable giving was under the umbrella of the whole council. There was a relatively modest amount of money included in the estimates for this and the branch also undertook some local fund-raising in aid of such charities as Guide Dogs for the Blind and MAGPAS (Mid-Anglia General Practitioners Accident Service). Later the Committee for Claims took over the responsibility of responding to appeals. In 1996 the Central Council agreed to give a greater role to the individual branches in dealing with requests for donations from charities active in their own localities. Charitable giving assumed a higher profile, all branches elected a separate committee and the post of Secretary to the Charities Committee was more clearly defined, being added to the responsibilities of the Clerk to the Branch Council. The amount available for local giving was increased substantially and the committee now adopts a local charity each year to be the recipient of a significant part of its giving. In 2003 other initiatives were put forward. In one such initiative a group of Partners gave their time and efforts to creating a garden for a local school. The branch committees have also taken on the further role of sifting applications from Partners who wish to be considered for an award from the Golden Jubilee Trust. This centrally-run scheme, launched in 2000 – the year of the Partnership's Golden Jubilee – allows Partners to work with charities while continuing to receive their full pay. Robert Sayle's first candidate, Gordon Bagnall, was accepted in 2002; he provided valuable help to the Arthur Rank Hospice.

Robert Sayle had a Young Partners' Council in 1970. It was established annually by a resolution of the Branch Council. All Partners under the age of 21 belonged to the council and they elected their own president, clerk and treasurer. They met regularly, both to discuss matters pertaining to the business and to arrange their own social events such as dances or outings. Young Partners were not members of their own departmental constituencies but formed their own branch council constituency with three representatives. Their council lasted until 1979 but by then the feeling had grown that they should be integrated with their own departments and, after considerable debate, the branch council decided against having a separate young Partners' council for the following year. While they had their own council young Partners organised charitable fund-raising events and community activities; at one time they had 'wood chopping' sessions on Mondays for the benefit of pensioners. For some years from the mid 1960s young Partners published their own monthly 'Mini-Chron' but support and interest in this waned and it was produced less and less frequently. It

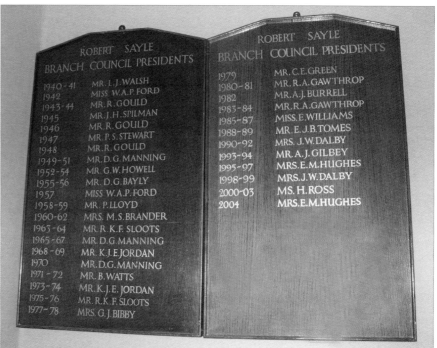

ceased altogether after 1972, although there was a brief but unsuccessful attempt to revive it in 1976.

The Branch Council holds an annual dinner. It has not been possible to hold it in the branch because of the lack of suitable facilities and a variety of outside venues has been used over the years, including King's College, the University Graduate Centre, the University Arms, the Arundel House Hotel and St John's College. However, in an innovative move in 2004 the dinner was held at the new service building at Trumpington.

Branch council spending has grown with the level of council activities since 1970. Its total expenditure in 1970/71 was £2,491. Thirty years later this figure had climbed to £47,936.

At the start of 2001 the councils faced a challenging year as the Partnership reviewed trading hours across the whole of its department store division and far-reaching changes were discussed. The council standing orders were also being scrutinised closely by an ad hoc committee of the Central Council and the structure of the Central Council changed. A divisional council was set up for the department stores, to mirror the Waitrose Branch

These boards, which hung in the branch, show the names of the Branch Council Presidents since Robert Sayle joined the Partnership in 1940

175

Council, which has now dropped 'Branch' from its title. Within these councils each division discusses issues relevant to its own business, rather than issues that affect both. The Partnership Council, which took over the role of the former Central Council and for which elections took place in early 2003, now looks at wider matters affecting the whole business. This followed the review of the Partnership's constitution, which was brought up to date and published in its new, current form in 2000.

36: All work and no play...

Miss Sieveking described in detail The Cambridge Experiment, which formed the framework of Robert Sayle's social and sporting activities during the 1950s and 60s. Many of these activities took place in the old Masonic Hall in Corn Exchange Street until it was pulled down in 1968. For a few years no alternative venue was available but, in 1970, Partners could still participate in a wide range of activities outside the branch. Clubs existed for bowls, darts, lawn tennis, badminton, table tennis and gardening. The sports clubs played in local leagues and the branch developed a close association with the Cambridge University Press, arranging social events with them and using their sports ground. This association with CUP petered out after 1980. Over the years interest in different activities has waxed and waned. Some clubs have come and gone – the crib club, art club, camera club, keep fit and, more recently, line dancing – others have enjoyed a longer-lasting popularity.

Swimming and football were both revived in 1970. Football has had a chequered history and it has not always been possible to field a full team although five-a-side has prospered. The swimming club negotiated the hire of the pool at the Leys School and it still uses it

30 years later. One new club started with a literal bang in 1971 – the rifle club. It used the TA range in Coldhams Lane but interest was short-lived and the club disbanded the following year. The provision of a new rest room in 1972 enabled a film club to start up. Attendance was limited to 32 each showing but the club showed up-to-date films throughout the autumn and winter months. It continued for many years although attendance gradually diminished. The social club committee took it over for a while and organised 'theme' evenings with refreshments; initially these were held once a month, then twice a year, but the club finally closed in 1987. The bowls club, one of the first to be set up in the Partnership, had a strong membership for a long time but bowled its last bowl in 1992.

Certain new clubs arrived and have continued to flourish. Golf started up in 1983 and is still going strong. The rambling club is very popular and, as well as arranging walks locally, has established a tradition of going to Ambleside for a weekend in early March each year. Another successful club is the theatre club. It was set up in 1985 and arranges trips to a variety of theatrical performances in many different venues. Badminton held onto its membership until 2002. The club used to play at Kelsey Kerridge Hall. The heyday of the clubs seems to have been in the late 1980s when 16 different activities flourished, but new interests still continue to emerge. A fishing club was set up in 1998 and an athletics club in 2000; the newest clubs are yoga and on-line gaming. Members of the athletics club have participated in local events such as the 'Chariots of Fire' relay race around the colleges in Cambridge. An annual rounders match is still held on Parker's Piece between management and 'the rest'.

One club that was very popular and enjoyed a great deal of support for many years was the sailing club. It had been rather dormant in the late 1960s but its fortunes revived in 1970. It had two dinghies and sailed at the Rosewell Pits near Ely. In 1975 the club applied to the Branch Council for £778 in order to buy a new Enterprise class dinghy and accessories. One of the club's dinghies was nine years old, the other 13, and the older boat was proving rather expensive to keep in good repair. The club had 40 members at the time, of whom 21 were regular sailors. 'Sayella Two' was launched at the Pits that year. Apparently during its second inaugural race it capsized. Despite its age, 'Sayella One' was sold. Later that year both 'Sayella Two' and the club's other dinghy, 'Undersayle', took

The Robert Sayle Running Club's team for the 'Chariots of Fire' race, 2000

part in the Partnership dinghy regatta. Another dinghy was acquired from Trewins in 1980 and the club passed 'Undersayle' on to the newly opened John Lewis Milton Keynes. Interest in the club continued. The Branch Council applied for funds to purchase a new dinghy in 1987 – the cost had risen to £2,500 by then – and another one in 1991, but within a few years membership waned, and the club closed in 1997. The dinghies were sold.

When Robert Sayle had had the use of the Masonic Hall the branch's dramatic society had been very popular, staging a string of successful productions over the years. Its final performance in 1968 was 'Ring Down the Curtain'. With the closure of the hall alternative premises were needed. These were found at the ADC Theatre and in 1970 the society produced 'Rock-a-Bye Sailor', a sequel to the 1963 offering of 'Sailor Beware'. Two years later the revue 'Up in Arms' was presented, again at the ADC Theatre. Forty Partners were involved either on or off the stage. The Gazette described the revue as an 'excellent achievement, full of fun and spectacle'. It included musical

Daryl Burchell, Robbie Barrett & Tracy Barrett in 'Noises Off', 1997

items such as 'Here Beginneth', a fun dig at the Partnership, and 'Much Binding Robert Sayle', a dig at local personalities. A production of 'Arsenic and Old Lace' was planned for 1973 but the ADC Theatre was unavailable and the play had to be cancelled. The following year a revue was put on, imaginatively entitled 'A Kind of Revue'. After that, drama lapsed into the doldrums until 1980 when the society was revived with play readings and a Christmas offering of 'Cindy-Jonella'. In 1981 Robert Sayle entered the Partnership's One Act Play Festival with 'The Small House of Uncle Thomas', an excerpt from 'The King and I'. The Gazette review commented on "a loving attention to detail in style of dance, costume, make-up, props, lighting and sound effects". Even so, the branch did not win. As well as entering the festival, the society staged local productions. 'Oliver' was played to great acclaim in 1981. For several years Christmas revues were popular although the one planned for 1983 was cancelled through lack of interest. The branch continued to enter the One Act Play Festival. The 1984 entry was Act I of 'Toad of Toad Hall'. 'Sequence of Events', a Victorian thriller put on in 1985, brought Robert Sayle

runner-up status and was highly praised for the dramatic atmosphere created on stage. The feeling in the auditorium was described as "electric". It was pipped at the post by John Lewis Peterborough's production of an excerpt from 'A Midsummer Night's Dream'. 'Seaside Postcard' in 1987 was played "in a lusty style"! Two years later the branch's entry was 'The Knight's Tale', based on one of Chaucer's Canterbury Tales. Thereafter drama productions lapsed for several years.

In 1994 the branch once again entered the Partnership's Drama Festival with 'What Men Live By' by local author Nick Warburton. A significant number of Partners wanted to take part, so a second play, 'Zartan', by the same author, was also rehearsed, and two performances of both plays were put on locally at the Robinson Theatre, Hills Road Sixth Form College. This stimulated a very successful revival of the drama group and annual local productions have continued ever since. The group has staged a wide variety of plays – 'Veronica's Room' (1995), 'The Ghost Train' (1996), 'Noises Off' (1997), 'A Murder is Announced' (1998), 'Habeas Corpus' (1999), 'The Importance of Being Earnest' (2000), 'Killers' (2001), 'When We Are Married' (2002), 'Rebecca' (2003) and 'Wyrd Sisters' (2004). A highlight of the 2001 production of 'Killers' was the acceptance by the playwright, Adam Pernak, of an invitation to attend a performance. He was pleased and impressed with the experience. 'Wyrd Sisters' in 2004 saw two innovations: the participation of a Partner from Waitrose

Cambridge in one of the leading roles and the partnership with the Penguin Club (local volunteers who give technical help to amateur theatrical societies) which enabled the group to use sophisticated stage and lighting effects.

Apart from the clubs, Robert Sayle has always enjoyed a busy programme of outings, trips and other social events. Foreign trips featured frequently in the 1970s. Twenty-seven Partners spent a week in Italy in 1972 and later that same year 31 had four days on Majorca. Other destinations over the years included Greece, Yugoslavia and Tunisia. By the late 1990s foreign visits were more likely to be weekend trips to a European city or to New York. Twenty to 30 years ago dances were held three or four times a year, frequently at the Dorothy Ballroom until it closed and then at the University Arms Hotel or the Graduate Centre in Mill Lane. Dances became less popular as the years went by and discos found favour among the younger generation. Partners have also been able to try out a host of different activities – gliding, parachute jumping, dry-slope skiing and health farms, to mention but a few.

The early sports and social link with the Cambridge University Press was furthered in 1971 by the advent of the Robert Sayle gala. This was a completely separate event from the Partnership gala, although teams from other branches were invited to participate. 'It's a Knockout' type games were organised and other attractions at that first gala included a dog obedience show, a model aeroplane display, children's fancy dress, a 'Miss Robert Sayle' contest, a flower show, and home brewing and angling exhibitions. The Cambridge Silver Band played, as did the Riverside Jazz Band. The event was a great success and a gala was organised again the following year. It retained its popularity for years but was never regarded as an alternative to the Partnership gala. In 1980 it was described at Central Council as "an event of long standing with a high reputation in the Partnership". In 1984 they called it "a local tradition". After 1974 it was held every other year and was themed. A Roman air permeated the 1978 gala, in 1980 it was the wild west, then the circus in 1982 and 'the good old days' two years later. The association with CUP continued

The cast of 'Habeas Corpus', 1999

One of the team games at the Robert Sayle Gala, 1974

deficit for the preceding year and the number of Partners using the room in the evenings had declined further. The darts club and crib club held their club nights in the room but did not find the facilities ideal. The room was not large and access was difficult. Councillors commented that many Partners did not want to stay in Cambridge for events after work, particularly if they lived a long way out of the city, but those who remembered the fight to get the club room in the first place argued that everything possible should be done to keep it. The decision was taken to persevere and try to attract more Partners.

Three years later a major project to improve the shop was undertaken. Included in the work was a new social club room, built on the roof above the soft furnishing workroom. The old club room became a stockroom and marking-off area for fashions. The new room was of a reasonable size to accommodate a games area and a bar, with shutters to divide the area if necessary. It was available during the day time as a rest room. The lift that had recently been installed provided access from the yard so that the club room could be reached at night without anyone having to go through the shop. Friday evening activities re-established themselves on a monthly basis. Over the years various themes have become popular, such as Trivial Pursuit, Pictionary, and A Question of Sport, to name a few. The original table tennis table fell into

until 1980 when the gala moved to Fison's sports ground at Hauxton. The last gala was held in 1984. The social committee discussed alternatives, such as a family sports day, but the event was not replaced.

Once the rebuilding at the rear of the shop had been completed during the early 1970s the possibility arose of the branch once again having its own clubroom, a facility Partners had long been asking for. The move of the fashion workroom to a new home enabled their old premises on the roof to be renovated for this purpose. Considerable refurbishment was carried out, including the installation of new heating, new floor covering, fixturing for a dart board and provision of a bar area. The club room opened its doors in October 1976 and a programme of events was organised for Friday evenings. The room was used during the day time by Partners who could play darts, cards and table tennis there. A pool table was installed, having been lifted onto the roof by crane. By 1979 interest in Friday evening activities had dropped off and the weekly events were replaced with monthly ones. In 1982 the Branch Council discussed the future of the club room. The bar account had shown a

disuse and was donated to a local special needs school in 1987. A pool table was rented for several years but then removed as it was not paying its way. Its exit was by way of a crane over the roof. More recently the branch purchased its own pool table, which proved popular.

Christmas festivities have been held at a variety of venues over the years; the Dorothy Ballroom was popular for many years but, after it closed, Partners were entertained at the Graduate Centre, the Guildhall, Chilford Hall Barns and, in 2003, at a city night club. In 1984 Partners joined in carol singing and a Christmas service in the department managers' rest room. Three years later the first city shop workers' carol service was held in Holy Trinity Church, initiated by Robert Sayle. It is now an annual event. It was organised by the branch in the early years but other retailers have since taken their turn.

Miss Sieveking, in her history, referred to the Waterloo Club. This was started in 1958 by Lewis Smith, the then General Manager, for Partners who had completed 25 years' service. For the next 40 years the club held an annual luncheon as near as possible to Waterloo Day (18 June), attended by both serving and retired Partners. However, it eventually became necessary to change its status. For a great many years the Branch Council had funded the club's activity, but by the end of the 1990s this no longer met the criteria adhered to throughout the Partnership for branch clubs. Thus the club has been

renamed the 25 Year Club and now has an annual luncheon, with a speaker, and an outing to a Partnership venue such as Leckford or Canary Wharf.

As Robert Sayle gets into the new century a varied programme of sports and social activities remain available. As well as the sports clubs, Partners can also enjoy events in the club room each month and a wide range of outings and trips to places far and wide. In recent years branches in the same part of the country have joined together for regional events such as a fun day at Norwich and a visit to Edinburgh. Early in 2001 'Snozone' at Milton Keynes was the venue for 200 Partners from several branches to try skiing at the largest indoor real snow centre in Europe. Later in the year over 400 Partners, including many from Robert Sayle, took over 'Wildtracks' near Newmarket.

One final event that continues in Cambridge, as it does throughout the Partnership, is the programme of concerts. As Miss Sieveking noted, these began in 1952 and were very successful. Since 1975 they have been given at two-year intervals and, more recently, have included a concert for young people from local schools, given in the afternoon prior to the main evening performance.

The 25 Year Club – previously the Waterloo Club – at Leckford

37: People

In a long-established branch it is not unusual to find a number of Partners who have notched up 40 and even 50 years' service by the time they retire. One such Partner was Teddy Potter, who retired in 1975. Mr Potter worked at Robert Sayle for 50 years and was one of the last strong links between the shop as it had been in the 1920s and 30s and its later existence as a branch of the John Lewis Partnership. He had started his career at the age of 15 in 1923 as a junior in the wholesale department when the formidable director, Mr Chaplin, still controlled the fortunes of the business. Known as "Chaplin's boy", the young Teddy Potter had to show his employer the marking-off book every morning: this book contained all entries of new goods. The Gazette report of Mr Potter's retirement relates the anecdote of how Mr Chaplin once said to him, "My boy, do you want to know how I made my money? I picked up every pin, saved every bit of string – and I use the oil from my sardine tins in my lawnmower"!

During the early days of his working life Mr Potter lived in the hostel and, in order to make himself comfortable, he papered his room, bought his own furniture and carpeted the floor, all at his own expense. He progressed as a salesman from wholesale goods to cottons, woollens and silks. In 1931 he left Robert Sayle to train for missionary work but returned a year later because, he said, his love for Greek was equalled by his lack of interest in learning Latin. Shortly after his return he became the shop's funeral director. At that time the business still conducted funerals and also supplied mourning wear and coffins made by its own carpenters.

In 1942 Mr Potter was conscripted into the RAF and sent to the Highlands to learn about radar. Three years later he was invalided out and returned to Robert Sayle to become department manager of soft furnishings and linens. As manager of linens during the days of austerity after the war he did a very good trade in second-hand linens from well-to-do households. Second-hand tablecloths sold particularly well as there was no limit on the amount of used cloth customers could buy, whereas they were allowed only 15 square yards of new material. Apparently old tablecloths were frequently dyed and made into curtains. Mr Potter later took on the job of outside representative in charge of contract work for Robert Sayle, the position he held until his retirement. Among notable contracts for which he was responsible were those for Christ's College and Anglesey Abbey. The curtains for the Abbey had to be specially woven in Holland from pure silk and the new stair carpets blended to match the wear in the old ones.

Another Partner who achieved 50 years' service was Basil Carroll. Mr Carroll retired in 1987. He had begun his career in 1937 in the display department at Tyrrell & Green. The Luftwaffe brought this first job to an end when Tyrrell & Green was bombed in 1940, and Mr Carroll then moved briefly to Blinkhorns in Gloucester before arriving at Robert Sayle in 1941, where he became assistant to the head window dresser. Evidently this was a rather drab job at the time as most shops had similar, limited merchandise owing to the restrictions imposed by the war. Once the situation in the country started to improve, Mr Carroll was involved with a display programme that regularly required dressing 26 arcade windows before they disappeared when the frontage was modernised in 1969. Mr Carroll remained in display for the whole of his career, becoming manager of the department. He also played a very active part in the social life of the branch: he set up and ran several of the clubs and was the leading figure on the social committee for a great many years, organising a great variety of outings, trips and other events.

After his retirement Mr Carroll recalled with great fondness the Masonic Hall – now lost to the Lion Yard car park – which Robert Sayle had leased during the 1950s and 60s. It had been used as a social club and as a rendezvous for Partners after work, as many were single and lived locally. The branch also staged three or four theatrical productions there each year – sometimes revues, sometimes straight plays, sometimes old time music hall. Mr Carroll was heavily involved with these productions and he and his team built a new stage and installed modern lighting in the theatre. He sometimes trod the boards himself but mostly preferred to work backstage, liking the mechanics of the theatre.

Among a number of Partners who achieved more than 40 years' service was Ted Grover – known to all his friends as

'Grove'. Mr Grover retired in 1984, having first joined the Partnership in the John Lewis Building Company in 1938. After active war service as a navigator, Mr Grover rejoined the Partnership in 1946 and was much involved in the rebuilding of John Lewis Oxford Street. In 1959 he became Service Manager at Robert Sayle. During his time in the branch Mr Grover presided over an almost continuous programme of alteration and refurbishment: the selling space almost doubled, virtually every department was enlarged and the Magnet was acquired.

As in the past, Robert Sayle still has a significant number of long-serving Partners: currently the one who has notched up the most years – 42 to date – is David Mayo, Section Manager in the audio and television department. David joined Robert Sayle straight from school and has a wealth of memories.

Teddy Potter (centre) at his retirement party in 1975. He had worked for the Partnership for 50 years

Appendix E: Mr Robert Sayle – a fresh insight

Since Miss Sieveking completed her book, fresh insight into the life of Mr Robert Sayle appeared in the Gazette in May 1987 in an article by the Partnership's then archivist, Lorna Poole. Mrs Poole had discovered a great deal of information about Robert Sayle's other face and the property negotiations in which he was involved. Much of this concerned the development of land near Cambridge railway station during the 1850s. When the first railway came to Cambridge in 1845 Mr Sayle was quick to realise that this could be a way to improve trade still further. In 1852 he applied to buy surplus land on the station site where he could erect warehouses and factories. In fact these did not materialise and were later constructed next to the shop in St Andrew's Street. What were actually built near the station were granaries. Mrs Poole posed the question of why Mr Sayle would want granaries. Miss Sieveking mentions that he came from a Norfolk farming family and rented land from Jesus College in the 1850s. Mrs Poole's research led her to conclude that he was dealing in grain in some way and possibly in livestock.

Further research by Mrs Poole confirmed that Robert Sayle was a man of wide interests. He was involved in the provision of student accommodation, with town improvements and with working-class housing schemes. Mrs Poole says that it is obvious that by the 1870s he had a considerable reputation as a middle man in property negotiations. When he died, the Cambridge Independent said that he was a man who took the liveliest interest in local matters "more so than appeared on the surface". Also, that "some of the best improvements that have taken place recently owed their inception and execution to his judgement and enterprise".

A further example of Robert Sayle's involvement in Cambridge has also come to light. On 18 October 1878 he purchased at auction, for the Evangelisation Society, the Barnwell Theatre on Newmarket Road. It was renamed the Barnwell Mission Hall and remained in use as such until around 1915, having had a congregation of 500 in its heyday. In 1926 it reverted to being a theatre and, as the Festival Theatre, enjoyed varying success until the end of World War II. In 1998 it was once again put to religious use, this time as the Cambridge Buddhist Centre, and it is still used on occasions for concerts and special theatrical events.

More detail about Robert Sayle's role in the purchase of the Leys estate for the Leys School in Cambridge and in the funding of the Wesleyan Chapel on the Hills Road appears in 'Partnership in Excellence' by Derek Baker, published by the Governors of the Leys School, Cambridge, in 1975.

A history of Robert Sayle

Part 3
2004-2007

by

Olivia Daly

38: New beginnings – into the future

The final chapter in the history of Robert Sayle is not, in fact, an end at all, but a transition between the past and an exciting future. In September 2004, with plans in place for the city-centre Grand Arcade – and a big, brand new shop – the 164-year-old department store in St Andrew's Street closed its doors for the last time. The sadness of that occasion, however, was vastly outweighed by the positive feeling that tingled in the air. The message that day was overwhelmingly "We'll be back!".

It would be almost exactly three years before that promise came true, with the opening of John Lewis Cambridge, the 'anchor' department store of the new

shopping centre and the first shop to open there. Meanwhile, Partners were off to take up residence in their temporary home in Burleigh Street, near the Grafton Centre.

Moving across town

Robert Sayle at Burleigh Street – or 'RS2', as the shop came to be known affectionately to Partners – was unlike any other John Lewis branch, created for a trading lifespan of just three years. The new building was designed for the Grosvenor firm of developers – which would also be behind the Grand Arcade – by Cambridge architects Barber Casanovas Ruffles, whose brief was to capture the spirit of the building that had previously stood on the site, with a similar red brick frontage and reconstituted stone. They added a glazed 'core' tower and aluminium-framed windows for a modern look.

The site had been home to the Cambridge Co-operative Society, whose shop started trading here in 1899 and closed in 1987 (then standing empty for a year before QD expanded into it from next door). Some remnants of this previous incarnation were preserved in the rebuilding: two stone panels were included in the front of the shop, bearing the Co-op's beehive motif and its motto, 'Unity is Strength', while some carved lettering stating 'Cambridge Co-operative, Est 1868, Central Premises' was used in the wall of the back yard.

The budget for fitting-out, decorating and amenities was tight, and the divisional and local teams creating the new shop saved money in innovative ways. For example, about 30 per cent of the fixtures and other equipment was 'recycled' from other branches, including perfumery

Long-serving supply chain Partner Simon Cassidy locks up the St Andrews Street shop for the last time, in September 2004

counters from Southampton, PCs from other branches and lighting tracks from the 'old' Robert Sayle. There was no expensive new flooring: vinyl was used on the ground floor, while on the upper storeys existing concrete floors were painted in different colours to denote the various departments.

The ceiling was also remarkable for its modern, 'industrial' look. "All the external services [were] exposed, so I went for an ambient lighting system that fitted in with the silver ducts and pipes," explained Barry Ayling, then Lighting Engineer, concepts, John Lewis. "Like everything else in Burleigh Street it was a big challenge on a limited budget."

The temporary shop opened on 29th September 2004 – just four days after St Andrew's Street closed – and introduced permanent seven-day trading for the first time in Robert Sayle's history. On opening day there was a very positive reaction from customers, who had been kept informed of the move, and plans for the Grand Arcade, through a number of special events and an effective advertising campaign, so they knew what to expect. And although the assortment was more limited at RS2 than in St Andrew's Street, the new premises did offer a few distinct advantages over the old shop: for one thing, everything was under one roof and there was no dashing across to toys and gardening in the rain, for Partners or customers.

"[In St Andrew's Street] Partners were struggling with outdated facilities that made their jobs far more difficult than they should be," said then MD Jenny Tomley at the time of the move. "Now, all these obstacles have been removed. Burleigh Street is stunning, both inside

and out, with all the latest selling support facilities, which will greatly improve the quality of Partners' working lives."

Life at Burleigh Street wasn't all plain sailing, however. In the early days, the lifts caused a few headaches for some Partners, not least Gerald Brackley, Branch Maintenance Manager. "After some problems early on, we upgraded one of the lifts, which helped a lot, but there was no goods lift so we had to move stock in the customer lifts instead," he explained. "Fortunately this turned out well and gave customers the chance to meet some more of our selling support Partners than they otherwise would! People do get used to things: after a

The temporary Robert Sayle shop in Burleigh Street, known as 'RS2'

Former Partner Jim Bullock on the central staircase at Burleigh Street

while no-one even noticed."

When the shop first opened, the Partners' Dining Room was only able to provide sandwiches and hot drinks, as it had been considered too difficult to supply enough power to the facility to run cookers, ventilation and fire suppression systems. However, the division's canny experts found a solution to this problem and the catering team could produce a limited range of hot, fresh food every day.

A new service building

While shop Partners were moving into their temporary Burleigh Street home, those over at the service building were already enjoying their new, state-of-the-art workplace. The multi-purpose facility – a vital piece in the jigsaw that would eventually be revealed as the new John Lewis Cambridge – opened on 15th March 2004, six months before RS2, incorporating the very latest technology and standards that would secure its efficient operation for years to come, supporting a much bigger shop than the 'old' Robert Sayle.

The service building is at Trumpington, near the M11 and next to Waitrose and one of Cambridge's Park & Ride sites, and this location was chosen partly to encourage customers to park there rather than driving into the city centre. "Cambridge has serious parking and traffic problems and any plans for developing a new shop had to take this into account," said Monica Starr, then Project Manager, Robert Sayle. "The Park and Ride system, which is extremely successful, is a vital element in the whole package." Additionally, there is now a Park & Ride pick-up point outside the new shop's Downing Street entrance.

The building is striking inside and out, with lots of glass and a 'brise-soleil' – like a giant aluminium venetian blind – and an attractive reception area where customers can browse the Partnership's website and get access to gift lists. Selling administration and office Partners from the shop's audio and television, electrical, furniture, flooring and furnishing fabrics departments work at the service building and take telephone enquiries from customers.

Naturally, the major part of the service building is taken up by the warehouse, the first purpose-built storage facility of this size for the branch and a very welcome arrival. "My team has waited a long time for a purpose-built warehouse – the Magnet, where we worked before, used to be a bowling alley," said Gary Stepney, then Goods Manager (Service

Building). "For the first time we are able to take overnight deliveries and have a loading bay big enough for the multi-deck trailers. That – and having all the latest equipment – is going to make a huge difference to our efficiency."

Getting fully involved

Life away from the selling floor carried on as normal during RS2's three-year life. The branch's active clubs and societies continued to offer Partners fun, worthwhile ways to enjoy themselves, although getting together regularly was more difficult because of increased opening hours – a Partnership-wide challenge. The Robert Sayle Drama Group, in particular, kept up its programme of regular performances, putting on 'The Matchmaker' (the play behind the musical 'Hello Dolly'), 'The Farndale Avenue Housing Estate Townswomen's Guild Dramatic Society's Production of Macbeth' and 'Bolt from the Blue' between 2004 and 2007. They also performed two short plays at 'Odfest' (the Odney Festival) in the summer of 2007. One was written by then Chronicle Assistant Jane Grant and set in The Grove at Odney, while the other was adapted by Sarah Ingram, Branch Forum Co-ordinator/Community Liaison Coordinator, from the Edith Wharton short story 'Roman Fever'.

The branch also produced enthusiastic teams each year for the city's 'Chariots of Fire' charity race. In 2007 it fielded four teams of six Partners – the most ever from Robert Sayle in more than a decade of

taking part in the event. Meanwhile, the Cricket Club also continued to play regularly, competing in the Cambridge Business House Cricket League.

The Partnership's democratic structure at branch level was dramatically reorganised in 2007 following the Partnership-wide 'Democracy Project', which first gathered Partners' views about what they wanted from their councils and committees. Local forums – called 'PartnerVoice' in Waitrose and branch forums in the John Lewis division – replaced Branch Councils and Committees for Communication, and the election system also changed, with Partners nominating someone they thought would make a good representative, rather than candidates putting themselves forward. At Cambridge this change was delayed until after the move to the Grand Arcade, although Partners continued to take their democratic commitments as seriously as ever.

The Charities Committee was particularly busy. The emphasis of its work

The new Robert Sayle Service Building, next to the Park & Ride site at Trumpington

189

did change, along with that of similar groups across the division. "Instead of just giving away money, we started to commit time, too," said Mark Chase, Charities Committee Chairman for much of the branch's time at Burleigh Street. "This proved hugely beneficial to the groups we were helping, and also got Partners involved with some exciting projects."

For instance, the committee teamed up with the branch's active 25-year Club (for Partners and retired Partners with at least 25 years' service) and Darwin Nurseries on Newmarket Road to create a sensory garden at the nursery for disabled people – particularly those with visual problems – to enjoy. "The adoption of St Phillip's School has also been very significant," said Mark. "It's a long-term arrangement, and Partners give their time to help in specific ways. For example, Eileen Hughes [Marketing Manager] has been along to give the school's management team useful advice on marketing, and our furnishing advisors have helped to revamp the visitors' reception area. Other Partners help the children with reading, painting and crafts, and the branch has benefited too – before Christmas 2006, the school choir came along to sing carols in the shop."

Into the future

Bovis Lend Lease, the principal contractors on the Grand Arcade scheme, started demolition work in St Andrew's Street soon after the opening of Burleigh Street. Although this process was extensive, taking in all the shops and offices up to the corner of Downing Street, it did leave some of the oldest, most interesting parts, as well as those that were listed, to be included in the new construction. These included the

The St Andrews Street frontage of the new John Lewis Cambridge department store

main front façade – 'propped up' while the new shopping centre was constructed behind it – and some of the older buildings once accessed from St Tibb's Row, which would be used as offices in the new shop and create attractive features visible from the main lifts and certain windows in John Lewis.

In June 2005, then-Partnership Chairman Sir Stuart Hampson, Cambridge City Council's Rob Hammond and the Duke Of Westminster, Chairman of Grosvenor, led a ceremony to mark the start of work on the Grand Arcade. Sir Stuart said that the ground-breaking – during which the Duke drove a pile into the ground – was "another exciting milestone towards the creation of a state-of-the-art John Lewis department store for Cambridge."

Over the next two years, the Grand Arcade – and John Lewis Cambridge – took shape, watched by the eager people of the city, until finally the new department store was ready. John Lewis was the first shop in the new centre to be revealed to the public; most of the remaining units opened – later than intended at the start of the project – on 27th March 2008. "We could have put back our opening but we decided to stick to our original date," said Tony Jacob, Head of Construction Management, John Lewis. "We moved into the basement while the developers were still working on other floors and we just had to find ways to work round each other."

The pre-opening marketing campaign featured images of a 40" plasma TV being taken down the River Cam on a punt, and in the weeks leading up to the opening the branch's pages on the johnlewis.com website included a blog by MD Robert

Hallam, detailing some of his thoughts and experiences as he prepared for the big day. Later, the site contained a clickable link to a short film showing the opening ceremonies. "It's interesting to reflect on the vastly different methods of communication for the successive generations involved with revising the landscape of Robert Sayle," he said.

An expectant crowd of shoppers waited outside on the morning of Thursday 8th November 2007, and at 9am specially invited guests cut the ribbons at each of the three entrances. Among them was Barbara Tomes, widow of John, whose Robert Sayle career spanned more than 30 years and included a long period as Department Manager of kitchenware before he retired. Other guests included customers

A customer walks across the bridge joining the new shop's two 'boxes'

building, with a total space of 280,000 sq ft. It covers five floors and has two main 'boxes' – a larger, central space built around the main escalator well, and a smaller area, holding haberdashery, fashion fabrics and floor coverings – which are joined by stylish glass bridges.

Beauty is in a third, single-storey area, with its own entrance from the Grand Arcade. There is a brasserie and a separate espresso bar, both on the fifth floor, from which customers can also enjoy spectacular views across the city. They are the branch's first customer catering facilities in 167 years of trading.

MD Robert Hallam (left) and floor coverings, furnishing fabrics and linens Partner Mark Chase alongside the plaque in the main entrance commemorating Robert Sayle

Mr and Mrs Geoffrey Lloyd, who have been shopping with John Lewis for 50 years, Cambridge University history student Helen Maduka, and 14-year-old Jordan Watson, a patient at Acorn House, the branch's charity of the year.

Before the public ceremonies, however, Partners had their own 'opening' inside the stunning new shop. Robert Hallam – Managing Director of Robert Sayle/John Lewis Cambridge since that June, joked: "We have waited for this day for so long. Some of you have waited years, some of you have waited decades. If you've waited centuries, I'm questioning our retention policy." He acknowledged that Partners from all over the business had helped to create the new shop; "But this day is for Cambridge Partners," he said, "and we are going to take it on from here."

The new department store is three times the size of the former Robert Sayle

John Lewis Cambridge – the first of the 'new generation' of the division's department stores, to be followed by the Liverpool relocation and the new shop in Leicester in 2008 – had the fastest fit-out yet achieved by the division, and came in well under budget. What's more, trade since opening has been phenomenal, surpassing all expectations and thrilling everyone involved.

Robert Hallam spoke with pride as he unveiled a plaque commemorating Robert Sayle in the St Andrew's Street entrance on 6th March 2008. "The enterprise of our business and our success since opening John Lewis Cambridge is a source of great delight for us all. Customers have trusted us over many generations, and we are at home here in Cambridge. It is our privilege to safeguard our reputation for many years to come."

Appendix F: Facts & figures since 1970

Partnership Bonus

Since 1970 Partnership Bonus has been paid wholly in cash. The rate of distribution has been as follows:

1970	10%	1971	11%	1972	15%	1973	18%
1974	15%	1975	13%	1976	13%	1977	15%
1978	18%	1979	24%	1980	20%	1981	14%
1982	16%	1983	16%	1984	21%	1985	19%
1986	20%	1987	24%	1988	24%	1989	22%
1990	17%	1991	12%	1992	9%	1993	8%
1994	10%	1995	12%	1996	15%	1997	20%
1998	22%	1999	19%	2000	15%	2001	10%
2002	9%	2003	10%	2004	12%	2005	14%
2006	15%	2007	18%	2008	20%		

Chairmen of the John Lewis Partnership

Sir Bernard Miller – 1955-1972 (knighted in 1967)

Peter Lewis – 1972-1993

Sir Stuart Hampson – 1993-2007 (knighted in 1998)

Charlie Mayfield – 2007-

Robert Sayle – heads of branch

Peter Miller – 1969-1977

Peter O'Ryan – 1977-1981

Chris Mitchell – 1981-1992

James Furse – 1992-1995

Simon Fowler – 1995-2001

Jenny Tomley – 2001-2004

David Barford – 2004-2006

Amanda Dammers – 2006-2007

Robert Hallam – 2007-

Registrars

Joy Henderson – 1966-1970

Eve France – 1970-1976

Joan Pridham (acting Registrar) – 1976

Veronica Bennett – 1976-1980

Mary Cavaco – 1980-1986

Alison Featherstone – 1986-1991

Jennifer Hutchings – 1991-1997

Jenny Josselyn – 1997-2004

Jane Pitchford – 2004-2008

Note: in 2004 the Partnership altered the Registry system and most Registrars are now responsible for two branches. Robert Sayle was twinned with John Lewis Norwich.

Appendix G: Expansion of the JLP department store division, 1970-2008

At the start of the 1970 trading year the Partnership had 20 department stores; at the start of 2008, 26.

1973 – John Lewis Edinburgh opens, the Edinburgh Silk Shop closes

1974 – Newcastle Silk Shop closes (Bainbridge is already trading in Eldon Square)

1975 – Bon Marché (Brixton) closes

1976 – John Lewis Brent Cross opens

1977 – Daniel Neal Bournemouth and Daniel Neal Cheltenham close

1979 – John Lewis Milton Keynes opens

1981 – John Barnes closes (food store becomes Waitrose Finchley Road)

1981 – Bonds (Norwich) opens

1982 – John Lewis Bristol opens

1982 – John Lewis Peterborough opens

1984 – John Lewis Welwyn opens

1988 – John Lewis High Wycombe opens

1989 – John Lewis Aberdeen opens

1990 – Pratts and Jones Bros. close

1990 – John Lewis Kingston opens

1990 – Trewins (Watford) relocates to Harlequin Centre

1995 – John Lewis Cheadle opens

1998 – John Lewis Cribbs Causeway opens (John Lewis Bristol closes)

1998 – John Lewis Glasgow opens

1999 – John Lewis Bluewater opens

2000 – John Lewis Southampton opens (Tyrrell & Green closes)

2001 – John Lewis Solihull opens

2005 – John Lewis Trafford opens

2006 – Caleys (Windsor) closes

By 2008 all the Partnership's department store branches, except two, had been renamed John Lewis .... (followed by the name of their location). The exceptions are Peter Jones and Knight & Lee. When Robert Sayle returned to the historic centre of Cambridge as part of The Grand Arcade it became John Lewis Cambridge.

Photos and illustrations, Parts II & III

Tony Jedrej: pp177, 178, 179, 190, 192

CODA Architects: p141

Ramsey & Muspratt: pp144, 145, 146

Peter Lofts/Frank Birch: p160

Olivia Daly: pp150, 154, 155, 157, 158

Mark Mackenzie: pp188, 189, 190, 193, back cover

Kevin Sansbury: p191, back cover

Other photographs are owned by John Lewis Cambridge or the Gazette.